MW01170224

# LEGAL ISSUES IN SPECIAL EDUCATION

## Allan G. Osborne, Jr.

*Snug Harbor Community School, Quincy, Massachusetts*
*Bridgewater State College*

**Allyn and Bacon**
Boston • London • Toronto • Sydney • Tokyo • Singapore

*To Debbie, my inspiration*

*Executive Editor:* Ray Short
*Editorial Assistant:* Christine Shaw
*Executive Marketing Manager:* Stephen Dragin
*Editorial-Production Service:* Susan McNally
*Composition Buyer:* Linda Cox
*Manufacturing Buyer:* Aloka Rathnam
*Cover Administrator:* Suzanne Harbison
*Cover Designer:* Jennie Burns

Copyright © 1996 by Allyn & Bacon
A Simon & Schuster Company
Needham Heights, MA 02194

**Library of Congress Cataloging-in-Publication Data**

Osborne, Allan G.
 Legal issues in special education / Allan G. Osborne, Jr.
  p. cm.
 Includes index.
 ISBN 0-205-18442-1
 1. Special education—Law and legislation—United States.
 2. Handicapped children—Education—Law and legislation—United
States.  I. Title.
 KF4210.O835  1996
 344.73é0791—dc20
 [347.304791]

                                            95-24024
                                              CIP

Printed in the United States of America

10  9  8  7  6  5  4  3        99  98

# CONTENTS

# PREFACE

In 1975 President Gerald Ford signed P.L. 94-142, the Education for All Handicapped Children Act, into law. The Act, which took effect two years later, mandates that school systems are to assure all students with disabilities a free appropriate public education in the least restrictive environment. That law has had a greater impact on the operation of our public schools than any other single piece of legislation. It also has generated more litigation than any other education law.

In the two decades since P.L. 94-142 was passed it has been amended several times. More significantly, however, thousands of court decisions have been handed down interpreting its provisions regarding the responsibility school districts have toward their special education students. The law, and the case law that has been generated since 1977, have changed the scope and purpose of the public schools and have added new responsibilities to the duties of school administrators at the building level as well as the central office level.

Teachers, principals, special education administrators, and superintendents must make critical decisions daily regarding the development and implementation of programs for students with disabilities. To make those decisions, school personnel need to consider the legal requirements of providing an appropriate program of special education and related services. To do so requires that they have the requisite knowledge and understanding of all pertinent legal issues. This is difficult in a era where new court decisions are being handed down daily.

This book is written for those who are responsible for planning, developing, and implementing educational programs for students with disabilities on a regular basis. Although it is written predominantly for those who are currently working in schools, it also is appropriate for those who are preparing to enter the field of education. The text could serve as a staff development resource for special education personnel, central office administrators, and building principals. It also would be appropriate as a text in courses on special education law and as a supplementary text in general special education and school law courses.

This book is designed to provide comprehensive information about the law and how the courts have interpreted it. Legal trends and developing legal principles in providing special education and related services have been extracted from the case law. The book is not designed to replace the school district's attorney. Rather, it is hoped that by providing school officials with information about what is, and is not, required, they will be able to make legally correct decisions that will withstand challenges in due process hearings and the courts. School officials who understand the law should make legally correct decisions and thus avoid costly litigation. The emphasis of this book, as outlined in the final chapter, is on preventive school law.

In 1990 the federal special education law was retitled the Individuals with Disabilities Education Act (IDEA). At the same time the law itself was amended to change the terminology used within it. The term *handicap* was replaced with the term *disability*. Thus, former usage of the term *handicapped student* has been changed to *student with disabilities* in the law. The intent of these changes was to stress the fact that students with disabilities are individuals first and that the disability is secondary. In this book attempts have been made to use terminology that reflects this philosophy. Therefore, for the sake of consistency, terminology used in pre-1990 court decisions has been edited to conform to the changes in the 1990 amendment. Also, to avoid confusion the author uses the title Individuals with Disabilities Education Act (IDEA) even when referring to the earlier version of the law titled the Education for All Handicapped Children Act.

The book has been organized around the major procedural and substantive issues in special education law. It is written for educators. In that respect, the author has attempted to keep legal terminology to a minimum. When it has been necessary to use legal terminology, attempts have been made to define the terms in language a layperson can understand. However, the author has taken great pains to use extensive footnotes so that the book also can be used as a research guide by scholars interested in education law.

A word about the overall format and style of the book is appropriate here. Most school law publications follow a footnoting style outlined in *A Uniform System of Citation* (known as the Bluebook) published by the Harvard Law Review Association. Since this book deals with legal issues it made sense to follow this format. However, since many educators may be unfamiliar with certain aspects of law review style, the author has deviated from strict use of this format. Elements of the American Psychological Association (APA) style have been incorporated in the references where it was felt that this format would provide greater clarity to educators. For example, journal articles and other publications have been footnoted using elements of the APA format rather than strict Bluebook format.

In Chapter 1 an historical perspective of the special education movement is presented. It begins with the exclusion of students with disabilities from educational programs in the early part of the nation's history and concludes with the passage of federal legislation that calls for integration of individuals with disabilities into all aspects of society. An overview of the equal educational opportunity movement and its effect on later legislation for students with disabilities is included.

Students with disabilities have an entitlement to receive a free appropriate public education. In Chapter 2 the specific rights students have to receive special education and related services are outlined. Information relative to who is eligible to receive services is presented.

One of IDEA's unique features is that it contains very elaborate due process safeguards to ensure that students with disabilities receive the free appropriate public education guaranteed by the law. Chapter 3 outlines the specific procedural rights students with disabilities and their parents have under IDEA regarding the identification of the student's disabilities and the development of individualized education programs.

When Congress passed IDEA, it envisioned a system whereby school officials and parents would work together to plan and develop the student's educational program. Congress was not naive, however. Congress realized that disputes would arise. The procedures contained in IDEA for dispute resolution are presented in Chapter 4.

More disputes have arisen over placement decisions than any other aspect of the federal law. In Chapter 5 all of the components of an appropriate education and the factors that must be considered when making placement decisions are discussed. Information is presented concerning when private day and residential school programs must be provided and when extended school year programs are warranted.

Students with disabilities are entitled to receive related, or supportive, services if those services are necessary for the students to benefit from their special education programs. Chapter 6 outlines the supportive services that qualify as related services that must be provided under IDEA and the circumstances under which they must be provided.

Unfortunately students with disabilities, like any other students, commit acts of misconduct. Special education students are not immune from discipline, but the disciplinary sanctions metered out must not deprive them of the free appropriate public education they are guaranteed by IDEA. In Chapter 7 the special procedures school officials must adhere to when disciplining special education students are discussed.

Parents have recourse when a school district fails to provide the free appropriate public education called for by the federal law. Over the years the courts have provided the parents with a number of compensatory remedies in addition to prospective relief. Chapter 8 outlines the remedies available to parents when a school district fails to live up to its responsibilities. Information regarding awards of tuition reimbursement, compensatory educational services, and attorney fees is presented along with general discussions of punitive damages and sovereign immunity.

There are a number of other miscellaneous issues that have been litigated under IDEA that did not warrant separate chapters of their own. These other issues have been placed together in Chapter 9. Among the issues discussed in this chapter are minimum competency tests, students with infectious diseases, third party payments, student records, and several regulatory issues.

IDEA is not the only federal law guiding the delivery of services to students with disabilities. Section 504 of the Rehabilitation Act and the Americans with Disabilities Act (ADA) also have many implications for special education as they prohibit discrimination against individuals with disabilities. Section 504 and ADA as they relate to students is the main focus of Chapter 10.

One of the more difficult aspects of a school administrator's job is managing the special education legal maze. The major goal of this book was to provide information that would make that maze easier to understand. If that goal has been met, administrators should be prepared to manage the legal system. The Epilogue deviates from the format of previous chapters in that it does not deal with the law itself; rather, it is concerned with how administrators can manage the legal conflicts that will arise. The emphasis is on preventing legal problems.

A book of this magnitude could not be written without the support, encouragement, and assistance of many friends and colleagues. It is impossible to acknowledge all who have in some way influenced me and, thus, contributed to this book. I wish, however, to offer my sincere appreciation to all those who have contributed to my knowledge and understanding of the subject matter of this book. This group includes many of my past and present teachers, colleagues, and graduate students. There are a number of people whose unique contributions warrant specific mention. Their immense contributions have added to the quality of this book and can never be adequately acknowledged.

My wife, Debbie, has been the major influence in my life and professional career. She has encouraged me to write and has shown great patience in listening to an endless monologue about special education court cases. Her contributions to my professional knowledge and thinking, and consequently to this book, are so great that she deserves co-author status. This book was written because of her and is dedicated to her with love.

Mr. Richard O'Brien, principal, and the staff, students, and parents of the Snug Harbor Community School in Quincy, Massachusetts have been a constant inspiration to me. Their quest for excellence has been the source of much of my enthusiasm and has provided me with many very rewarding professional experiences.

Pat Smith, a very special friend and colleague also has provided me with much inspiration. Her love of children and teaching has shown me that everything we do is worthwhile. If all teachers ran their classrooms the way Pat does, inclusion would be a reality, not a goal!

Mr. Eugene Creedon, Dr. Carol Lee Griffin, Dr. Richard DeCristofaro, and Mr. Louis Tozzi of the Quincy Public Schools have provided much encouragement in my research and writing endeavors. They have allowed and encouraged me to pursue my interest in educational law in numerous ways.

Dr. Philip DiMattia, my mentor in my doctoral program at Boston College, was the person who initially encouraged me to research these issues. He has remained a close friend who constantly challenges me to not let these issues rest.

Dr. Tracy Baldrate and my colleagues at Bridgewater State College have given me many opportunities to teach courses concerned with legal and public policy issues in special education, thus providing me with a forum to explore these issues in depth. In teaching these courses I have come in contact with many graduate students who have challenged my thinking and questioned my analysis. The final result is that the ideas in this book have undergone critical review prior to being put on paper.

My appreciation to my parents, Allan G. and Ruth L. Osborne, can never be adequately expressed. Their influence over a lifetime has been profound. My father can be credited with teaching me how to write and providing me with many opportunities to practice the art. My mother, by her example, taught me how to persevere. I will never forget that lesson.

*A. G. O.*

# 1

# SPECIAL EDUCATION LAW: AN INTRODUCTION

When public schools first came into being in colonial America, students with disabilities were virtually excluded. The only education and training they received, if any, was provided by the family. However, in the nineteenth century special schools and classes began to emerge for the visually impaired, hearing impaired, and individuals with physical disabilities. Toward the end of that century and early in the twentieth century classes were developed for students who were mentally retarded. Unfortunately, these programs were segregated from the mainstream and often were taught by insufficiently trained personnel.

This chapter begins with a brief overview of the United States legal system. This introductory section will help the reader who is unfamiliar with general principles of educational law better understand the discussions in subsequent chapters. Also in this chapter, the history of the movement to obtain equal educational opportunity rights for students with disabilities will be outlined. Important court cases that led to federal and state legislation mandating a free appropriate public education for students with disabilities will be highlighted. Following a review of that legislation, an explanation of the dispute resolution procedure established by federal law and a discussion of the role courts play in enforcing the rights established by law will be presented. Readers unfamiliar with legal terminology may want to consult the glossary at the end of this book.

## SOURCES OF LAW

In the United States there are basically three sources of law: constitutions, statutes, and court decisions. However, these sources of law exist at both the federal and state level. A constitution is the fundamental law of a nation or state.[1] A statute is an act of the legislative body;[2] basically, a law that the Congress or a state legislature has passed. Statutes must be consistent with the controlling constitutions. Most statutes are accompanied by implementing regulations. These regulations are guidelines that have been written by the agency charged with the implementation and enforcement of the statute. They are written with greater specificity than are the statutes. Finally, the many decisions of the courts interpreting the constitutions and statutes comprise a body of law known as case, or common, law.

The federal judicial system has three levels. The lowest level, the trial court, is known as the district court. Each state has at least one district court and some states have as many as four. The district court is the basic trier of fact in a legal dispute. As the trier of fact in a special education lawsuit the district court would review the record of any administrative hearings, review additional evidence, and hear the testimony of witnesses. The court would render a decision based on the evidence presented by the parties to the lawsuit. Any party not satisfied with the decision of a district court may appeal to a circuit court of appeals; however, the appeals court is not required to hear all appealed lawsuits. A circuit is comprised of the districts of several states. For example, the First Circuit Court of Appeals consists of Maine, New Hampshire, Massachusetts, Rhode Island, and Puerto Rico. There are 13 federal judicial circuits in the United States. Any party not satisfied with the decision of the court of appeals may appeal to the U.S. Supreme Court; however, that Court does not hear all cases brought before it on appeal. Cases may come before the Court either on appeal or by a request for a *writ of certiorari*.[3] The high Court may determine, for whatever reason, that a case is not worthy of review. Generally, if the high Court wishes to hear an appeal it will grant a writ of certiorari. At least four of the nine justices must vote to grant certiorari in order for a case to be heard.[4] Denying the writ has the effect of leaving the lower court's decision unchanged.[5]

Each of the states has a similar arrangement except that the names of the courts vary. Generally speaking, there are three levels of state courts: a trial court, an appellate court, and a court of last resort. One has to be careful with the names of state courts. For example, we generally think of the supreme court as being the name given to a state's highest court; however, in New York, the trial court is known as the supreme court.

When a court hands down a decision, that decision is binding only within that court's jurisdiction. For example, a decision of the federal district court for New Hampshire is binding only in New Hampshire. The federal district court in Massachusetts might find a decision of the New Hampshire court persuasive, but it is not bound by it. However, a decision of the First Circuit Court of Appeals would be binding on all states within its jurisdiction and lower courts in those states must rule consistently. A decision by the U.S. Supreme Court is enforceable in all 50 states and U.S. territories.

## HISTORY OF THE EQUAL EDUCATIONAL OPPORTUNITY MOVEMENT

The federal government did not require states to provide special education services to students with disabilities until 1975.[6] Prior to that some states had enacted legislation providing special education services to students with disabilities, but those states were in the minority. Before the enactment of these laws school districts routinely excluded students who were difficult to educate. When challenged, these exclusionary practices were upheld by the courts until the early 1970s.

The federal initiative came after a long battle by advocates of the disabled to gain equal rights. At first, the battle was fought in the courts and much of it came about as a result of the civil rights movement.

### Exclusionary Practices Upheld

In the early years of public education the schools' programs were not generally available to students who had disabilities. The exclusion of these students frequently was upheld by the courts. The Supreme Judicial Court of Massachusetts in 1893 upheld the exclusion from the public schools of a student who was mentally retarded.[7] The student had been excluded because he was too "weak minded" to profit from instruction. School records indicated that he was "troublesome" and was unable to care for himself physically. The court ruled that the school committee, by law, had general charge of the schools and refused to interfere with their judgment. The court stated that if acts of disorder interfered with the operation of the schools, whether committed voluntarily or because of imbecility, the school committee should be able to exclude the offender without being overruled by a jury that lacked expertise in educational matters.

The Wisconsin Supreme Court also upheld the exclusion of a student with a form of paralysis in 1919.[8] The student, who had normal intelligence but whose condition caused him to drool and make facial contortions, attended the public schools through grade five. He was excluded because school officials claimed his physical appearance nauseated teachers and other students, his disability required an undue amount of his teacher's time, and he had a negative impact on the discipline and progress of the school. School officials had suggested that he attend a day school for students with hearing impairments and defective speech, but the student refused and was supported by his parents. The school board refused to reinstate the student in the public schools and the court upheld that decision. The court ruled that the student's right to attend the public schools could not be insisted on when his presence there was harmful to the best interests of the school. The court even indicated that since his presence was not in the best interests of the school, the school board had an *obligation* to exclude him.

The dilemma between exclusionary practices and compulsory education statutes was recognized by a state appellate court in Ohio; however, the authority of school officials to exclude certain students was upheld.[9] State law required children between the ages of 6 and 18 to attend school but the Department of Education was given the authority to determine if certain children were incapable of profiting from instruction. The school board in one community adopted a rule excluding any child with an IQ score below 50. A student with IQ scores ranging from 45 to 61 was subsequently excluded. Although the court held that the Department of Education had the authority to exclude some students, it ordered the school board to reinstate the student involved in this case since it had been the local school board, not the state, that had excluded the student. In reaching its decision, the court noted that education was so essential that it was compulsory between certain ages.

## Effect of the Civil Rights Movement

The greatest advancements in special education have come since World War II. These advancements have not come easily, but have resulted from improved professional knowledge, social advancements, and legal mandates initiated by concerned parents, educators, and citizens.

The civil rights movement in the United States provided the initial impetus for the movement to secure educational rights for students with disabilities. In *Brown* v. *Board of Education*,[10] the landmark school desegregation case, the U.S. Supreme Court unknowingly laid the foundation for future right to education cases on behalf of students with disabilities. Chief Justice Warren, writing for the majority, characterized education as the most important function of government. Noting that education was necessary for citizens to exercise their most basic civic responsibilities, Warren stated:

> *In these days, it is doubtful that any child may reasonably be expected to succeed in life if he is denied the opportunity of an education. Such an opportunity, where the State has undertaken to provide it, is a right that must be made available to all on equal terms.*[11]

This statement often has been either directly quoted or paraphrased by other courts in subsequent cases seeking equal educational opportunities for students with disabilities. Students with disabilities became known as the other minority as special educators and parents demanded that they be accorded the same rights to an equal educational opportunity that had been gained by racial and ethnic minorities.

## Equal Educational Opportunity Movement

The movement to procure equal educational opportunities for students with disabilities picked up more ammunition in the late 1960s and early 1970s when lawsuits were filed seeking such opportunities for the poor, language minorities, and racial minorities. All of these lawsuits were not successful; however, as with the *Brown* decision, much of the language that emerged from the courts' opinions had direct implications for the plight of students with disabilities.

### Discriminatory Tracking

The tracking system, as used by the public schools in the District of Columbia, was held to be discriminatory in 1967. Students had been placed in tracks, or curriculum levels, as early as elementary school based on an ability assessment that relied heavily on nationally normed standardized aptitude tests. Once placed, it was difficult for a student to ever move out of the assigned track. The federal district court ordered the school district to abolish the tracking system after hearing testimony indicating that the tests could give inaccurate and misleading results when used with populations other than white middle-class students.[12] Using these tests with poor minority students often resulted in their being placed according to environmental and psychological factors rather than innate ability.

The court found that the school district lacked the ability to determine accurately the innate learning abilities of a majority of its students and that their placement in lower tracks was not justified. Certain classes of students were thus denied an equal educational opportunity as students in the lower tracks received a limited curriculum. The district further denied students in the lower tracks an equal educational opportunity by failing to provide compensatory educational services that would help bring them back into the mainstream of public education according to the court's opinion.

### Culturally Biased Testing
Placement of students in segregated programs on the basis of culturally biased assessments was prohibited on two other occasions. In one case, a Spanish-speaking student was placed in a class for the mentally retarded on the basis of an IQ test administered in English.[13] The issue was similar in the second case except that the student was black.[14] In this case the courts held that standardized IQ tests that had not been validated for black students caused a disproportionate placement of minority students in special education classes. In each of these cases the school districts were ordered to develop nondiscriminatory procedures for placing students in special education classes. However, in a separate action a federal district court held that standardized IQ tests commonly in use in schools were not culturally or racially biased.[15]

### Language Minorities
In 1974 the U.S. Supreme Court held that the failure to provide remedial English language instruction to non–English-speaking students violated section 601 of the Civil Rights Act of 1974.[16] A class action lawsuit had been filed on behalf of Chinese students in the San Francisco school system who did not speak English and who had not been provided with English language instruction. The Court found that the lack of remedial instruction denied the students a meaningful opportunity to participate in public education. The Court held that, as a recipient of federal funds, the school district was bound by Title VI of the Civil Rights Act of 1964 and a Department of Health, Education, and Welfare regulation that required school districts to take affirmative steps to rectify language deficiencies.

### Equal Expenditure of Funds
Several cases have come before the courts claiming that the poor were discriminated against in that the quality of education provided was based on the wealth of the district. In most of these cases a property tax was used to finance education, resulting in great disparities in educational expenditures among a state's school districts. The differences in expenditure levels, it was claimed, resulted in differences in the quality of education provided.

The U.S. Supreme Court held that these disparities did not violate the federal Constitution.[17] Holding that the poor were not a suspect class and that education was not a fundamental right, the Court stated that at least where wealth was concerned, the Constitution did not require absolute equality.

In reaching this decision the Court delineated the criteria for what constitutes a suspect class: a group "saddled with such disabilities or subjected to such a history of purposeful unequal treatment, or relegated to such a position of political powerlessness as to command extraordinary protection from the majoritarian political process."[18] Categorization as a suspect class requires the courts to use what is known as the strict scrutiny test. The strict scrutiny test imposes a higher standard on governmental units to justify unequal treatment. In practical terms, delineation as a suspect class would make it easier for a plaintiff class to show that disparate treatment was discriminatory.

The California Supreme Court used the strict scrutiny test to declare that the state's school finance system violated the equal protection clause of the state constitution.[19] Several other states have been involved in similar lawsuits. Overall, the state courts are fairly evenly split on the issue. Most decisions depend on the state's own constitutional provisions.

## A New Era for Students with Disabilities

State and federal court decisions concerning equal educational opportunities for the poor, language minorities, and racial minorities have been persuasive in subsequent decisions regarding access to public school programs for students with disabilities. The legal principles remain the same regardless of reasons why a particular class of students may be classified as a minority. Advocates for students with disabilities used the equal educational opportunity decisions discussed above to lobby for the passage of laws mandating equal educational opportunities for these students. Several lawsuits were filed and won by these advocates. Although these lawsuits were decided in lower courts, some are considered landmark cases in that they provided the impetus for Congress to pass sweeping legislation that granted an entitlement to a free appropriate public education for students with disabilities, regardless of the severity or nature of the disability. Other cases are important in that they helped establish many of the legal principles that shaped the federal legislation.

### Wolf v. State of Utah

One of the first court cases decided in favor of students with disabilities was handed down by a state court in Utah.[20] The lawsuit was filed on behalf of two children with mental retardation who had been denied admission to the public schools. The children had been enrolled in a private day-care center at their parents' expense.

The Utah Constitution provided that the public school system should be open to all children in the state. That provision previously had been interpreted broadly by the state supreme court. State statutes further stipulated that public education would be provided at taxpayers' expense for all children between the ages of 6 and 21 who had not completed high school. The court in *Wolf* declared that children who were mentally retarded were entitled to a free appropriate public education under the state constitution. The court's opinion reads remarkably similar to portions of the *Brown* desegregation opinion.

## *Pennsylvania Association for Retarded Children* v. *Commonwealth of Pennsylvania*

In 1972 two class action suits were brought before the federal courts that, when taken together, had a profound effect on the education of students with disabilities in the United States. The first of these cases was brought by the Pennsylvania Association for Retarded Children[21] against the state on behalf of all mentally retarded individuals between the ages of 6 and 21 who had been excluded from the public schools. The exclusions were justified on the basis of four state statutes that relieved the state of any obligation to educate a child certified as uneducable and untrainable by a school psychologist, allowed postponement of admission to any child who had not attained a mental age of 5 years, excused a child from compulsory attendance who had been found unable to profit from education, and defined compulsory school age as 8 to 17 (but was used to exclude mentally retarded children not between those ages). The plaintiff class sought a declaration that the statutes were unconstitutional and preliminary and permanent injunctions against the enforcement of the statutes.

The dispute was settled by a stipulation and consent agreement between the parties that was endorsed by the court. The stipulation stated that no mentally retarded child, or child thought to be mentally retarded, could be assigned to a special education program or be excluded from the public schools without due process. The consent agreement stated that Pennsylvania had an obligation to provide each mentally retarded child with a free appropriate public education and training program appropriate to the child's capacity.

## *Mills* v. *Board of Education*

The Pennsylvania case helped to establish that students who were mentally retarded were entitled to receive a free appropriate public education. The second 1972 case extended that right to other classes of students with disabilities and established the principle that a lack of funds was not a sufficient reason for denying services.[22] This decision provided much of the due process language included in later federal legislation.

The *Mills* case also was a class action lawsuit brought on behalf of children who had been excluded from the public schools in the District of Columbia after having been classified as being behavior problems, mentally retarded, emotionally disturbed, and hyperactive. The plaintiff class sought a declaration of rights and an enjoinment ordering the school district to provide a publicly supported education to all students with disabilities either within the public schools or at any alternative program at public expense. It was estimated that approximately 18,000 out of 22,000 students with disabilities in the district were not receiving special education services.

School officials admitted the school district had the responsibility to provide a publicly supported education to meet the needs of all children within its boundaries and that it had failed to do so. However, school officials claimed that it was impossible to afford the plaintiff class the relief it sought due to a lack of funds. School authorities also admitted that they had not provided the plaintiffs with due process procedures prior to their exclusion.

The court found that the school district was required by the U.S. Constitution, the District of Columbia Code, and its own regulations to provide a publicly supported education to all children, including those with disabilities. The court ruled that the school district must expend its available funds equitably so that all students would receive a publicly funded education consistent with their needs and abilities. If sufficient funds were not available, the court held that existing funds would have to be distributed in such a manner that no child was entirely excluded, and the inadequacies could not be allowed to bear more heavily on one class of students. The school district also was ordered to provide due process safeguards before any child was excluded from the public schools, was reassigned, or had special education services terminated. In its opinion, the court outlined elaborate due process procedures that were to be followed. These procedures later formed the foundation for the due process safeguards that were mandated in the federal special education statute.

### *Hairston v. Drosick*

In 1976 a federal district court in West Virginia held that the exclusion of a minimally disabled student from the public schools without a legitimate educational reason was a violation of federal law.[23] The student, who had spina bifida, had been excluded from general public school classes even though she had the mental competence to attend them. Her exclusion was enforced without any prior written notice or other due process safeguards. The court held that an exclusion from general education and placement in special education absent prior written notice, the opportunity to be heard, and other basic procedural safeguards violated the due process clause of the fourteenth amendment.

### In re Downey
A 1973 decision by the Family Court of New York City helped establish the principle that special education programs must be free of cost to the child's parents.[24] The lawsuit was filed on behalf of a student with disabilities who attended an out-of-state school because the city did not have an adequate public facility that could meet his instructional needs. The student's parents were required to pay the difference between the actual tuition costs and the state aid received. The court held that requiring parents to contribute to the costs of the child's education violated the equal protection clauses of both the U.S. and New York constitutions. In ordering reimbursement for the parents' out-of-pocket expenses, the court stated that it was the child who was given the right to an education, not the parent, and that this right should not be limited by the parents' willingness to pay.

### Panitch v. State of Wisconsin
A district court in Wisconsin held that to not provide an appropriate education at public expense to mentally retarded students would be a violation of the equal protection clause of the fourteenth amendment to the U.S. Constitution.[25] The state had implemented legislation in 1973 that would have provided the relief the plaintiffs sought; however, by 1977, when the court issued its order, the state law had not been implemented. The court held that this delay was a sufficient indication of intentional discrimination in violation of the equal protection clause. The state was ordered to provide an appropriate education at public expense to the students in question.

### In re G.H.
The North Dakota Supreme Court in 1974 held that a student with disabilities had a constitutional right to an education under the state's constitution.[26] The child's parents had moved out of state leaving her behind at the residential school she had been attending. The school district that had been paying her tuition and the welfare department disputed which party was responsible for her educational expenses. The court concluded that the school district was liable after determining that the child had the right to have her tuition paid because special education students were entitled to no less than other students under the state's

constitution. The court suggested that students with disabilities constituted a suspect class because their disabilities were characteristics that
were determined solely by the accident of birth. The court reasoned that
the deprivation of an equal educational opportunity to a student with
disabilities was a similar denial of equal protection as had been held to
be unconstitutional in racial discrimination cases.

### Fialkowski v. Shapp

In another Pennsylvania case the federal district court helped to define what constituted an adequate program for a student with disabilities.[27] The parents of two students with severe disabilities claimed that
their children were not getting an appropriate education in that they
were being taught academic subjects instead of self-help skills. The
state, relying on the U.S. Supreme Court's *Rodriguez* decision argued that
the parents had no claim because there was no fundamental right to
an education. However, the district court held that *Rodriguez* was not
controlling and that the students were not being given an adequate
education because their program was not giving them the tools they
would need in life. The parents had argued that mentally retarded
students constituted a suspect class and the district court agreed that their
argument had appeal. Reviewing the U.S. Supreme Court's criteria for a
suspect class, the district court stated that such a test could include
retarded students. However, the district court saw no need to determine if
they were in fact a suspect class as it was able to resolve the case without
doing so.

### Frederick L. v. Thomas

One year later that same court heard a class action lawsuit filed on behalf
of students with specific learning disabilities who, it was alleged, had been
deprived of an education appropriate to their specialized needs.[28] The
complaint alleged that students with specific learning disabilities who
were not receiving instruction suited to their needs were being discriminated against in that children who did not have disabilities were receiving
a free public education appropriate to their needs, that mentally retarded
children were being provided with a free public education suited to their
needs, and that some children with specific learning disabilities were
receiving special instruction. Therefore, it was claimed, specific learning
disabled students who were not receiving an education designed to
overcome their disabilities were being denied an equal educational opportunity. The court found that the students in question were not being
provided with appropriate educational services in violation of state special education statutes and regulations and section 504 of the Rehabilitation Act of 1973. The appeals court upheld the decision.

## LEGISLATIVE MANDATES

Special education in the United States is governed by three federal laws and numerous state laws. The federal laws are known as the Individuals with Disabilities Education Act, section 504 of the Rehabilitation Act, and the Americans with Disabilities Act. Each is discussed in the following sections.

### Individuals with Disabilities Education Act

In 1975 Congress passed Public Law (P.L.) 94-142, which at that time was known as the Education for All Handicapped Children Act.[29] In 1990 this landmark statute was amended and retitled the Individuals with Disabilities Education Act (IDEA).[30] P.L. 94-142 was not an independent act, rather it was an amendment to previous legislation that had provided funds to the states for educating students with disabilities.[31] The important aspect of P.L. 94-142 is that it is permanent legislation, whereas previous laws required periodic reauthorization.

IDEA mandates a free appropriate public education in the least restrictive environment for all students with disabilities between the ages of 3 and 21. The law provides that an Individualized Education Program (IEP) is to be developed in conference with the student's parents for any child who requires special education and related services. The statute is very specific as to how the IEP is to be developed and what is to be contained therein. The law contains very elaborate due process safeguards to protect the rights of students and ensure that its provisions are enforced. The act contains a funding formula that allows all school districts to qualify for funds; however, districts receiving funds are subject to fairly rigid auditing and management requirements.

IDEA has been amended several times since its original enactment in 1975. The important amendments have added clauses that allow parents who prevail in a lawsuit against a school district to recover their legal expenses[32] and provide grants to states that wish to provide services to children with disabilities from birth to age 2.[33]

### Section 504, The Rehabilitation Act

Section 504 of the Rehabilitation Act of 1973 states:

*No otherwise qualified individual with a disability in the United States . . . shall, solely by reason of her or his disability, be excluded from the participation in, be denied the benefits of, or be subjected to discrimination under any program or activity receiving Federal financial assistance or under any program or activity conducted by any Executive agency or by the United States Postal Service.*[34]

Section 504 was the first civil rights legislation that specifically guaranteed the rights of individuals with disabilities. The provisions that individuals with disabilities could not be discriminated against in programs receiving federal funds were similar to nondiscrimination provisions that previously had been granted on the basis of race and sex. Section 504 effectively prohibits discrimination by any recipient of federal funds in the provision of services or employment.

An individual is considered to have a handicap under section 504 if he or she has a physical or mental impairment that substantially limits one or more of the person's major life activities, has a record of such an impairment, or is regarded as having an impairment.[35] Major life activities are "functions such as caring for oneself, performing manual tasks, walking, seeing, hearing, speaking, breathing, learning, and working."[36]

## Americans with Disabilities Act

The Americans with Disabilities Act (ADA),[37] passed in 1990, prohibits discrimination against individuals with disabilities in the private sector. According to the preamble to the law, its purpose is "to provide a clear and comprehensive national mandate for the elimination of discrimination against individuals with disabilities."[38] Basically, the intent of the ADA is to extend the protections afforded by section 504 to programs and activities that are not covered by section 504 because they do not receive federal funds.

Although the ADA is aimed primarily at the private sector, public agencies are not immune to its provisions. Compliance with section 504 does not automatically translate to compliance with the ADA. The legislative history of the ADA indicates that it also addresses what the judiciary had perceived as shortcomings or loopholes in section 504.[39]

## State Statutes

Since education is a function of the states, special education is governed by state statutes as well as the federal laws discussed above. Each state's special education laws must be consistent with the federal laws; however, differences do exist. Most states have laws that are similar in scope, and even language, to IDEA. Several states, however, have provisions in their legislation that go beyond IDEA's requirements. Some states have higher standards of what constitutes an appropriate education for a student with disabilities. Other states have stricter procedural requirements. Most have established procedures for program implementation that are either not covered by federal law or have been left to the states to determine for themselves. If a conflict develops between provisions of the federal law and a state law, the federal law is considered to be supreme.[40]

A comprehensive discussion of the laws of each of the 50 states, the District of Columbia, and various U.S. possessions and territories is beyond the scope of this book. Each of these governmental entities has its own terminology, laws, regulations, funding schemes, and legal systems. Indeed an entire book could be written on the special education laws of each state. The purpose of this book is to provide comprehensive information on the federal mandate, the law that encompasses the entire nation. However, the reader is cautioned that one cannot have a complete understanding of special education law if one is not familiar with state law. The reader is advised to seek out a source of information on the pertinent laws of the state in which he or she resides to supplement this book.

## ENFORCEMENT

IDEA has established an elaborate system of due process safeguards to ensure that students with disabilities are properly identified, evaluated, and placed.[41] These safeguards provide for parental participation throughout the process in such a way that the parents become a vital component of the school district's multidisciplinary evaluation and placement team. However, if the parents disagree with any of the school district's recommendations regarding a proposed IEP or any aspect of a free appropriate public education, they may request an impartial due process hearing. IDEA allows states to establish their own administrative hearing process. Some states have established a two-tier system whereby the initial hearing decision may be appealed to a state level hearing officer or hearing panel.

If either the parents or the school district is dissatisfied with the results of the administrative appeals, they may file legal action in either the state or federal courts. The only stipulation is that all administrative remedies must be exhausted prior to seeking redress in the courts unless it is futile to do so.

The courts have been empowered to review the record of the administrative proceedings, hear additional evidence, and grant whatever relief the court determines is appropriate, based on the preponderance of evidence standard. In this respect the courts have been given wide latitude in making decisions; however, the U.S. Supreme Court has cautioned judges not to substitute their views of proper educational methodology for that of competent school authorities.[42]

## SUMMARY

IDEA and its implementing regulations specifically provide for the identification, evaluation, and placement of students with disabilities. A companion law, section 504 of the Rehabilitation Act, also prohibits the exclusion of students with disabilities from programs and activities in the public schools. Together, these laws guarantee students with disabilities a free appropriate public education in the least restrictive environment.

Although IDEA and section 504 and their implementing regulations are comprehensive, they do not cover all possible situations. The courts have frequently been asked to interpret these laws as they apply to specific situations. As a result of court involvement, we now have a tremendous amount of case, or common, law regarding the education of students with disabilities. These issues are still being litigated; however, the common law that we now have must be used by school administrators as they make decisions regarding the placement of students with disabilities as the common law is equally as important as the statutes themselves.

## ENDNOTES

1. Black, H. C. (1979). *Black's Law Dictionary* (5th ed.). St. Paul, MN: West Publishing Co.
2. *Id.*
3. Alexander, K. (1980). *School law.* St. Paul, MN: West Publishing Co.
4. Morris, A. A. (1980). *The Constitution and American education.* St. Paul, MN: West Publishing Co.
5. Black, H. C. (1979). *Black's Law Dictionary* (5th ed.). St. Paul, MN: West Publishing Co.
6. P.L. 94-142, the Education for All Handicapped Children Act, 20 U.S.C. § 1400 et seq.
7. *Watson* v. *City of Cambridge,* 157 Mass. 561 (Mass. 1893).
8. *State ex rel. Beattie* v. *Board of Education of Antigo,* 169 Wis. 231 (Wis. 1919).
9. *Board of Education* v. *Goldman,* 47 Ohio App. 417 (Ohio Ct. App. 1934).
10. 347 U.S. 483 (1954).
11. *Id.* at 493.
12. *Hobson* v. *Hansen,* 269 F. Supp. 401 (D.D.C. 1967), *aff'd* 408 F.2d 175 (D.C. Cir. 1969).
13. *Diana* v. *State Board of Education,* Civ. No. C-70-37 RFP (N.D. Cal. 1970 & 1973).

14. *Larry P. v. Riles,* 343 F. Supp. 1306 (N.D. Cal. 1972), *aff'd* 502 F.2d 963 (9th Cir. 1974), *further action* 495 F. Supp. 926 (N.D. Cal. 1979), *aff'd* 793 F.2d 969 (9th Cir. 1984).
15. *Parents in Action on Special Education v. Hannon,* 506 F. Supp. 831 (N.D. Ill. 1980).
16. *Lau v. Nichols,* 414 U.S. 563 (1974).
17. *San Antonio v. Rodriguez,* 411 U.S. 1 (1973).
18. *Id.* at 28.
19. *Serrano v. Priest,* 5 Cal.3d 584 (Cal. 1971).
20. *Wolf v. State of Utah,* Civ. No. 182646 (Utah Dist. Ct. 1969).
21. *Pennsylvania Association for Retarded Children v. Commonwealth of Pennsylvania,* 343 F. Supp. 279 (E.D. Pa. 1972).
22. *Mills v. Board of Education,* 348 F. Supp. 866 (D.D.C. 1972).
23. *Hairston v. Drosick,* 423 F. Supp. 180 (S.D.W.V. 1976); citing section 504 of the Rehabilitation Act of 1973, 29 U.S.C. § 794.
24. *In re Downey,* 72 Misc.2d 772 (N.Y. Fam. Ct. 1973).
25. *Panitch v. State of Wisconsin,* 444 F. Supp. 320 (E.D. Wis. 1977).
26. *In re G.H.,* 218 N.W.2d 441 (N.D. 1974).
27. *Fialkowski v. Shapp,* 405 F. Supp. 946 (E.D. Pa. 1975).
28. *Frederick L. v. Thomas,* 408 F. Supp. 832, 419 F. Supp. 960 (E.D. Pa. 1976), *aff'd* 557 F.2d 373 (3d Cir. 1977).
29. Codified as 20 U.S.C. § 1400 et seq.
30. 1104 Stat. 1103 (1990). For the sake of clarity the federal special education law will be referred to by its new title throughout this book.
31. P.L. 93-380 which was an amendment to Title IV-B of the Elementary and Secondary Education Act.
32. The Handicapped Children's Protection Act, P.L. 99-372 (1986).
33. Education of the Handicapped Amendments, P.L. 99-457 (1986).
34. 29 U.S.C. § 794.
35. 29 U.S.C. § 706(7)(B).
36. 28 C.F.R. § 41.31.
37. 42 U.S.C. § 12101 et seq.
38. 42 U.S.C. § 12101.
39. Marczely, B. (1993). The Americans with Disabilities Act: Confronting the Shortcomings of Section 504 in Public Education. *Education Law Reporter, 78,* 199–207.
40. *The Constitution of the United States,* Article VI.
41. 20 U.S.C. § 1415.
42. *Board of Education of the Hendrick Hudson Central School District v. Rowley,* 458 U.S. 176, 102 S.Ct. 3034, 73 L.Ed.2d 690, 5 Ed.Law Rep. 34 (1982).

# 2

# RIGHTS TO ACCESS AND RECEIVE SERVICES

The Individuals with Disabilities Education Act (IDEA)[1] mandates that school districts provide students with disabilities with a free appropriate public education (FAPE), consisting of any needed special education and related services.[2] However, the law does not establish any substantive standards by which those services can be judged to be adequate. The act requires that the student be provided with specially designed instruction[3] in conformance with the student's Individualized Education Program (IEP).[4] The U.S. Supreme Court has held that a student with disabilities is entitled to personalized instruction with support services sufficient to permit the student to benefit from the instruction provided.[5] The lower courts have been cautioned not to impose their views of preferable educational methods on school districts;[6] however, they frequently are asked to determine what level of services is required to meet IDEA's minimum standards.

IDEA provided students with disabilities with unprecedented access to the public schools in the United States. As the first chapter indicated, prior to the passage of IDEA, students with disabilities routinely were denied access to public school programs. Those who were not excluded generally were relegated to second-class citizen status in that they were not provided adequate services.

In this chapter information will be presented on who is eligible to receive special education and related services. Questions of eligibility often arise as students must fit into one of IDEA's disability categories to be eligible for services in most states. Additionally, the specific rights of access to services and programs in the public schools will be delineated along with those for students who may not be enrolled in the public schools.

## DEFINITIONS

IDEA defines *children with disabilities* as children:

> *(i) with mental retardation, hearing impairments including deafness, speech or language impairments, visual impairments including blindness, serious emotional disturbance, orthopedic impairments, autism, traumatic brain injury, other health impairments, or specific learning disabilities; and (ii) who, by reason thereof, need special education and related services.*[7]

Under this definition a student is not considered disabled, for purposes of IDEA, unless that student requires special education services. Special education is defined as "specially designed instruction, at no cost to the parents or guardians, to meet the unique needs of a child with a disability."[8] Students between the ages of 3 and 21 are eligible for services.[9]

## ENTITLEMENT TO SERVICES

The regulations implementing IDEA make it very clear that the states are to ensure that all children between the eligible ages receive a FAPE.[10] A FAPE cannot be denied, regardless of the severity of the child's disability. The First Circuit Court of Appeals has held that the language of IDEA is unequivocal and does not include an exception for those with severe disabilities nor does it require that a child demonstrate an ability to benefit from services to be eligible.[11] In making its decision, the court referred to the original title of the law, the Education for All Handicapped Children Act, to support its proposition that none could be excluded. In the same decision, the court also defined education in a broad sense, encompassing training in basic life skills. The U.S. Supreme Court also has indicated that even students with disabilities who are dangerous cannot be excluded from the benefits of IDEA.[12] However, not all students with disabilities need be educated within a public school setting. IDEA allows for placement of students, whose needs require it, in residential or institutional settings.[13]

Students with disabilities also are entitled to access programs and activities that are available to the general student population as long as they qualify for participation. To deny such access would violate section 504 of the Rehabilitation Act.[14] Furthermore, IDEA's regulations state that students with disabilities are to be provided with nonacademic and extracurricular services and activities[15] and that students with disabilities are to participate in these activities with nondisabled children to the maximum extent appropriate.[16] Section 504 further requires all recipients of federal funds to provide reasonable accommodations to any child with a disability who would be otherwise qualified to participate in any of these programs.[17]

The courts have held that there was no entitlement prior to the effective date of IDEA (October 1, 1977) and that students who were already beyond the age of eligibility on that date did not have any valid claims to receive services.[18] Courts also have held that it is the students who have the entitlement to services and that this entitlement cannot be conditioned on the residence of their parents.[19]

IDEA requires states to provide special education services to students between the ages of 18 and 21 if they provide educational services to nondisabled students between those ages.[20] A state court in Indiana has ruled that students with disabilities over the age of 18 in that state are entitled to receive services.[21] The court specifically struck down a state law that had the effect of automatically terminating services for some special education students at the age of 19 and which gave school districts the option of providing services to others over the age of 18.

Students may not continue to receive services until the age of 21 if they no longer require those services. A district court in Michigan upheld a school district's decision to graduate a student with disabilities and terminate special education services after determining that the student had received a free appropriate public education and had been provided with adequate transition services.[22] The court found that the student had completed all graduation requirements and had shown exceptional performance in mainstream classes and was, thus, no longer eligible for special education services. However, a school district may not graduate a student who has not met the normal requirements and simply terminate special education services. The Supreme Judicial Court of Massachusetts held that a school had inappropriately graduated a student who had not met all of the usual graduation standards.[23]

Although these regulations seem to be straightforward, there has been some legal controversy over who is, and is not, eligible for special education and related services. Much of that controversy has evolved over the specified disability categories defined in the statute and regulations.

However, the most controversial eligibility lawsuits have been those concerned with the provision of special education or related services to students attending private schools at their parents' option.

## Eligibility

Students who may be classified under any of the categories of disabilities specifically listed in IDEA[24] are eligible for services as long as they require those services. Students are generally considered to require services if their educational performance is adversely affected by their disability. Individual states may specify disability categories in addition to those listed in IDEA or may provide special education services on a noncategorical basis. The U.S. Supreme Court has indicated that only a level of services as is required so that the student will receive educational benefit is required.[25] The Court also has indicated that a student who receives passing marks and advances from grade to grade is receiving educational benefit.

One court has ruled that gifted students do not fall within the protections of IDEA.[26] The lawsuit arose over a dispute concerning the educational program for the student. After all issues were settled the student's parent sought reimbursement of attorneys fees and other expenses, claiming entitlement under IDEA. The court held that IDEA was not controlling in this case.

One of the disability categories listed in IDEA is seriously emotionally disturbed. IDEA's implementing regulations indicate that in order to be classified as seriously emotionally disturbed, a student's educational performance must be adversely affected by the condition.[27] The definition lists characteristics of emotional disturbance as an inability to learn that cannot be explained by other factors, an inability to build and maintain interpersonal relationships, inappropriate behavior or feelings under normal circumstances, a general pervasive mood of unhappiness or depression, or a tendency to develop physical symptoms or fears. That definition includes schizophrenia but specifically excludes children who are socially maladjusted from the classification as seriously emotionally disturbed.

Courts have frequently been called upon to determine if a given student qualified for services under the category of seriously emotionally disturbed. One court held that a gifted student who had been hospitalized because of emotional concerns was not seriously emotionally disturbed and was not entitled to special education services.[28] The court found that although the student had some emotional difficulties, these difficulties did not adversely affect his educational performance.

The Tenth Circuit Court of Appeals held that a student who experienced problems with peer interaction, impulse control, and excessive anxiety was not seriously emotionally disturbed even though she had attempted suicide.[29] The court stated that the fact that the child was socially maladjusted was not by itself evidence that she was seriously emotionally disturbed. The appeals court upheld the district court's finding that the student had a conduct disorder but, again, that did not warrant classification as seriously emotionally disturbed.

Academic failure appears to be the key to determining whether or not a student can be classified as seriously emotionally disturbed. The students in the cases cited above did not experience academic failure in spite of their emotional difficulties. Conversely, the Sixth Circuit Court of Appeals held that a student who had average intelligence, but had a long history of academic failure, difficulty making and maintaining friendships, and an inability to create normal social bonds, was seriously emotionally disturbed and entitled to services under IDEA.[30] The court stated that school officials had failed to properly make the determination that the student was disabled in that they failed to fully examine his academic, emotional, and psychological profile.

The District Court for the District of Columbia upheld a school district's determination that a student who had an attention deficit hyperactivity disorder (ADHD) was not eligible for special education services.[31] The district had determined that the student's educational performance had not been adversely affected by the ADHD since his academic performance was superior. The court found that the evidence supported this conclusion. Although attention deficit disorder is not currently a disability category under IDEA, the 1990 amendment to the Act called for a Notice of Inquiry to be published in the *Federal Register* soliciting public comments concerned with whether the disorder should be categorized as a disability under IDEA.[32]

Another disability classification that has been controversial is that of other health impairment. Students so classified must have "limited strength, vitality, or alertness" caused by chronic or acute health problems.[33] The health problems must adversely affect the student's educational performance to entitle the student to receive services.

One question that has arisen is whether having AIDS would qualify a student as being other health impaired. The answer would depend on how far the disease has progressed and the effect it has had on the student. A state court in New York held that a student is not disabled merely because he or she has AIDS but could become disabled as the disease progresses.[34] In order to qualify as disabled, according to the court, the student's educational performance must be adversely affected as a result of limited strength, vitality, or alertness resulting from the AIDS.

Another court held that IDEA would apply to students with AIDS only if their physical condition adversely affected their ability to learn and do the required classroom work.[35] Using the language of IDEA's regulations, the court established a three-part test for determining if a student could be classified as other health impaired. Under that test each of the following conditions must be met: 1) the student must have limited strength, vitality, or alertness due to chronic or acute health problems; 2) the health problem must adversely affect school performance; and 3) the student must require special education and related services.

## Health Exclusion

Students with disabilities cannot be excluded from the public schools because of health problems, even when afflicted with a contagious disease, if the risk of transmission of the disease is low. Excluding students with health problems from the public schools would violate section 504 as well as IDEA. The Second Circuit Court of Appeals has held that students who were carriers of the hepatitis B virus could not be excluded from the public schools or segregated within those schools because of their medical condition.[36] Similarly, a state court in Illinois held that a student with hepatitis B was entitled to be educated in a mainstream setting.[37] In each of these cases the courts found that the risk of transmission was low and could be reduced further through the use of proper prophylactic procedures.

The reasoning in the hepatitis cases also can be applied to situations where students have AIDS. The Eleventh Circuit Court of Appeals has held that a court must determine if reasonable accommodations could reduce the risk of transmission before a student could be excluded.[38] The student in question was classified as mentally retarded and had been excluded from the public schools in part because she was incontinent and drooled. On remand, the district court found that the risk of transmission from the student's bodily secretions was remote and ordered the school district to admit the student to a public school special education classroom.

## State-Operated Facilities

IDEA applies to all students with disabilities between the ages of 3 and 21. IDEA's regulations state that the act applies to all agencies within the states that are involved in the education of students with disabilities, including state correctional facilities.[39] This means that a student with disabilities would not lose his or her eligibility due to incarceration. The federal district court in Massachusetts has held that inmates of county correctional institutions below the age of 22 who had not yet received a high school diploma[40] were entitled to special education services under IDEA and state law.[41] The court found that their incarcerated status would require adjustments in the delivery of services, but it did not eviscerate their entitlement to receive those services.

IDEA also applies to individuals between the eligible ages who may reside in state institutions. One federal district court held that IDEA's provisions apply to state-operated facilities for individuals with disabilities.[42] The state had argued that IDEA did not apply to students receiving services in state-operated programs funded by federal legislation other than IDEA. The court disagreed, finding that IDEA imposed an obligation to educate all children with disabilities, including those in state institutions, and that once a state received federal funds under IDEA, all children within the state received IDEA's entitlements.

## Other Public Facilities

IDEA specifically states that its provisions apply to United States territories and possessions, Indian reservation schools, and correctional facilities[43] but gives little guidance as to other public facilities that do not fall within the jurisdiction of a state government. The District Court for the District of Columbia has held that students attending government-operated schools overseas are entitled to the benefits and protections of IDEA.[44] The case involved two students with learning disabilities who had been attending a school operated by the Department of Defense. After finding that the programs offered by this school were not sufficient to meet the students' needs, the court ordered the department to provide and pay for residential placements. This decision indicates that all government-operated programs would come under the auspices of IDEA.

## Extracurricular Activities

Under the nondiscrimination provisions of section 504 and the Americans with Disabilities Act, students with disabilities are entitled to participate in any programs operated by the school district as long as they meet the qualifications for participation. In addition, IDEA's regulations state:

> *Each public agency shall take steps to provide nonacademic and extracurricular services and activities in such manner as is necessary to afford children with disabilities an equal opportunity for participation in those services and activities.*[45]

These regulations further define nonacademic and extracurricular activities to include athletics, recreational activities, and special interest groups or clubs. Another regulation indicates that nonacademic and extracurricular services and activities are to be provided in the mainstream to the maximum extent appropriate.[46]

The Sixth Circuit Court of Appeals has interpreted the above provision narrowly.[47] A lower court had ordered a school district to provide one hour of extracurricular activities per week to a student with severe disabilities. The appeals court reversed, holding that the school district was not obligated to provide the extracurricular activities since the student would receive no significant benefit from them. This ruling indicates that school districts are obligated to provide nonacademic and extracurricular activities to students only if a benefit can be derived from them.

Many state athletic associations have rules prohibiting transfer students from playing sports for a certain period of time after their transfer, generally one year. However, if the student's transfer occurred for special education purposes, the rule may not be enforceable. A federal district court in Tennessee issued an order that had the effect of prohibiting a secondary school athletic association from barring a transfer student who had learning disabilities from participating in sports.[48] The student had transferred from a private school to a public high school in order to avail himself of special education services. The athletic association declared that he was ineligible to participate in sports, invoking a rule that prohibited transfer students from playing for one year. The student filed suit after his request for exemption from the rule was denied by the association. The court held that the association had interfered with the student's rights as guaranteed by IDEA by not allowing him to play.

Students with disabilities frequently repeat grades so that they are older than other students at the same grade level. A state court in Texas ruled that an athletic association could not enforce a rule prohibiting students over the age of 19 from participating in interscholastic sports when the students involved had disabilities.[49] The students were over the age of 19 in their senior year because they had repeated grades due to their disabilities. The court held that waiving the over-19 rule was a reasonable accommodation under section 504 that would allow the students to have meaningful access to the schools' programs. However, a student may not invoke the protections of IDEA to contravene eligibility rules if the student does not have a formal written IEP, even if the student claims to be disabled and had received remedial educational services.[50]

These decisions indicate that rules or policies concerning eligibility for extracurricular activities may not be enforceable if they have the effect of limiting the involvement of students with disabilities. One question that remains is whether students with disabilities who fail courses would be ineligible for participation under "no pass, no play" rules. The answer likely would depend on the individual circumstances of the situation. If the failure is a direct result of the student's disability or of an inappropriate IEP, enforcement of the rule could be discriminatory.

## Nontraditional Program Schedules

At this writing students in most states typically attend school 6 hours a day, 180 days a year, for 12 years. Several courts have held that students with disabilities are entitled to programming arrangements and schedules that deviate from this pattern if necessary for them to receive an appropriate education. IDEA requires that IEPs be individually tailored to meet the unique needs of the student[51] and this provision sometimes requires nontraditional schedules for the delivery of services.

Students with disabilities sometimes repeat a grade or several grades. Consequently, they may require more than 12 years to complete the general program of studies. The Tenth Circuit Court of Appeals ruled that students with disabilities are entitled to more than the standard 12 years of schooling if necessary.[52] The school district terminated educational services for the student in this case after she had completed 12 years of school, even though she was not yet 21 years of age and had been classified as a tenth grader. The school district was ordered to provide her with two more years of schooling.

Many courts also have held that students with disabilities are entitled to educational programming that extends beyond the parameters of the traditional school year if the combination of regression during a vacation period and recoupment time required prevents meaningful progress. This is discussed at greater length in Chapter 5.

Some students, due to the nature of their disabilities, may not be able to tolerate long periods of instruction and thus may require a shortened school day. A school district is not required to provide a full day of educational programming if a full day is not in the student's best interests according to a ruling by the Fifth Circuit Court of Appeals.[53] This lawsuit was filed on behalf of a student with multiple disabilities whose educational programming consisted of basic sensory stimulation. Due to his inability to sustain prolonged stimulation, special educators in the school district recommended a reduction in his program to two hours per day. His guardian protested and the district court held that a four-hour day was appropriate. The appeals court, noting that IEPs must be individually tailored, held that there was no requirement that students with disabilities be provided with a full school day.

## Parochial and Private School Students

IDEA states that local school districts must provide special education and related services to students with disabilities who are enrolled in private schools.[54] IDEA's implementing regulations further stipulate that if a student with disabilities is enrolled in a parochial or other private school, the local school district is responsible for developing, reviewing, and revising the student's IEP.[55] These sections of the law and regulations make it clear that students with disabilities who attend parochial schools are entitled to receive special education and related services from their local public school district.

In 1985, in a case involving the provision of Chapter I services to parochial school students, the U.S. Supreme Court ruled that providing remedial services on the premises of a parochial school violated the establishment clause[56] of the U.S. Constitution.[57] Although the decision in *Aguilar v. Felton* involved Chapter I services, school law experts generally felt that the legal principle applied to the special education situation as well.[58]

Since the *Aguilar* decision most school districts have met their obligation by providing special education services to parochial school students off-site, either in a nearby public school building or at a neutral site. This arrangement may be inconvenient but it is an acceptable alternative for the vast majority of special education students attending parochial schools. However, for some students with disabilities, off-site services are not a viable alternative. For example, sign-language interpreter services for hearing impaired students can only be provided on-site.

The U.S. Supreme Court has held that the provision of a sign-language interpreter on the premises of a parochial school is not unconstitutional.[59] This decision reversed a ruling by the Ninth Circuit Court of Appeals which held that the provision of a sign-language interpreter for parochial school students with hearing impairments violated the establishment clause.[60] In *Zobrest v. Catalina Foothills School District* the appellate court held that since religious doctrine permeated every aspect of the curriculum in the parochial school, the sign-language interpreter would be conveying the religious message of the school along with the secular content of the instruction. The local school district had offered to provide the services if the student enrolled in the local public schools. The court held that even though this arrangement would burden the student's free exercise of religion, the burden was justified by a compelling state interest: avoidance of an establishment clause violation.

However, a slim majority of the Supreme Court disagreed, holding that the establishment clause did not bar the school district from providing the sign-language interpreter. The Court stated that IDEA was a general government program that distributed benefits neutrally to any student with disabilities, regardless of whether the school the student attended was public or private, sectarian or nonsectarian. The Court found that since parents had the freedom to select a school of their choice, a publicly financed interpreter would be present in a sectarian school only as the result of parental decision making. The Court did not see that any financial incentive was created for parents to choose a parochial school or that the interpreter's presence at a parochial school could be attributed to government decision making.

Finding that the parochial school would not be relieved of any financial burden if the school district provided the interpreter, the Court stated that the only economic benefit it received would be indirect. The Court held that the student with disabilities would be the primary beneficiary of the services and that the only benefit received by the school, if any, would be incidental.

The Court did not specifically rule that the school district had an obligation under IDEA to provide the requested sign-language interpreter. The Court's decision was limited to a ruling that it would not be unconstitutional to do so. The Court's opinion is narrow, in that it applies only to services such as a sign-language interpreter. In fact, the Court made a distinction between a sign-language interpreter and a teacher or guidance counselor. The Court viewed the interpreter's task as one of accurately translating whatever was presented in class without adding or subtracting from the message. Teachers and counselors, on the other hand, could inculcate the student with their own religious philosophies while performing their duties.

As stated above, the *Zobrest* decision does not require school districts to provide services on the premises of a parochial school. It also does not indicate that all services may be provided on-site without violating the establishment clause. The Court's opinion indicates that direct instructional services should not be provided on-site. Several courts have held that a school district is required only to make services available to students who attend private schools by parental choice.[61] If the services are available off-site, and the parents reject that arrangement, the school district has met its obligation.

If a school district makes arrangements for a student to receive services at a neutral site or at a nearby public school, the school district is responsible for transporting the student to the site where the services will be provided. Transportation is a related service that school districts must provide in conjunction with special education if the student requires it in order to access the special education services.[62] The U.S. Supreme Court has held that the establishment clause does not prohibit school districts from providing transportation to parochial school students.[63] A district court in Missouri has held that a parochial school student is entitled to be transported from the sidewalk in front of the parochial school to special education classes at a public school.[64] According to the court, providing transportation serves an important state interest without violating the establishment clause.

Off-site services also were not a viable alternative for a sect of Hasidic Jews in New York who operated their own school system because their religious beliefs and cultural background dictated that their children be isolated from children of dissimilar backgrounds. Prior to the Supreme Court's *Aguilar* decision, the local public schools provided special education services to the sect's children on the premises of the parochial school; however, after the decision the services were provided in a mobile unit off-site by order of a state trial court. A state appellate court held that this practice violated the establishment clause; however, the state's highest court held that the school district was not compelled to make services available only in public school buildings nor without the authority to provide them in another manner.[65] The high Court emphasized that the parochial school students' entitlement to special education did not carry with it the right to dictate where those services would be offered.

In an attempt to compromise this dispute, the state legislature created a special school district whose boundaries matched the village inhabited by the sect. The sole purpose of the newly created district was to provide educational services to students with disabilities who resided within the village. The state courts found that this arrangement violated the establishment clause in that it was enacted to meet the religious needs of the sect.[66] The U.S. Supreme Court affirmed the decisions of the state courts because it found that the state law departed from the constitutional mandate of neutrality toward religion in that it delegated authority over public schools to a religious community. The Court held that the state law resulted in a forbidden fusion of governmental and religious functions and crossed the line from permissible accommodation to impermissible establishment of religion.

Not all private schools are sectarian. Parents may choose to send their children to private nonsectarian schools as well. Of course, the establishment clause does not create any problems regarding the provision of services to nonsectarian private school students. The issue, when it comes to private schools, concerns the extent to which the school district is obligated to provide services to students who have been placed by their parents.

IDEA's regulations state that services must be made available to students placed in private schools by their parents.[67] However, several courts have held that this does not mean that the services must be provided at the private school. If the services are readily available within the public schools, courts have held that the school district has complied with the requirement to make services available. In two cases involving students who were unilaterally enrolled in private schools by their parents, courts held that the school district was not required to provide transportation to those schools.[68] Courts also have held that school districts are not responsible for the costs of speech therapy[69] or other related services[70] for students whose parents have chosen private schools.

## Least Restrictive Environment

Students with disabilities are entitled to have all special education and related services provided in the least restrictive environment.[71] The courts have held that under this provision of IDEA, students with disabilities may not be removed from the general education environment unless such removal is necessary to provide the student with appropriate special education services.[72] Students with disabilities also must be provided with access to any general education programs, either academic or nonacademic, in which they are able to participate and receive benefit. The least restrictive environment issue is discussed at greater length in Chapter 5 in the discussion of factors to consider in making placement decisions.

## SUMMARY

IDEA provides students with disabilities with an entitlement to receive a free appropriate public education, consisting of special education and related services, in the least restrictive environment. These students also have specific procedural rights that dictate how they are to be identified, evaluated, and served. IDEA ended a long period in which students with disabilities, especially those with severe disabilities, were excluded from the public schools.

In this chapter, the specific rights associated with the students' entitlement to access and receive services from the public schools were outlined. Issues concerned with who is entitled to receive services, what services are required, and where they may be provided were discussed. Other entitlements such as procedural rights, appropriate placement alternatives, and related services are the subjects of separate chapters.

Any student who meets the criteria for classification in one of the disability categories defined by IDEA's regulations is eligible for the benefits and protections of IDEA as long as that student requires special education services in order to receive an appropriate education. Students are not eligible if they are able to obtain an appropriate education, despite the disability, without special education services. For example, a student with serious emotional problems would not be eligible for special education services under IDEA if he or she were making adequate academic progress without the services.

Students may not be excluded from the scope of services provided under IDEA due to the severity of the disability, disciplinary reasons, or health reasons. Students who attend state-operated facilities, other public facilities, and even private schools are entitled to receive services. In addition to educational services, students with disabilities are entitled to participate in nonacademic and extracurricular programs. State statutes may provide additional entitlements.

School districts are required to make special education services available to students who attend private schools at their parents' option. However, courts have held that this does not mean that services must be provided at the private school site. Courts have consistently held that if the services are available within the public schools, the school district has met its obligation under IDEA.

Parochial schools create additional problems due to the establishment clause of the U.S. Constitution, which creates a wall of separation between church and state. Several court decisions indicate that school districts may not provide remedial services on the premises of a parochial school. Although the U.S. Supreme Court has held that the establishment clause does not create a bar to providing sign-language services on the premises of a parochial school, it is generally felt that school districts are not required to provide any on-site services. In view of other Supreme Court rulings, this decision has not been interpreted to allow the provision of other on-site services at a parochial school such as direct tutoring, speech therapy, or counseling.

## ENDNOTES

1. 20 U.S.C. § 1401 et seq.
2. 20 U.S.C. § 1401(a)(18).
3. 20 U.S.C. § 1401(a)(16).
4. 20 U.S.C. § 1401(a)(18)(D). An IEP is a written statement that outlines the student's current levels of performance, annual goals and short-term objectives, and the specific educational services to be provided to the student. 20 U.S.C. § 1401(a)(20). For more information on IEPs, see Chapter 3.
5. *Board of Education of the Hendrick Hudson Central School District v. Rowley,* 458 U.S. 176, 102 S. Ct. 3034, 73 L. Ed.2d 690, 5 Ed.Law Rep. 34 (1982). See Chapter 4 for a complete discussion of this case.
6. *Id.*
7. 20 U.S.C. § 1401(a)(1)(A).
8. 20 U.S.C. § 1401(a)(16).
9. 20 U.S.C. § 1412(2)(B).
10. 34 C.F.R. § 300.300(a).
11. *Timothy W. v. Rochester, N.H. School District,* 875 F.2d 954, 54 Ed.Law Rep. 74 (1st Cir. 1989).
12. *Honig v. Doe,* 484 U.S. 305, 108 S. Ct. 592, 98 L. Ed.2d 686, 43 Ed.Law Rep. 857 (1988).
13. 34 C.F.R. § 300.302 & § 300.551.
14. 29 U.S.C. § 794.
15. 34 C.F.R. § 300.306.

16. 34 C.F.R. § 300.553.
17. 34 C.F.R. § 104.12(a).
18. *Gallagher v. Pontiac School District,* 807 F.2d 75, 36 Ed.Law Rep. 553 (6th Cir. 1986); *Alexopulos v. Riles,* 784 F.2d 1408 (9th Cir. 1986).
19. *Rabinowitz v. New Jersey State Board of Education,* 550 F. Supp. 481, 7 Ed.Law Rep. 590 (D.N.J. 1982); *Sonya C. v. Arizona School for the Deaf and Blind,* 743 F. Supp. 700, 62 Ed.Law Rep. 947 (D. Ariz. 1990).
20. 20 U.S.C. § 1412(2)(B).
21. *Evans v. Tuttle,* 613 N.E.2d 854, 82 Ed.Law Rep. 1204 (Ind. Ct. App. 1993).
22. *Chuhran v. Walled Lake Consolidated Schools,* 839 F. Supp. 465, 88 Ed.Law Rep. 588 (E.D. Mich. 1993).
23. *Stock v. Massachusetts Hospital School,* 467 N.E.2d 448, 19 Ed.Law Rep. 637 (Mass. 1984).
24. 20 U.S.C. § 1401(a)(1)(A)(i). Definitions for each disability classification can be found at 34 C.F.R. § 300.7.
25. *Board of Education of the Hendrick Hudson Central School District v. Rowley,* 458 U.S. 176, 102 S. Ct. 3034, 73 L. Ed.2d 690, 5 Ed.Law Rep. 34 (1982).
26. *Huldah A. v. Easton Area School District,* 601 A.2d 860, 72 Ed.Law Rep. 575 (Pa. Commw. Ct. 1992).
27. 34 C.F.R. § 300.7(b)(9).
28. *Doe v. Board of Education of the State of Connecticut,* 753 F. Supp. 65, 65 Ed.Law Rep. 109 (D. Conn. 1990).
29. *A.E. v. Independent School District No. 25 of Adair County, Oklahoma,* 936 F.2d 472, 68 Ed.Law Rep. 278 (10th Cir. 1991).
30. *Babb v. Knox County School System,* 965 F.2d 104, 75 Ed.Law Rep. 767 (6th Cir. 1992).
31. *Lyons v. Smith,* 829 F. Supp. 414, 85 Ed. Law Rep. 803 (D.D.C. 1993).
32. 104 STAT. 1105 (1990).
33. 34 C.F.R. § 300.7(b)(8).
34. *District 27 Community School Board v. Board of Education of the City of New York,* 502 N.Y.S.2d 325, 32 Ed.Law Rep. 740 (N.Y. Sup. Ct. 1986).
35. *Doe v. Belleville Public School District No. 118,* 672 F. Supp. 342, 42 Ed.Law Rep. 1125 (S.D. Ill. 1987).
36. *New York State Association for Retarded Children v. Carey,* 612 F.2d 644 (2d Cir. 1979).
37. *Community High School District 155 v. Denz,* 463 N.E.2d 998, 17 Ed.Law Rep. 885 (Ill. App. Ct. 1984).
38. *Martinez v. School Board of Hillsborough County, Florida,* 861 F.2d 1502, 50 Ed.Law Rep. 359 (11th Cir. 1988), *on remand* 711 F. Supp. 1066, 53 Ed.Law Rep. 1176 (M.D. Fla. 1989).
39. 34 C.F.R. § 300.2.
40. In Massachusetts state law grants entitlement to special education until a student reaches his or her 22nd birthday or earns a high school diploma. 71B M.G.L.A. § 1 et seq.
41. *Green v. Johnson,* 513 F. Supp. 965 (D. Mass. 1981). *Also see Donnell C. v. Illinois State Board of Education,* 829 F. Supp. 1016 (N.D. Ill. 1993).
42. *Association for Retarded Citizens in Colorado v. Frazier,* 517 F. Supp. 105 (D. Col. 1980).

43. 20 U.S.C. § 1411.

44. *Cox* v. *Brown,* 498 F. Supp. 823 (D.D.C. 1980).

45. 34 C.F.R. § 300.306.

46. 34 C.F.R. § 300.553.

47. *Rettig* v. *Kent City School District,* 788 F.2d 328, 31 Ed.Law Rep. 759 (6th Cir. 1986). For a previous decision in the same case, see 720 F.2d 328, 14 Ed.Law Rep. 445 (6th Cir. 1983).

48. *Crocker* v. *Tennessee Secondary School Athletic Association,* 735 F. Supp. 753, 60 Ed.Law Rep. 502 (M.D. Tenn. 1990), *aff'd without pub. opinion sub nom. Metropolitan Government of Nashville and Davidson County* v. *Crocker,* 908 F.2d 973, 61 Ed.Law Rep. 1187 (6th Cir. 1990). A subsequent lawsuit seeking damages against the association was dismissed by the district court and affirmed by the appeals court, *Crocker* v. *Tennessee Secondary School Athletic Association,* 980 F.2d 382, 79 Ed.Law Rep. 389 (6th Cir. 1992).

49. *University Interscholastic League* v. *Buchanan,* 848 S.W.2d 298, 81 Ed.Law Rep. 1145 (Tex. Ct. App. 1993).

50. *J.M., Jr.* v. *Montana High School Association,* 875 P.2d 1026, 91 Ed.Law Rep. 1165 (Mont. 1994).

51. 20 U.S.C. § 1401(a)(20).

52. *Helms* v. *Independent School District,* 750 F.2d 820, 21 Ed.Law Rep. 1208 (10th Cir. 1984).

53. *Christopher M.* v. *Corpus Christi Independent School District,* 933 F.2d 1285, 67 Ed.Law Rep. 1048 (5th Cir. 1991).

54. 20 U.S.C. § 1413(a)(4)(A) *and* 34 C.F.R. § 300.452.

55. 34 C.F.R. § 300.348.

56. *Constitution of the United States, Amendment I.* The first amendment states: "Congress shall make no law respecting an establishment of religion, or prohibiting the free exercise thereof; . . ." It has been interpreted to establish a wall of separation between the church and state. *See Lemon* v. *Kurtzman,* 403 U.S. 602, 91 S. Ct. 2105, 29 L. Ed.2d 745 (1971).

57. *Aguilar* v. *Felton,* 473 U.S. 402, 105 S. Ct. 3232, 87 L. Ed.2d 290, 25 Ed.Law Rep. 1022 (1985). However, in a recent decision five justices (O'Connor, Kennedy, Scalia, Thomas, and Rehnquist) have indicated that they felt the Court's decision in *Aguilar* may be erroneous; *Board of Education of Kiryas Joel Village School District* v. *Grumet,* ___ U.S. ___, 114 S. Ct. 2481, ___ L. Ed.2d ___, 91 Ed.Law Rep. 810 (1994).

58. Mawdsley, R. (1989). EHA and parochial schools: Legal and policy considerations. *Education Law Reporter, 51,* 353–364. Osborne, A. G. (1988). Providing special education services to handicapped parochial school students. *Education Law Reporter, 42,* 1041–1046. However, then Secretary of Education William Bennett disagreed in a policy letter to chief state school officers in which he indicated that the *Aguilar* decision did not automatically apply to special education programs. Policy Letter (1985). *Education of the Handicapped Law Report, 211,* 372–373.

59. *Zobrest* v. *Catalina Foothills School District,* ___ U.S. ___, 113 S. Ct. 2462, 125 L. Ed.2d 1, 83 Ed.Law Rep. 930 (1993).

60. *Zobrest* v. *Catalina Foothills School District,* 963 F.2d 190, 75 Ed.Law Rep. 178 (9th Cir. 1992). *See also Goodall* v. *Stafford County School Board,* 930 F.2d 363, 67 Ed.Law Rep. 79 (4th Cir. 1991).
61. *See, for example, Dreher* v. *Amphitheater Unified School District,* 797 F. Supp. 753, 77 Ed.Law Rep. 211 (D. Ariz. 1992), aff'd 22 F.3d 228, 91 Ed.Law Rep. 32 (9th Cir. 1994); *Tribble* v. *Montgomery County Board of Education,* 798 F. Supp. 668, 77 Ed.Law Rep. 784 (M.D. Ala. 1992); *Wright* v. *Saco School Department,* 610 A.2d 257 (Me. 1992).
62. 20 U.S.C. § 1401(a)(17). See Chapter 6 for a discussion of related services.
63. *Everson* v. *Board of Education,* 330 U.S. 1, 67 S. Ct. 504, 91 L. Ed.2d 711 (1947).
64. *Felter* v. *Cape Girardeau School District,* 810 F. Supp. 1062, 80 Ed.Law Rep. 595 (E.D. Mo.).
65. *Board of Education of the Monroe-Woodbury Central School District* v. *Wieder,* 522 N.Y.S.2d 878, 43 Ed.Law Rep. 1115 (N.Y. App. Div. 1987), aff'd as modified 531 N.Y.S.2d 889, 48 Ed.Law Rep. 894 (N.Y. 1988).
66. *Grumet* v. *New York State Education Department,* 579 N.Y.S.2d 1004, 72 Ed.Law Rep. 998 (N.Y. Sup. Ct. 1992), aff'd 592 N.Y.S.2d 123, 80 Ed.Law Rep. 685 (N.Y. App. Div. 1992); aff'd sub nom. *Grumet* v. *Board of Education of Kiryas Joel Village School District,* 601 N.Y.S.2d 61, 85 Ed.Law Rep. 209 (N.Y. 1993), aff'd sub nom. *Board of Education of Kiryas Joel Village School District* v. *Grumet,* ___ U.S. ___, 114 S. Ct. 2481, ___ L. Ed.2d ___, 91 Ed.Law Rep. 810 (1994).
67. 34 C.F.R. § 300.403(a).
68. *McNair* v. *Cardimone,* 676 F. Supp. 1361, 44 Ed.Law Rep. 236 (S.D. Ohio 1987), aff'd sub nom. *McNair* v. *Oak Hills Local School District,* 872 F.2d 153, 52 Ed.Law Rep. 950 (6th Cir. 1989); *Work* v. *McKenzie,* 661 F. Supp. 225, 40 Ed.Law Rep. 233 (D.D.C. 1987).
69. *Dreher* v. *Amphitheater Unified School District,* 797 F. Supp. 753, 77 Ed.Law Rep. 211 (D. Ariz. 1992), aff'd 22 F.3d 228, 91 Ed.Law Rep. 32 (9th Cir. 1994).
70. *Tribble* v. *Montgomery County Board of Education,* 798 F. Supp. 668, 77 Ed.Law Rep. 784 (M.D. Ala. 1992).
71. 20 U.S.C. § 1412(5)(B).
72. Osborne, A. G. (1992). The IDEA's least restrictive environment mandate. *Education Law Reporter, 71,* 369–380. Osborne, A. G. & DiMattia, P. (1994). The IDEA's least restrictive environment mandate: Legal implications. *Exceptional Children, 61,* 6–14.

# 3

# PROCEDURAL DUE PROCESS

One of the more unique features of the Individuals with Disabilities Education Act (IDEA)[1] is that it contains an elaborate system of due process safeguards to ensure that students with disabilities are properly identified, evaluated, and placed according to the procedures outlined in the act.[2] The main purpose of these safeguards is to make the parents equal partners with the school district in the education of the child. Never before have parents been given such rights.

IDEA requires the development of an Individualized Education Program (IEP) for every child found to need special education and related services.[3] The regulations promulgated under IDEA state that the parents or guardian of a child with disabilities must be provided with the opportunity to participate in the development of the IEP for their child.[4]

Prior to IDEA, school districts could make placement decisions concerning the child without regard for the parents' wishes. This led to many of the exclusionary policies outlined in the first chapter. IDEA's regulations ensure that no action is taken without parental knowledge by requiring school districts to obtain parental consent prior to evaluating the student or making an initial placement[5] and by requiring proper notice before any change in placement is initiated after the original placement has been made.[6]

Although the framers of IDEA envisioned parents and school officials working together, they were realistic enough to know that agreements regarding classification and placement would not always be reached. For that reason Congress created a dispute resolution process that allows parents to bring grievances to an impartial hearing officer and eventually to the courts, if necessary. The dispute resolution process is outlined in Chapter 4.

In this chapter, the due process mechanism of IDEA as it relates to the identification, evaluation, and placement of a student with disabilities will be discussed. An emphasis will be placed on the procedural rights that students and parents must be afforded. The importance of procedural compliance cannot be overemphasized. The U.S. Supreme Court has indicated that an educational program is not appropriate if it is not developed according to the act's procedures.[7]

## EVALUATION PROCEDURES

IDEA requires the states to establish procedures to ensure that all children with disabilities are properly identified and evaluated.[8] All testing and evaluation materials and procedures must be selected and administered in a manner that is not racially or culturally biased.[9] Students whose language or other mode of communication is not English must be evaluated in their native language or other mode of communication.[10] The evaluation process must be multidisciplinary; that is, no single procedure can be the sole criterion for determining eligibility or placement,[11] and eligibility decisions are made by a group of persons, at least one of whom must have knowledge in the suspected area of disability.[12] The evaluation also must be individualized.[13] All assessments must be administered by trained personnel in conformance with the instructions provided by their producer.[14] All assessment instruments must be validated for the specific purpose for which they are used.[15]

As stated before, parental consent must be obtained prior to conducting the evaluation. A complete reevaluation must be conducted at least every three years for each child found to have a disability.[16] The parents have the right to obtain an independent evaluation of the child if they disagree with the school district's evaluation.[17] The independent evaluation will be at public expense if it can be shown that the school district's evaluation was not appropriate. The school district must consider the results of the independent evaluation in any decisions it makes regarding the provision of services.

An IEP can be invalidated if it is not based on a proper evaluation of the child. One federal district court held that a proposed IEP for a deaf student was not appropriate because school district personnel failed to follow proper evaluation procedures.[18] The court found that the school district's evaluation team based its conclusions regarding placement on simple observations. Personnel did not use validated instruments to measure the child's aptitude and the procedures used tended to be biased against students with hearing impairments. Also, an expert on the education of hearing impaired students was not included on the evaluation team.

State law dictates the timelines for completing an evaluation. Depending on how the state law is worded, school districts may be required to conduct evaluations over the summer vacation period if necessary to complete the evaluation within prescribed time limitations. A district court in Maryland, whose laws require evaluations to be completed within 45 calendar days of referral, held that a school district had violated a student's rights by not conducting the evaluation within that time frame.[19] The student's mother had requested the evaluation in May but school officials informed her that they could not do it over the summer months.

In a case involving the education of students with emotional problems resulting in acting out and aggressive behavior, a district court found that the students' placement was based on vague criteria that tended to discriminate against minorities.[20] Once placed, students were not reevaluated as mandated by state and federal law. To remedy the situation the parties implemented a nondiscriminatory assessment procedure that was approved by the court.

IDEA requires school districts to consider the results of an independent evaluation but this does not mean that the independent evaluator's recommendations must be adopted. In fact, the First Circuit Court of Appeals has held that the requirement that school districts consider the results of an independent evaluation does not mean that there needs to be a substantive discussion of those findings.[21] Similarly, the district court in Connecticut held that IDEA does not require school districts to accept the recommendations of an independent evaluation or that the evaluation be accorded any particular weight.[22] The Second Circuit Court of Appeals affirmed that decision ruling that the plain meaning of the word consider is to reflect or think about with care. These decisions indicate that school districts satisfy the requirement to consider independent evaluations if the results are reviewed at the IEP conference.

School district personnel are not required to leave the state to evaluate a student that has been unilaterally placed in an out-of-state facility by his or her parents. A district court in Michigan held that a school district had the right to evaluate a student whose parents had requested payment of tuition for an out-of-state residential school, but were not required to leave the state to conduct the evaluation.[23] The student had been enrolled in the school by his parents without the knowledge or consent of the school district.

Under IDEA's regulations a student must be evaluated before an initial placement in special education and must be reevaluated at least every three years. However, a school district may not insist on evaluating a student if the evaluation procedures would present a risk to the student's health or welfare. A federal district court in Texas held that a school district could not premise a student's continued eligibility for special education on a reevaluation when his doctor had indicated that an evaluation would push the student's anxiety level to panic proportions.[24] The parents had provided several third party evaluations but the school district had determined that these evaluations did not meet state criteria. The court found, however, that the benefits of an evaluation conducted by the school district were outweighed by the risks it presented.

## DEVELOPMENT OF INDIVIDUALIZED EDUCATION PROGRAMS

IDEA defines an IEP as a written statement for each child with a disability that includes statements of the student's current educational performance, annual goals and short-term objectives, the specific educational services to be provided, the extent to which the student can participate in the general education program, the date of initiation and duration of services, and the evaluation criteria to determine if objectives are being met.[25] An IEP must be developed before special education and related services can be provided.[26]

The IEP is to be developed at a meeting that includes a representative of the school district qualified to provide or supervise special education, the student's teacher, the parents (and student if appropriate), and a person knowledgeable about evaluation procedures.[27] Other persons may be present at the request of either the parents or school district. This meeting is to be held within 30 calendar days of a determination that the child needs special education and related services.[28] The school district is required to take steps to ensure the participation of at least one of the student's parents at the meeting.[29] If necessary, the school district must provide translators to facilitate parental participation.[30] If the student attends a private school, a representative of the private school also must be present.[31]

An overriding theme of IDEA is that IEPs and educational programs for students with disabilities must be individualized. This means that they must be designed according to the unique characteristics of each individual child, taking into consideration the child's strengths and weaknesses. Programs must be developed to fit the child. Courts have held that IEPs that are not individualized are not appropriate. For example, one federal court ruled that an IEP that did not contain academic objectives and methods of evaluation that addressed the student's unique needs and abilities was not appropriate.[32] Another court criticized an IEP that was not specific to the student but, rather, was assembled using portions of IEPs that had been developed for other students.[33]

Parental input into the IEP process cannot be minimized. One of IDEA's unique features is its provisions for parental participation. Parents cannot simply be provided with token opportunities for participation. Their input into the process must be genuine. The Ninth Circuit Court of Appeals affirmed a lower court's ruling that an IEP that was developed without input from the student's parents and his parochial school teacher was invalid.[34] The court stated that procedural violations that infringe on the parents' opportunity to participate in the formulation of an IEP result in denial of a free appropriate public education. Similarly, a federal district court held that the failure of public school officials to attend an IEP meeting held at the private school a student was attending rendered their proposed placement invalid.[35] Informal contacts between parents and school officials do not fully meet IDEA's parental participation requirements. A state court in Pennsylvania held that impromptu meetings between a student's mother and school officials did not satisfy IDEA's requirement of affording parents the opportunity to participate in the development of an IEP.[36]

An IEP does not have to be written perfectly to pass a court's inspection. Courts generally will allow some flaws as long as those flaws do not compromise the appropriateness of the student's educational program. Courts are generally more forgiving if the missing information was available or provided in another form. For example, the Sixth Circuit Court of Appeals held that an IEP that did not specifically state current levels of performance or the objective criteria for evaluating progress was appropriate since that information was known to all concerned.[37] The court was unwilling to exalt form over substance and stated that the emphasis on procedural safeguards referred to the process by which an IEP was developed, not the myriad of technical items that are to be included in the written document. Another district court found that an IEP that contained present levels of performance and objective evaluation criteria and schedules was not defective as claimed by the parents.[38] On the other hand, a district court in California invalidated an IEP that did not address all areas of the student's disabilities and that did not contain any statement of the specific services to be provided.[39] An IEP with those defects would compromise the integrity of the student's educational program.

Another of the major tenets of IDEA is that the student's placement must be based on the IEP, not the other way around. Placements are to be developed that fit the unique, individual needs of the student. The practice of writing an IEP to fit the placement has been invalidated by the courts. The Fourth Circuit Court of Appeals held that a school district violated IDEA when it decided to educate a student in a county facility and then wrote an IEP to carry out that decision.[40] The district court in Connecticut also held that a school district violated IDEA when it proposed a placement without first evaluating the child or writing an IEP.[41] However, the First Circuit Court of Appeals ruled that a school district that considered various options along a continuum from least restrictive to most restrictive did not determine the student's placement prior to formulating the IEP.[42]

This does not mean that school district personnel cannot present a draft IEP at the conference for purposes of discussion. The federal district court in Rhode Island held that presenting the parents with a completed IEP at the conference was not an indication that the parents were denied a meaningful opportunity to participate in the development of the IEP.[43] Similarly, the First Circuit Court of Appeals held that it is acceptable for one person to draft an IEP as long as the parents and other members of the IEP team had the opportunity to provide input into its contents.[44] The Third Circuit Court of Appeals also affirmed a district court ruling that a draft IEP did not violate IDEA's parental participation requirement when there was evidence that the parents made suggestions for changes and some of those changes were incorporated into the final IEP.[45]

The courts, however, certainly would frown on any attempt by school officials to develop an IEP beforehand and then force that IEP on the parents without any meaningful discussion of the child's educational needs. A district court in Virginia stated that school officials must come to the IEP conference with open minds but that this does not mean they must come with blank minds.[46] The court emphasized that a school district may not finalize its placement decision before the IEP meeting, but school officials should have given thought to the placement issue prior to the meeting. School district representatives must remain receptive to all concerns raised by the parents, however.

School districts sometimes develop an interim IEP for a student to cover a short period of time while a permanent IEP is being prepared. This may occur, for example, so that the student can be placed in a special education program while an evaluation is being conducted or to cover a short period of time while a permanent IEP is being prepared. However, such a practice is not consistent with IDEA. A district court in Alabama held that the act does not contain any provision for an interim IEP.[47] The court stated that school districts are required to hold meetings and develop IEPs prior to the beginning of the school year, even if that means meeting over the summer. The district court in Maryland also ruled that school district personnel must meet over the summer months, if necessary, to develop an IEP within 30 days of the determination that a student needs special education and related services.[48]

IEPs for students with disabilities must be reviewed and revised, if necessary, at least annually.[49] Reviews and revisions should occur more frequently if needed. Procedures for reviewing and amending an IEP generally are similar to the procedures for developing an initial IEP. All of IDEA's procedural and notification rights apply to any meetings held to review and possibly revise an IEP. Naturally, parents must be given input into the process just as they are with the initial IEP.

IEPs should be reviewed if parents express any dissatisfaction with the student's educational program. One court has held that a parent's request for a due process hearing put the school district on notice that she was dissatisfied with the student's placement status and that the school district was obligated to review and possibly revise the student's IEP.[50] However, the First Circuit Court of Appeals has held that a school district had no obligation to review and revise an IEP for a student who had been unilaterally placed in a private school by his parents.[51]

## PARENTAL RIGHTS

When Congress passed IDEA it intended for parents to become partners in the development of appropriate educational programs for their children. To accomplish this goal, Congress provided parents with substantial procedural due process rights. The provision of these rights was unprecedented in federal education legislation. In IDEA, parents were given the rights to examine all records relative to the special education process, to have an independent evaluation conducted if they disagree with the school district's evaluation findings, and to receive written notification of any plans by the school district to initiate or change, or refuse to initiate or change, the student's educational placement.[52] In addition, parents were given the right to participate in all meetings in which the child's evaluation or educational placement is to be discussed.[53] Parents also are provided with avenues through which they can dispute any recommendations or decisions made by school authorities concerning the provision of a free appropriate public education.[54]

The courts recognize the importance Congress placed on parental participation. Although the courts have not insisted on absolute compliance with the letter of the law regarding parental rights, they have been diligent in upholding the rights of parents in the special education process. The courts will allow school district proposals to stand if the procedural violations did not prejudice the process in any way and did not result in a detriment to the student, but have not tolerated egregious violations of parental rights.[55]

## Parental Notification

Parents cannot exercise their rights if they are not aware of them. IDEA stipulates that school districts must inform parents fully of their rights under the law.[56] Failure to do so limits parental participation. The purpose of notifying parents of their rights is to provide them with sufficient information to protect their rights, allow them to make informed decisions, and fully participate in due process hearings, if necessary.[57]

Parents also must be provided with notification of any action the school district proposes or any actions it refuses to initiate along with an explanation of why the action is proposed or refused. Furthermore, a description of any options that were considered and rejected and the reasons for rejection must be provided. Parents also must be given information relative to evaluation procedures that were used as part of the school district's decision-making process. All notices must be written in language that can be understood by the general public and, if necessary, must be translated into the parents' native language or primary mode of communication. Oral notification may be given in situations where written notification is not feasible.[58]

A federal district court in Illinois held that the school district's failure to notify a student's parents of their right to review psychological evaluations and obtain an independent evaluation and failure to notify them of meetings in which the student's educational placement was discussed violated IDEA.[59] These procedural violations had the effect of denying the parents the opportunity to participate in the development of the student's IEP. In another case, the Fourth Circuit Court of Appeals held that a school district's failure to notify parents of their rights resulted in a failure to provide a free appropriate public education under the U.S. Supreme Court's *Rowley* decision.[60] The lower court had found that the school district consistently failed to comply with federal and state statutes concerning parental notification of rights. The appeals court reasoned that this failure relegated parental participation to little more than acquiescence.

The purpose of IDEA's notice requirements is to give the parents information that will allow them to actively participate in the educational planning process. In a District of Columbia case, parents challenged the notice provided by the school district, but the district court held that the school district's notices were statutorily sufficient.[61] The court found that the notices informed parents about where the school district proposed to place the student and why that placement was chosen. The court held that the information supplied was sufficient to provide the parents with the opportunity to have a meaningful role in the decision-making process and draw informed conclusions about whether the proposed placement would confer an appropriate education.

Naturally, a misleading notice will be problematic for a school district. The district court for the District of Columbia held that a misleading notice violated the procedural rights of parents under IDEA.[62] The school district had notified the parents that they had 15 days in which to request a due process hearing. No such limitation is contained in IDEA.

## Procedural Errors

Procedural errors on the part of school district personnel may or may not render their recommendations concerning an IEP inappropriate. The courts examine the effect of the violations to determine if, and to what extent, the violations interfered with the development of the student's IEP. If the letter of the law is violated but the error does not interfere with parental participation in the IEP process, the courts generally do not find the IEP to be invalid. However, if the violations prevent active parental participation in the development of the IEP, the errors generally are cause for the courts to invalidate the IEP.

Egregious disregard for IDEA's basic provisions will provide the courts with sufficient grounds to invalidate a school district's proposed IEP. The Fourth Circuit Court of Appeals held that a school district that failed to conduct an annual review of the student's program, as required by law, and failed to involve the parents in the IEP process failed to provide an appropriate education.[63]

The Sixth Circuit Court of Appeals stated that strict compliance with IDEA's procedural safeguards was the best way to assure that the act's substantive provisions were enforced.[64] However, in spite of that pronouncement the court did not find that the school district's failure to provide written notice was prejudicial since the student's mother received adequate oral notice and participated in the IEP conference. Similarly, a district court in New York held that a school district's violation of the letter of the law did not prejudice the student or his parents in any way since the parents were involved in planning and executing the student's IEP.[65] Also, the Eleventh Circuit Court of Appeals held that deficiencies in the notices provided to parents that had no impact on their full and effective participation in the IEP process did not cause any harm.[66] In each of these cases the courts reasoned that the procedural errors did not result in substantive deprivations and thus were not sufficient to render otherwise appropriate IEPs invalid.

## The IEP Conference

The IEP conference provides parents with the best opportunity to participate in the development of an appropriate educational program for their child. It is at this meeting that evaluation results are shared, the IEP is developed, and placement decisions are made. Prior to this conference parents may have attended meetings where the student's school problems were discussed and may have provided information about the child; however, the IEP conference is where most decisions regarding the student's future education are made. IDEA's regulations stipulate that school personnel must take steps to ensure that at least one of the student's parents is present at this conference.[67]

Parental participation is meaningless if the parents do not understand the proceedings of the IEP conference. School officials are required to take necessary steps to ensure that the parents do understand the proceedings. This may require the provision of an interpreter if the parents' primary mode of communication is not standard English.[68] Other steps also must be taken to ensure that the parents fully understand the proceedings. In two separate cases, the federal district court in Connecticut has held that parents have the right to tape-record the IEP conference. In the first case the student's mother had limited English proficiency and requested permission to tape-record the proceedings so that she could better understand and follow what was said at the meeting.[69] In the second case the mother could not take notes at the meeting due to a disabling hand injury.[70] In each case the court ruled that IDEA's intent of parental participation meant more than mere presence at the IEP conference and that tape recordings would allow the parents to become active and meaningful participants.

School districts also may have the right to make a record of IEP proceedings. The First Circuit Court of Appeals has held that school districts have the right to employ a court reporter at administrative hearings to secure a verbatim record of those proceedings.[71] Although the nature of an administrative hearing is different than an IEP conference, in some instances the need for a verbatim record may exist. In those instances the school district would likely have the right to create a verbatim transcript of the meeting.

As several of these cases illustrate, procedural errors can be fatal to a school district in that they may cause a court to rule in favor of a parent in a dispute involving the IEP. However, as a Sixth Circuit Court of Appeals decision indicates, parents may give up some of their rights by failing to participate in the process.[72] The parents in this litigation challenged the adequacy of an IEP because all of the required participants were not present at the IEP conference; however, they rejected the school district's offer to convene a properly constituted IEP meeting. The court ruled that the parents relinquished their right to a procedurally correct IEP conference by rejecting the school district's offer to schedule one.

## IEP Revisions

From time to time a school district may need to make alterations to the student's educational program. These alterations may be necessary due to changing circumstances within the educational environment or changes in the student's needs. Minor adjustments that do not result in a change in the student's placement are of little consequence. However, any change that would alter the IEP substantially or result in the IEP not being implemented as written would trigger the procedural protections of IDEA. Parents must be notified of any change in the student's educational placement and must be given the opportunity to object.[73]

The appeals court for the District of Columbia Circuit held that the school district's failure to notify a surrogate parent of the curtailment of a student's instructional program constituted a denial of an appropriate education.[74] The student lived in a children's hospital and was transported to a school district facility to receive educational services. His educational program was halted for several months because medical problems prohibited his being transported. However, alternative services were not provided and his surrogate parent was never notified that educational services were no longer being provided. However, the Third Circuit Court of Appeals affirmed a district court ruling that IDEA was not violated when an IEP was modified as a result of discussions that had taken place pursuant to a rejected IEP, even though the normal IEP revision process had not been followed.[75] The district court found that the modifications had been made in the spirit of compromise.

## Noncustodial Parents

In today's world many students do not live with both parents. The parental rights granted by IDEA also apply to parents who do not have custody of the child due to divorce. One court has ruled that a divorced parent's right to be involved in the child's education was basic unless a restraining order indicated otherwise.[76] The mother in this situation had legal custody but the father had financial responsibility for the child. The school district held several meetings with the mother to develop an IEP but the father was never invited to attend any of those meetings. The father later rejected the IEP the mother had accepted and requested a due process hearing. A hearing officer rejected the father's claim reasoning that a noncustodial parent was not authorized to accept or reject an IEP. However, the district court held that a noncustodial parent had standing and that the school district could not rely solely on the mother's acceptance of the IEP since the father had not been notified of the IEP meetings.

## Adult Students

Many students continue to receive special education services after their eighteenth birthday. Although these students assume rights of their own on reaching the age of majority, their parents do not lose their own rights under IDEA just because the students have reached this milestone. The Second Circuit Court of Appeals held that the procedural safeguards of IDEA apply to students between the ages of 18 and 21 even if they have not been determined to be incompetent.[77] In this case special education services for a 20-year-old student had been terminated, with the student's consent, but without the parent being notified of the contemplated change. The court held that the termination of services without parental notification violated IDEA.

## Privacy Rights

IDEA's regulations prohibit a school district from disclosing any personally identifiable information about a student with disabilities[78] and require school boards to protect the confidentiality of personally identifiable information.[79] One court held that a school district violated the parents' privacy rights when it released the names of the student and his parents to a local newspaper after a due process hearing.[80] The Eighth Circuit Court of Appeals has held that court proceedings brought pursuant to IDEA can be closed to the public to protect the privacy of the student.[81]

## CHANGE IN PLACEMENT

Once a student with disabilities has been placed in a program, that placement may not be changed unless the student's parents have been notified in writing of the planned action and have been given the opportunity to contest the proposed change in placement.[82] IDEA further provides that while any administrative hearings or judicial proceedings are pending, the student shall remain in his or her "then current placement" unless the parents and school district agree otherwise.[83] This particular section of the law has become known as the *status quo* or *stay put* provision and has been the subject of much litigation.

## Then Current Placement

Generally, the placement the student was in at the time the action in question arose would be considered to be the then current placement. One court defined the then current placement as the operative placement actually functioning at the time the dispute first arises.[84] The court made it clear that a proposed placement that had never been implemented did not qualify as the status quo.

Sometimes a school district may make a placement with the intent that it is to be a temporary placement only. If that is the case, the school district is obliged to make its intentions very clear or the courts will consider the placement to be the then current placement. Several cases involving the District of Columbia public schools illustrate this point. In one case an IEP was developed by the private facility a student had been attending calling for a transfer to a residential school. The school district agreed to the new placement, but one year later notified the student's parents that it saw no need for continued placement there and it would no longer assume financial responsibility for the placement. The district court held that the residential school was the student's then current placement since the school district had assumed responsibility for it and had given no indication at the time that it intended to do so for one year only.[85] In a separate case the same court held that any limitation on a placement must be spelled out clearly and described in a settlement agreement.[86] The student in this case had been placed by mutual consent of the school district and parents in a private school pending resolution of a placement dispute. The school district argued that the private school was an interim placement only, but the court held that it was the then current placement since its interim status had not been articulated clearly. In another case, the appeals court held that a private school placement ceased to be the then current placement at the end of the school year since a hearing officer's order indicated clearly that the placement was to be for one year only.[87] A New York court also held that a private school placement that a hearing officer had ordered a school district to fund for one year only was not the then current placement.[88]

A unilateral placement made by parents can be the then current placement if the school district failed to propose an appropriate program in a timely fashion. The district court for the District of Columbia held that since the school district had not proposed a program by the deadline established by a hearing officer, the parents were justified in placing the student in a private school and it thus became his current educational placement.[89]

If a parent unilaterally removes a student from a program, that program does not cease to become the then current placement. The Eighth Circuit Court of Appeals held that the public school placement a student had been attending when his parents removed him from the school was the status quo.[90] The parents had enrolled the student in another school district but one month later he was re-enrolled in his former district. The student's mother tried to re-enroll him as a regular education student rather than a special education student but the court held that a one month term as a regular education student in another school district did not negate his special education history. Similarly, an Illinois district court held that the stay put provision does not apply to students who are unilaterally placed in private schools by their parents.[91]

## Placement Pending Appeals

The First Circuit Court of Appeals held that Congress did not intend to freeze an arguably inappropriate placement for the length of time it takes for review proceedings to culminate.[92] The question then arises as to when parents or a school district would be entitled to change a placement based on the decision of a hearing officer or judge. Some judges feel that a change in placement can occur once an administrative hearing decision is issued, even if that decision is appealed. The Ninth Circuit Court of Appeals held that once a state educational agency decided that a parents' chosen placement was correct, it became the then current placement under IDEA and the school district was required to maintain that placement pending court review.[93] The District Court in Massachusetts held that if a state agency, such as the Bureau of Special Education Appeals, and the student's parent agreed on a placement, the school district's approval was not required to make a change in placement.[94] Similarly, a New York federal court held that a school board was not relieved of its obligation to fund an alternative school placement until final administrative review procedures had been completed.[95] The court held, however, that the school board was financially responsible only until the date the final decision was handed down and not until the end of the school year.

IDEA calls for agreement either by the state or local education agency and the parents to effectuate a change in placement during the pendency of any review proceedings. The U.S. Supreme Court, in dicta, stated that a state-level hearing decision in favor of the parents' chosen placement would seem to constitute agreement by the state to a change in placement.[96]

However, the District of Columbia Court of Appeals held that IDEA's status quo provision requires that a student's placement shall remain the same until all administrative hearings and trial court action has been completed.[97] The court ruled that IDEA did not entitle a student to remain in a private school at public expense pending review by an appeals court. In this case the hearing officer and the district court had found that IEPs offered by the school district were appropriate. The District of Columbia trial court held that the school district was required to fund a private school placement during the pendency of the parents' appeal of a hearing officer's decision.[98] The court further held that it would be inappropriate, insensitive, and indefensible for a court to order a change in placement one semester before a student completed his or her schooling and ordered the school district to fund the private school until the student's graduation, even though a hearing officer found that the school district's proposed change in placement was appropriate. Similarly, a New York court held that the status quo provision prohibited a school district from graduating a student during the pendency of administrative appeals.[99]

IDEA's status quo provision states that during the pendency of any appeals regarding a student who is applying for initial admission to a public school, the student is to be placed in the public school program until all appeals have been completed.[100] The law does not specify whether that placement should be in a general education classroom or a special education program. A New York district court held that Congress's goal could be satisfied by the provision of a public school placement, regardless of whether it was in special education or general education.[101] The parents of the student in this case preferred placement in a regular kindergarten class, but school officials had recommended a special class placement. The court found that the school district's recommendation would provide the student with a free appropriate public education.

Students who have not yet been placed by a school district are not protected by the status quo provision. An Illinois district court held that IDEA's status quo provision did not apply to a student who was unilaterally placed by his parents before the school district had the opportunity to educate the student.[102] The court stated that the status quo provision was designed to prevent interruptions in a student's program but was not intended to protect a student who had not yet been placed by the state.

## Change in Program Location

The courts have held that the general rule of IDEA is that the term *change in placement* refers to changes that affect the form of educational instruction provided, not the location where that instruction takes place. For various reasons, such as school closings, school districts may be required to move a special education program from one building to another. Courts have held that such transfers of entire classes or programs do not constitute a change in placement that would trigger IDEA's due process procedures.[103]

However, when a program is moved from one location to another, the program must remain substantially the same. The elimination of a major component of the program would be sufficient cause to trigger IDEA's due process mechanism. For example, a federal district court in New York held that the elimination of the summer component of what had been a year-round residential program was of such critical magnitude that it constituted a change in placement.[104] Similarly, a district court in Pennsylvania nullified the proposed transfer of two students from one program to another that would involve a change in the method of instruction.[105] The court noted that once a student was making progress in a program any change must be considered with caution.

Even when a transfer involves moving a single student, it may not be considered a change in placement if the new program is almost identical to the former program. The appeals court for the District of Columbia held that at a minimum a student must show that a fundamental change in or an elimination of a basic element of the education program took place for a change in placement to have occurred.[106] The Fifth Circuit Court of Appeals held that a transfer from one school building to another did not constitute a change in placement since the student's IEP was fully implemented following the transfer.[107] Failure to implement the IEP completely following a change of location would constitute a change in placement. The District of Columbia Court of Appeals held that the school district violated IDEA's change in placement provisions when it failed to notify a student's surrogate parent that the student's educational program had been curtailed for medical reasons.[108] Due to the student's medical condition he could no longer be transported to his special education program, but no attempt was made to provide alternate services.

## Graduation Is a Change in Placement

As indicated previously, major changes to a student's IEP would be considered a change in placement. Courts have held that a student's graduation is a change in placement since it terminates all educational services. The Supreme Judicial Court of Massachusetts held that the failure to provide parents with formal written notice of a decision to graduate a student violated IDEA and state law.[109] Using a similar reasoning a district court in New York stated that graduation was analogous to an expulsion since it resulted in the total exclusion of the student from the educational placement.[110]

## Adjustments to an IEP

Although the general rule is that changes to an IEP would constitute a change in placement, minor adjustments are allowable. The Third Circuit Court of Appeals held that the important element in determining whether a change in placement has occurred is whether the change is likely to affect the student's learning in some significant way.[111] In this case the court found that a minor change in the student's transportation arrangements was not a change in placement but warned that under some circumstances transportation could have an effect on the child's learning. The district court in Massachusetts echoed the Third Circuit's criteria that a child's learning experience must be affected in some significant way in determining that an adjustment to an IEP that was more superficial than substantive was not a change in placement.[112]

## Services Not in the IEP

School districts sometimes provide a student with disabilities with auxiliary services that are not specified in the student's IEP. If the service is not being provided under the terms of the IEP it can be changed without providing the due process safeguards called for by IDEA. The Ninth Circuit Court of Appeals ruled that a tutoring program that was not provided under an IEP was not a special education service and, thus, a change in tutors was not a change in placement.[113] Ironically, the tutoring was provided after the student's parents rejected the school district's offer to provide special education services. Similarly, the Sixth Circuit Court of Appeals held that a school district did not violate IDEA's stay put provision when it refused to maintain a student in an extended school year program that had never been included in the child's IEP.[114]

IDEA's change in placement procedures do not apply to placements that are not made pursuant to IDEA. For example, if a residential placement was made by a state agency for social purposes, IDEA's change in placement requirements could not be invoked if that agency attempted to transfer the student to another facility or otherwise remove the student from the residential facility.[115] IDEA's change in placement procedures are applicable only to services called for in an IEP. Similarly, IDEA's change in placement provision may not be invoked by a service provider in license revocation proceedings.[116]

## Programs that Are No Longer Appropriate

A special problem regarding IDEA's status quo provision exists when it is no longer appropriate for a student to remain in the program he or she has been attending. This may occur for a variety of reasons: the program may lose its state approval, it may be found to be lacking in quality, or the program may no longer be able to serve the student. Generally, in this situation the courts will approve a placement in a similar facility. Once again, the key element is that the new facility must be able to implement the student's IEP fully to pass muster under the status quo provision. Several key court decisions illustrate this point.

A district court in New York held that the transfer of several students from a private school that had been found to be lacking to alternate facilities was not a change in placement.[117] The school board had terminated its contract with the private school after an audit had disclosed several problems including mismanagement of funds and serious educational deficiencies. However, the Second Circuit Court of Appeals held that a placement in a facility that had lost state approval must be maintained until an appropriate alternative could be found.[118]

The Sixth Circuit Court of Appeals held that the transfer of several students from a treatment facility that closed due to budgetary constraints to dissimilar alternate facilities was a change in placement.[119] However, the court held that since the closing occurred for financial reasons IDEA's procedural safeguards did not apply. The students could, however, contest their new placements through IDEA's administrative hearing process. In another case where the private school a student had been attending closed, the district court for the District of Columbia upheld a hearing officer's order that the school district fund a placement at another private school.[120] When the school closed, the school district offered a public school placement but failed to execute a complete IEP. When no IEP had been presented to them by the start of the next school year, the parents unilaterally enrolled the student in another private school.

In two separate cases the appeals court for the District of Columbia held that when a private school determines that it can no longer serve a student, the school district is obligated to locate and fund a similar program.[121] In one of those rulings where the private school placement was no longer available, the court allowed the school district to make an interim placement in a public school program that was not inherently dissimilar until a final placement decision had been made.[122]

## Placements Must Be Reviewed Annually

IDEA requires school districts to review special education placements at least annually.[123] For that reason hearing officers and courts cannot order a school district to maintain a given placement for longer than one year. Of course, each year's IEP is subject to IDEA's due process requirements. The district court for the District of Columbia denied a parental request that the school district be prohibited from changing a private school placement for two years, stating that the school district must be free to determine that the private school was no longer appropriate during that time frame.[124]

## Parental Placement Changes

Although the school district is prohibited from changing a student's placement during the pendency of any due process procedures initiated under IDEA, the parents are always free to exercise their traditional authority over their child and make a placement change to a private school. If they do so, however, it is at their own financial risk. Unless their choice of programs is eventually determined to be the appropriate placement for the child, the parents must bear the costs of the private placement. This issue is discussed at greater length in Chapter 8.

## Placement Changes for Disciplinary Reasons

A comment to IDEA's regulations states that the status quo provision does not preclude the school district from using its normal procedures to deal with special education students who present a danger to themselves or others.[125] However, the courts have placed limitations on the authority of school officials to administer disciplinary sanctions that would permanently exclude students with disabilities from their special education programs. This is discussed at greater length in Chapter 7.

## SUMMARY

IDEA and its implementing regulations provide students with disabilities and their parents with specific procedural rights. Those rights were included in the statute because Congress intended parents to be equal partners in the development of appropriate educational programs for their children. Prior to the implementation of IDEA, school officials made decisions about students with disabilities with little or no input from their parents. Parents also had little recourse if they did not agree with those decisions. The U.S. Supreme Court has stated that Congress, when it passed IDEA, was well aware that school districts had all too often denied students with disabilities an appropriate education without consulting their parents. To remedy that situation Congress emphasized the importance and necessity of parental participation throughout the statute.[126]

 IDEA provides specific safeguards throughout the process from the identification stage through final placement. Once placed, a student's program cannot be substantially altered unless IDEA's safeguards are again implemented. Students are entitled to a fair assessment of their disabilities, and parents are guaranteed input into the evaluation and placement process. Under IDEA school district personnel may not make unilateral decisions regarding the child.

The status quo provision of IDEA, which states that a student's placement may not be altered while a placement decision is being contested, has generated significant litigation. The entire dispute resolution process can take years before a final settlement is obtained. It is safe to say that Congress did not intend for a student to remain in what could be an inappropriate placement for several years while the parents and school district battled it out in court. However, it is not clear as to exactly at what point in the process either party may make a change in placement. Most courts have held that a change in placement can occur after a final administrative decision has been issued; however, one court indicated that the change cannot take place until a trial court has made a placement determination. Of course, a placement can be changed at any time if the parents and school district agree to it. Also, a placement change can be implemented at any stage in the appeals process if the losing party decides not to appeal. Courts may use their traditional powers of equity to determine an interim placement pending appeals.

Failure to provide parents with the rights enumerated in the law and its regulations will compromise the school district's position during litigation. Courts have scrupulously enforced IDEA's procedural protections by rendering proposed IEPs invalid that were not developed in accordance with proper legal procedure. However, the courts have not gone overboard in this regard. Judges recognize the intricate nature of IDEA and have allowed minor transgressions to pass if they did not effectively prevent parental participation in the development of the student's IEP.

The school district's intent may be an important consideration in a court's determination of whether an error is sufficient to invalidate an IEP. If the school personnel proceed in good faith, afford parents a genuine opportunity to participate in the development of the IEP, and do not intentionally seek to thwart parental participation, the courts generally will not reprimand them for an occasional error. However, egregious procedural errors will be costly.[127]

## ENDNOTES

1. 20 U.S.C. § 1400 et seq.
2. IDEA's due process procedures can be found at 20 U.S.C. § 1415.
3. 20 U.S.C. § 1414(a)(5).

4. 34 C.F.R. § 300.345.
5. 34 C.F.R. § 300.504(b).
6. 20 U.S.C. § 1415(b)(1)(C).
7. *Board of Education of the Hendrick Hudson Central School District v. Rowley,* 458 U.S. 176, 102 S. Ct. 3034, 73 L. Ed.2d 690, 5 Ed.Law Rep. 34 (1982).
8. 20 U.S.C. § 1412(2)(C).
9. 20 U.S.C. § 1412(5)(C).
10. *Id.*
11. *Id.*
12. 34 C.F.R. § 300.532(e).
13. 34 C.F.R. § 300.531.
14. 34 C.F.R. § 300.532(3).
15. 34 C.F.R. § 300.532(2).
16. 34 C.F.R. § 300.534.
17. 34 C.F.R. § 300.503.
18. *Bonadonna v. Cooperman,* 619 F. Supp. 401, 28 Ed.Law Rep. 430 (D.N.J. 1985).
19. *Gerstmyer v. Howard County Public Schools,* 850 F. Supp. 361, 91 Ed.Law Rep. 569 (D. Md. 1994).
20. *Lora v. Board of Education of the City of New York,* 456 F. Supp. 1211 (E.D.N.Y. 1978), *aff'd in part* 623 F.2d 248 (2d Cir. 1980), *final order* 587 F. Supp. 1572, 19 Ed.Law Rep. 133 (E.D.N.Y. 1984).
21. *G.D. v. Westmoreland School District,* 930 F.2d 942, 67 Ed.Law Rep. 103 (1st Cir. 1991).
22. *T.S. v. Ridgefield Board of Education,* 808 F. Supp. 926, 80 Ed.Law Rep. 115 (D. Conn. 1992), *aff'd sub nom. T.S. v. Board of Education of the Town of Ridgefield,* 10 F.3d 87, 87 Ed.Law Rep. 386 (2d Cir. 1993).
23. *Lenhoff v. Farmington Public Schools,* 680 F. Supp. 921, 45 Ed.Law Rep. 1093 (E.D. Mich. 1988).
24. *Andress v. Cleveland ISD,* 832 F. Supp. 1086, 86 Ed.Law Rep. 773 (E.D. Tex. 1993).
25. 20 U.S.C. § 1401(a)(20).
26. 34 C.F.R. § 300.342.
27. 34 C.F.R. § 300.344.
28. 34 C.F.R. § 300.343(c).
29. 34 C.F.R. § 300.345.
30. 34 C.F.R. § 300.345(e). *See also Rothschild v. Grottenthaler,* 907 F.2d 286, 61 Ed.Law Rep. 490 (2d Cir. 1990).
31. 34 C.F.R. § 300.349.
32. *Chris D. v. Montgomery County Board of Education,* 753 F. Supp. 922, 65 Ed.Law Rep. 355 (M.D. Ala. 1990).
33. *Gerstmyer v. Howard County Public Schools,* 850 F. Supp. 361, 91 Ed.Law Rep. 569 (D. Md. 1994).
34. *W.G. and B.G. v. Board of Trustees of Target Range School District No. 23, Missoula, Montana,* 789 F. Supp. 1070, 75 Ed.Law Rep. 254 (D. Mont. 1991), *aff'd* 960 F.2d 1479 (9th Cir. 1992).
35. *Smith v. Henson,* 786 F. Supp. 43, 73 Ed.Law Rep. 951 (D.D.C. 1992).

36. *Big Beaver Falls Area School District* v. *Jackson,* 615 A.2d 910, 78 Ed.Law Rep. 888 (Pa. Commw. Ct. 1992).
37. *Doe* v. *Defendant I,* 898 F.2d 1186, 59 Ed.Law Rep. 619 (6th Cir. 1990).
38. *French* v. *Omaha Public Schools,* 766 F. Supp. 765, 68 Ed.Law Rep. 638 (D. Neb. 1991).
39. *Russell* v. *Jefferson,* 609 F. Supp. 605, 25 Ed.Law Rep. 769 (N.D. Cal. 1985).
40. *Spielberg* v. *Henrico County Public Schools,* 853 F.2d 256, 48 Ed.Law Rep. 352 (4th Cir. 1988).
41. *P.J.* v. *State of Connecticut Board of Education,* 788 F. Supp. 673, 74 Ed.Law Rep. 1117 (D. Conn. 1992).
42. *G.D.* v. *Westmoreland School District,* 930 F.2d 942, 67 Ed.Law Rep. 103 (1st Cir. 1991).
43. *Scituate School Committee* v. *Robert B.,* 620 F. Supp. 1224, 28 Ed.Law Rep. 793 (D.R.I. 1985), *aff'd without pub. opinion* 795 F.2d 77 (1st Cir. 1986).
44. *Hampton School District* v. *Dobrowolski,* 976 F.2d 48, 77 Ed.Law Rep. 1109 (1st Cir. 1992).
45. *Fuhrmann* v. *East Hanover Board of Education,* 993 F.2d 1031, 83 Ed.Law Rep. 71 (3d Cir. 1993).
46. *Doyle* v. *Arlington County School Board,* 806 F. Supp. 1253, 79 Ed.Law Rep. 498 (E.D. Va. 1992).
47. *Myles S.* v. *Montgomery County Board of Education,* 824 F. Supp. 1549, 84 Ed.Law Rep. 264 (M.D. Ala. 1993).
48. *Gerstmyer* v. *Howard County Public Schools,* 850 F. Supp. 361, 91 Ed.Law Rep. 569 (D. Md. 1994).
49. 34 C.F.R. § 300.343.
50. *Edwards-White* v. *District of Columbia,* 785 F. Supp. 1022, 73 Ed.Law Rep. 943 (D.D.C. 1992).
51. *Amann* v. *Stow School System,* 982 F.2d 644, 80 Ed.Law Rep. 42 (1st Cir. 1992).
52. 20 U.S.C. § 1414.
53. 34 C.F.R. § 300.345.
54. 20 U.S.C. § 1415.
55. Osborne, A. G. (1993). Parental rights under the IDEA. *Education Law Reporter, 80,* 771–777.
56. 34 C.F.R. § 300.505(a)(1).
57. *Kroot* v. *District of Columbia,* 800 F. Supp. 977, 78 Ed.Law Rep. 324 (D.D.C. 1992).
58. 34 C.F.R. § 300.505.
59. *Max M.* v. *Thompson,* 566 F. Supp. 1330, 12 Ed.Law Rep. 761 (N.D. Ill. 1983).
60. *Hall* v. *Vance County Board of Education,* 774 F.2d 629, 27 Ed.Law Rep. 1107 (4th Cir. 1985).
61. *Smith* v. *Squillacote,* 800 F. Supp. 993, 78 Ed.Law Rep. 65 (D.D.C. 1992).
62. *Smith* v. *Henson,* 786 F. Supp. 43, 73 Ed.Law Rep. 951 (D.D.C. 1992).
63. *Board of Education of the County of Caball* v. *Dienelt,* 843 F.2d 813, 46 Ed.Law Rep. 64 (4th Cir. 1988).
64. *Thomas* v. *Cincinnati Board of Education,* 918 F.2d 618, 64 Ed.Law Rep. 43 (6th Cir. 1990).

65. *Hiller v. Board of Education of Brunswick Central School District*, 743 F. Supp. 958, 62 Ed.Law Rep. 974 (N.D.N.Y. 1990).

66. *Doe v. Alabama State Department of Education*, 915 F.2d 651, 63 Ed.Law Rep. 40 (11th Cir. 1990). *See also Myles S. v. Montgomery County Board of Education*, 824 F. Supp. 1549, 84 Ed.Law Rep. 264 (M.D. Ala. 1993).

67. 34 C.F.R. § 300.345.

68. 34 C.F.R. § 300.345(e). The Second Circuit Court of Appeals has held that school districts must provide sign-language interpreters so that hearing impaired parents can participate in meetings and conferences that are important to their child's education. Although the children in this situation were not receiving special education services, and the case was decided under section 504 of the Rehabilitation Act, 29 U.S.C. § 794, the legal principles are applicable for IEP meetings. *Rothschild v. Grottenthaler*, 907 F.2d 286, 61 Ed.Law Rep. 490 (2d Cir. 1990).

69. *E.H. and H.H. v. Tirozzi*, 735 F. Supp. 53, 60 Ed.Law Rep. 478 (D. Conn. 1990).

70. *V.W. and R.W. v. Favolise*, 131 F.R.D. 654, 62 Ed.Law Rep. 618 (D. Conn. 1990).

71. *Caroline T. v. Hudson School District*, 915 F.2d 752, 63 Ed.Law Rep. 56 (1st Cir. 1990).

72. *Cordrey v. Euckert*, 917 F.2d 1460, 63 Ed.Law Rep. 798 (6th Cir. 1990).

73. 20 U.S.C. § 1415 and 34 C.F.R. § 300.504.

74. *Abney v. District of Columbia*, 849 F.2d 1491, 47 Ed.Law Rep. 460 (D.C. Cir. 1988).

75. *Fuhrmann v. East Hanover Board of Education*, 993 F.2d 1031, 83 Ed.Law Rep. 71 (3d Cir. 1993).

76. *Doe v. Anrig*, 651 F. Supp. 424, 37 Ed.Law Rep. 511 (D. Mass. 1987).

77. *Mrs. C. v. Wheaton*, 916 F.2d 69, 63 Ed.Law Rep. 93 (2d Cir. 1990).

78. 34 C.F.R. § 300.571.

79. 34 C.F.R. § 300.572.

80. *Sean R. v. Board of Education of the Town of Woodbridge*, 794 F. Supp. 467, 76 Ed.Law Rep. 785 (D. Conn. 1992).

81. *Webster Groves School District v. Pulitzer Publishing Co.*, 898 F.2d 1371, 59 Ed.Law Rep. 630 (8th Cir. 1990).

82. 34 C.F.R. § 300.504.

83. 20 U.S.C. § 1415(e)(3).

84. *Thomas v. Cincinnati Board of Education*, 918 F.2d 618, 64 Ed.Law Rep. 43 (6th Cir. 1990).

85. *Jacobson v. District of Columbia Board of Education*, 564 F. Supp. 166, 11 Ed.Law Rep. 885 (D.D.C. 1983).

86. *Saleh v. District of Columbia*, 660 F. Supp. 212, 40 Ed.Law Rep. 157 (D.D.C. 1987).

87. *Leonard v. McKenzie*, 869 F.2d 1558, 52 Ed.Law Rep. 498 (D.C. Cir. 1989).

88. *Zvi D. v. Ambach*, 520 F. Supp. 196 (E.D.N.Y. 1981), *aff'd* 694 F.2d 904, 8 Ed.Law Rep. 10 (2d Cir. 1982).

89. *Cochran v. District of Columbia*, 660 F. Supp. 314, 40 Ed.Law Rep. 161 (D.D.C. 1987).

90. *Digre* v. *Roseville Schools Independent School District No. 623,* 841 F.2d 245, 45 Ed.Law Rep. 523 (8th Cir. 1988).
91. *Joshua B.* v. *New Trier Township High School District 203,* 770 F. Supp. 431, 69 Ed.Law Rep. 797 (N.D. Ill. 1991).
92. *Doe* v. *Brookline School Committee,* 722 F.2d 910, 15 Ed.Law Rep. 72 (1st Cir. 1983).
93. *Clovis Unified School District* v. *California Office of Administrative Hearings,* 903 F.2d 635, 60 Ed.Law Rep. 728 (9th Cir. 1990).
94. *Grace B.* v. *Lexington School Committee,* 762 F. Supp. 416, 67 Ed.Law Rep. 660 (D. Mass. 1991).
95. *Board of Education of the City of New York* v. *Ambach,* 612 F. Supp. 230, 26 Ed.Law Rep. 622 (E.D.N.Y. 1985).
96. *Burlington School Committee* v. *Department of Education of the Commonwealth of Massachusetts,* 471 U.S. 359, 105 S. Ct. 1996, 85 L. Ed.2d 385, 23 Ed.Law Rep. 1189 (1985).
97. *Anderson* v. *District of Columbia,* 877 F.2d 1018, 54 Ed.Law Rep. 784 (D.C. Cir. 1989).
98. *Holmes* v. *District of Columbia,* 680 F. Supp. 40, 45 Ed.Law Rep. 688 (D.D.C. 1988).
99. *Cronin* v. *Board of Education of East Ramapo Central School District,* 689 F. Supp. 197, 48 Ed.Law Rep. 461 (S.D.N.Y. 1988).
100. 20 U.S.C. § 1415(e)(3).
101. *Logsdon* v. *Board of Education of the Pavilion Central School District,* 765 F. Supp. 66, 68 Ed.Law Rep. 346 (W.D.N.Y. 1991).
102. *Joshua B.* v. *New Trier Township High School District 203,* 770 F. Supp. 431, 69 Ed.Law Rep. 797 (N.D. Ill. 1991).
103. *Brown* v. *District of Columbia Board of Education,* EHLR 551:101 (D.D.C. 1978); *Concerned Parents and Citizens for the Continuing Education at Malcolm X.* v. *New York City Board of Education,* 629 F.2d 751 (2d Cir. 1980); *Middlebrook* v. *School District of the County of Knox, Tennessee,* 805 F. Supp. 534, 79 Ed.Law Rep. 85 (E.D. Tenn. 1991).
104. *Gebhardt* v. *Ambach,* EHLR 554:130 (W.D.N.Y. 1982).
105. *Visco* v. *School District of Pittsburgh,* 684 F. Supp. 1310, 47 Ed.Law Rep. 142 (W.D. Pa. 1988).
106. *Lunceford* v. *District of Columbia Board of Education,* 745 F.2d 1577, 20 Ed.Law Rep. 1075 (D.C. Cir. 1984).
107. *Weil* v. *Board of Elementary and Secondary Education,* 931 F.2d 1069, 67 Ed.Law Rep. 482 (5th Cir. 1991). *See also Sherri A.D.* v. *Kirby,* 975 F.2d 193, 77 Ed.Law Rep. 665 (5th Cir. 1992) where the court approved a magistrate judge's transfer of a student from one location to another but did not alter the IEP.
108. *Abney* v. *District of Columbia,* 849 F.2d 1491, 47 Ed.Law Rep. 460 (D.C. Cir. 1988).
109. *Stock* v. *Massachusetts Hospital School,* 467 N.E.2d 448, 19 Ed.Law Rep. 637 (Mass. 1984).
110. *Cronin* v. *Board of Education of East Ramapo Central School District,* 689 F. Supp. 197, 48 Ed.Law Rep. 461 (S.D.N.Y. 1988).
111. *DeLeon* v. *Susquehanna Community School District,* 747 F.2d 149, 21 Ed.Law Rep. 24 (3d Cir. 1984).

112. *Brookline School Committee* v. *Golden,* 628 F. Supp. 113, 30 Ed.Law Rep. 1156 (D. Mass. 1986).
113. *Gregory K.* v. *Longview School District,* 811 F.2d 1307, 37 Ed.Law Rep. 1104 (9th Cir. 1987).
114. *Cordrey* v. *Euckert,* 917 F.2d 1460, 63 Ed.Law Rep. 798 (6th Cir. 1990).
115. *Corbett* v. *Regional Center for the East Bay, Inc.,* 676 F. Supp. 964, 44 Ed.Law Rep. 222 (N.D. Cal. 1988).
116. *Corbett* v. *Regional Center for the East Bay, Inc.,* 699 F. Supp. 230, 50 Ed.Law Rep. 414 (N.D. Cal. 1988).
117. *Dima* v. *Macchiarola,* 513 F. Supp. 565 (E.D.N.Y. 1981). *Also see Cohen* v. *Board of Education of the City of New York,* 454 N.Y.S.2d 630, 6 Ed.Law Rep. 1048 (N.Y. Sup. Ct. 1982) for a similar decision.
118. *Vander Malle* v. *Ambach,* 673 F.2d 49, 3 Ed.Law Rep. 293 (2d Cir. 1982).
119. *Tilton* v. *Jefferson County Board of Education,* 705 F.2d 800, 10 Ed.Law Rep. 976 (6th Cir. 1983).
120. *Block* v. *District of Columbia,* 748 F. Supp. 891, 63 Ed.Law Rep. 876 (D.D.C. 1990).
121. *McKenzie* v. *Smith,* 771 F.2d 1527, 27 Ed.Law Rep. 465 (D.C. Cir. 1985); *Knight* v. *District of Columbia,* 877 F.2d 1025, 54 Ed.Law Rep. 791 (D.D.C. 1989).
122. *Id. Knight* v. *District of Columbia.*
123. 20 U.S.C. § 1414(a)(5) and 34 C.F.R. § 300.343(d).
124. *Kattan* v. *District of Columbia,* 691 F. Supp. 1539, 48 Ed.Law Rep. 1218 (D.D.C. 1988).
125. 34 C.F.R. § 300.513 Note.
126. *Honig* v. *Doe,* 484 U.S. 305, 108 S. Ct. 592, 98 L. Ed.2d 686, 43 Ed.Law Rep. 857 (1988).
127. School districts may be required to reimburse parents for the costs of unilaterally obtained services and their legal expenses if the courts determine that the school district failed to offer an appropriate education. See Chapter 8 for additional information on the remedies courts will order when it is found that a school district did not provide a free appropriate public education.

# 4

# COMPLAINT RESOLUTION

Although Congress envisioned school districts and parents working together to develop an appropriate educational program for students with disabilities, it recognized that agreements could not be reached in all situations. Therefore, Congress included provisions within the Individuals with Disabilities Education Act (IDEA)[1] for the resolution of any disputes that may arise regarding any aspect of the special education process.

If the parents of a student with disabilities disagree with any of the school district's actions regarding a proposed Individualized Education Program (IEP), or any aspect of the provision of a free appropriate public education, they may request an impartial due process hearing.[2] Any party not satisfied with the outcome of administrative hearings may appeal to the state or federal courts.[3] Prior to resorting to the courts, however, a litigant must exhaust all administrative remedies unless it clearly is futile to do so. As was discussed in the previous chapter, while administrative or judicial action is pending, the school district may not change the student's placement without parental consent[4] or a court order.[5]

IDEA empowers the courts to review the record of the administrative proceedings, hear additional evidence, and "grant such relief as the court determines is appropriate" based on the preponderance of the evidence standard.[6] However, the U.S. Supreme Court has cautioned judges not to substitute their views of proper educational methodology for that of competent school authorities.[7] No statute of limitations for filing a lawsuit under IDEA is contained within the act; therefore, courts must turn to applicable state statutes to determine whether or not a given lawsuit is timely.

# ADMINISTRATIVE DUE PROCESS HEARINGS

Parents have the right to request an administrative due process hearing on any matter concerning the provision of a free appropriate public education to their child, including the identification, evaluation, and educational placement of that child.[8] The hearing must be impartial and may be conducted by either the school district or the state educational agency.[9] Employees of the agency conducting the hearing, or any agencies involved with the education of the child, cannot serve as hearing officers.[10]

If the initial hearing is conducted by the school district or local educational agency, an appeal to a state-level review hearing must be provided.[11] Each state is free to establish either a one-tiered or two-tiered administrative due process mechanism. Procedures vary from state to state, but most states that have established a two-tiered system provide for a local-level hearing conducted by a single hearing officer or administrative law judge with an appeal to either a reviewing officer or reviewing panel. If a two-tiered system is established, both tiers cannot be at the state level.[12]

Any party involved in an administrative due process hearing has the right to be represented by counsel and advised by individuals who are experts in the education of children with disabilities.[13] The due process hearing is a quasi-judicial forum whereby the parties may present evidence, compel the attendance of witnesses, and cross-examine witnesses.[14]

## Issues Subject to a Hearing

IDEA's stipulation that a due process hearing can be requested on any matter relating to the provision of a free appropriate public education gives wide latitude as to the issues that are subject to a hearing. Basically, parents have the right to request a hearing if they disagree with any finding or recommendation made by the school district, feel that their rights have been violated, or are dissatisfied with the implementation of an IEP. State laws and regulations may provide parents with additional rights regarding the content and structure of a due process hearing.

Although hearing officers are given some discretion regarding the conduct of the hearing itself, they only may consider issues that have been raised by the parties. In a state-level appeal, only the issues that have been appealed may be considered by the reviewing officer. For example, a district court in New York held that a reviewing officer exceeded the scope of his authority by considering the issue of whether the student had a disability and reversing the hearing decision on that issue when it had not been raised on appeal.[15]

A hearing also may be requested on a school district's refusal to classify a student as disabled and provide special education services. The Ninth Circuit Court of Appeals held that even though a student was not identified by the school district as disabled, he could challenge that determination in an administrative hearing under IDEA.[16] The school district had claimed that the hearing officer lacked jurisdiction because the student was not a special education student.

Students still may request a hearing after their eligibility for special education services has ended since they may be entitled to compensatory educational services if it is found that they were denied a free appropriate public education. The Supreme Court of Ohio held that a student was entitled to a hearing even though the request for the hearing was submitted one day before the student's eligibility for special education services ended under state law.[17] The school district had objected to the hearing since the student was no longer eligible for services, but the court disagreed, reasoning that since it was possible to award compensatory services to students who had been denied an appropriate education, the student was entitled to the hearing.

## Impartiality

Those serving as hearing officers must be impartial. Naturally, persons who are involved in the student's education, who have a personal or professional interest in the student, or who are employees of the student's school district cannot serve as hearing officers.[18] IDEA further stipulates that hearing officers may not be employees of the state educational agency.[19] In states that have opted for a two-tiered due process mechanism, the appeal hearing also must be impartial.

Impartiality requires that anyone connected with the school district involved in the dispute may not serve as a hearing officer. However, a Michigan district court held that an attorney who represents school districts is not automatically biased to serve as a hearing officer in a dispute that does not involve a school district he or she had represented.[20] The fact that a school board may appoint and pay a hearing officer does not make that person an employee of the school district or an impartial person. A federal district court in New York has held that IDEA does not prohibit school districts from appointing or paying for hearing officers.[21]

Several states established a two-tiered administrative hearing process whereby the appeal was heard by the head of the state educational agency. Courts have held that this arrangement does not meet IDEA's impartiality requirements. A district court in New York has held that the Commissioner of Education, as a state employee, is not impartial.[22]

Similarly, the Third Circuit Court of Appeals has ruled that the Pennsylvania Secretary of Education is not impartial[23] and that employees of the Delaware Department of Public Instruction cannot serve as state level review officers.[24] A district court in Mississippi also held that a state review team comprised of officials from local school districts was not impartial.[25] However, a state court in New York has held that state review officers, appointed specifically for the purpose of reviewing hearing officers' decisions, are impartial even though they are subordinate to the Commissioner of Education.[26]

## Burden of Proof

IDEA and its regulations are silent as to which party bears the burden of proof in a special education administrative hearing. Thus, the determination of which party is to bear the burden of proof lies with state law or the discretion of the courts if state law also is silent. This is one area where the courts are in disagreement.

Several courts have held that the party attacking the terms of the IEP and the placement it calls for or the party seeking to change the student's educational placement bears the burden of proof.[27] In these decisions, the courts assign a presumption in favor of the IEP as long as it was developed according to the procedures outlined in IDEA. However, some courts have placed the burden of proof on the school district regardless of whether it or the parents sought to alter the IEP.[28] The reasoning behind this line of thinking is that the school district has the obligation to provide a free appropriate public education, is responsible for identifying students with disabilities and developing the IEP, is better able to meet the burden of proof, and has better access to relevant information and that parents lack the expertise to formulate an appropriate program.

## Authority of Hearing Officers

In an administrative due process hearing, the hearing officer's main tasks are to sort out the facts leading up to the controversy and apply the law to the factual situation. As such, the hearing officer's authority is similar to that of the judge in a court trial. Hearing officers are empowered to issue orders regarding the provision of a free appropriate public education. In general, the hearing officer has the same power as a judge to grant equitable relief.

However, there are limitations on the power of the hearing officer. Disputes that involve only questions of law are generally left to jurists. For example, hearing officers do not have the authority to rule on the constitutionality of a given statute. IDEA also reserves the awarding of attorney fees to a prevailing parent in a special education dispute to the discretion of the federal district court.[29]

There has been a question of whether hearing officers have the authority to grant awards of compensatory services to students who have been denied a free appropriate public education. The Third Circuit Court of Appeals held that the administrative process was powerless to address the issue of compensatory education.[30] However, the district court in New Hampshire held that a hearing officer's conclusion that he lacked the authority to grant an award of compensatory services was erroneous.[31] That court reasoned that given the importance Congress placed on the administrative process, a hearing officer's authority to grant relief was coextensive with that of the courts. Since hearing officers routinely grant awards of tuition reimbursement, it seems logical that they also would have the power to grant awards of compensatory educational services.[32]

Hearing officers may rule only on the issues that are presented to them. Similarly, a review officer may rule only on the issues that have been appealed. A New York court held that the Commissioner of Education exceeded the scope of his authority by considering the question of whether a student was disabled when the school district had not raised that issue on appeal.[33]

A state agency that does not receive funds under IDEA and is not charged with the responsibility of providing special education and related services under IDEA cannot be subjected to a due process hearing held pursuant to that act. A state court in New Jersey held that an administrative law judge did not have the authority to order a state agency to pay a portion of the costs associated with a special education placement.[34] The court ruled that under state law the obligation to provide a free appropriate public education was imposed exclusively on local boards of education.

## Exhaustion of Available Administrative Remedies

Prior to resorting to the courts, parties to a special education dispute first must exhaust all possible administrative remedies unless it clearly is futile to do so, an agency has adopted a policy or practice of general applicability that violates the law, it is impossible to obtain adequate relief through the administrative process, or the administrative process is powerless to address the issues involved in the dispute.[35] Basically, this means that a party may not bring a lawsuit to the courts until the matter has been brought before an administrative due process hearing and all administrative appeals have been pursued. When a lawsuit is brought before the court, issues that were not completely exhausted at the administrative level will not be entertained by the court.[36]

## Exhaustion Required

There are numerous cases in which the courts have refused to hear a case after determining that the party bringing the lawsuit simply had not first exhausted all available administrative remedies.[37] On some occasions courts have been asked to address unique situations to determine whether exhaustion was required.

Courts require exhaustion for a variety of reasons. Judges consider themselves to be generalists with no particular expertise in the educational needs of students with disabilities, whereas hearing officers are more experienced in fact-finding and have an expertise in these matters.[38] The administrative due process mechanism provides a system whereby knowledgeable professionals review special education placement decisions.[39]

Courts have held that administrative remedies under IDEA must be exhausted when parents are challenging the application of other laws or rules to students with disabilities along with their IDEA claims. The Sixth Circuit Court of Appeals ruled that IDEA's administrative procedures were adequate to provide parents who protested an athletic association's rule barring a transfer student from playing sports for one year the relief they sought.[40] The court also stated that the need for swift action could justify an exception to the exhaustion rule but not when the emergency was of the parents' own making by failing to request a hearing in a timely fashion. In another sports-related case, a state court in Texas held that the parents of students with disabilities who challenged the application of the state's "no pass, no play" rule were required to exhaust administrative remedies under IDEA.[41]

Most courts have held that class action suits are subject to the exhaustion requirements[42] and one court has held that all members of a class are required to exhaust their remedies prior to bringing suit.[43] However, other courts have held that filing several representative claims would serve the purposes of exhaustion.[44] Class actions generally challenge policies and procedures that have widespread application. The Tenth Circuit Court of Appeals stated that the issue of whether a state's policies had denied students with disabilities a free appropriate public education entailed a factually intensive inquiry into the circumstances of the students' cases, which was the type of issue the administrative process was designed to address.[45] One court, however, has held that plaintiffs representing a class are not required to exhaust administrative remedies because class action administrative hearings are not permitted.[46]

The exhaustion doctrine requires a litigant to exhaust all claims at the administrative level before raising them in court. In other words, a litigant cannot bring a claim at the court level that has not already been raised and acted on at the administrative level. The Second Circuit Court of Appeals held that a student could not raise the claim that the school district had committed procedural violations when he had not raised that issue at a due process hearing held to consider his request for compensatory educational services.[47] Similarly, a district court in New York held that parents could not raise the issue of the appropriateness of an evaluation facility at the court level when they had failed to appeal the hearing officer's decision regarding that issue to a state-level review officer.[48]

Exhaustion also is required when claims are made under other statutes in addition to IDEA,[49] when classroom procedures are being challenged,[50] or when enforcement of an administrative order is sought if state regulations provide for enforcement through the administrative process.[51]

### Exhaustion Not Required

The administrative process may be bypassed when the parents' complaint is that they have been denied access to that process. An Arizona district court held that exhaustion would be futile when a parent's claim was that she was denied meaningful access to IDEA's due process procedures.[52] Similarly, the Ninth Circuit Court of Appeals held that parents had no option except resorting to the courts after they were denied a requested due process hearing.[53]

Courts also have considered exhaustion to be futile when the hearing officer lacked authority to grant the relief sought. The Second Circuit Court of Appeals ruled that a parent's complaint regarding the method by which hearing officers were selected was not subject to the exhaustion requirement since the hearing officer lacked the authority to alter that procedure.[54] A district court in New York also held that exhaustion was not required when the requested relief was placement in a school that was not on the state's list of approved schools since the hearing officer was not permitted to order a placement at an unapproved facility.[55] Similarly, another New York court held that exhaustion was not required to challenge a decision of state education department officials who had considered the parents' request but declined to make an exception to general procedures.[56]

Hearing officers generally do not have the power to provide remedies when broad policies or procedures that affect a large number of students are challenged. The Ninth Circuit Court of Appeals held that a hearing officer lacked the authority to address the legislature's failure to appropriate sufficient funds for special education programs.[57] Similarly, a district court in Indiana held that a hearing officer did not have the authority to rule on the legality of a state-required application review process for students who required residential placements or to provide an appropriate remedy.[58] A district court in Florida held that exhaustion was not required in a case that alleged broad-scale misclassification on the basis of race.[59]

Since hearing officers do not have the authority to award attorney fees,[60] parents filing an attorney fees reimbursement petition are not required to exhaust administrative remedies.[61]

The exhaustion requirement compels parties to a dispute to exhaust all due process remedies. In a state that has established a two-tiered administrative procedure, appeals must be made to the second level before resorting to the courts. However, an appeal to the second level would not be required if it would be futile to do so. Futility may be established when it can be shown that the school district failed to respond appropriately to a hearing officer's previous order.[62]

In the previous section several cases were cited where it was held that class action lawsuits are subject to the exhaustion requirement. However, as with individual cases class action lawsuits may fall within the allowed exceptions to the exhaustion requirement. Exhaustion of administrative remedies may not be required in a class action lawsuit where the plaintiffs' claim is systemic in nature and the hearing officer would not have the authority to order relief. The Second Circuit Court of Appeals held that exhaustion was not required in a class action suit when the hearing officer could not order a system-wide change to correct the alleged wrongs.[63]

Since the time it takes to resolve a special education dispute often takes longer than the time period covered by the disputed IEP, a new IEP may be proposed before the dispute over the original IEP is resolved. The Fourth Circuit Court of Appeals has held that parents are not required to exhaust administrative remedies for the subsequent IEP in such a situation.[64]

Exhaustion also may not be necessary in an emergency situation if requiring it would cause severe or irreparable harm to the student. However, the Third Circuit Court of Appeals has stated that mere allegations of irreparable harm are not sufficient to excuse completion of the administrative process; hard evidence of irreparable harm must be presented.[65]

When the litigation involves issues that are purely legal rather than factual, exhaustion may not be required.[66] Exhaustion also may not be required if the state persistently fails to render expeditious decisions regarding a child's educational placement.[67]

In an interesting case a Tennessee district court held that the U.S. Attorney General was not required to exhaust administrative remedies prior to bringing a lawsuit in federal court against the state for alleged denial of a free appropriate public education to institutionalized persons.[68] The court held that the exhaustion requirement applied only to parents and school districts.

Courts also have held that exhaustion is not required when the students involved in the dispute do not require special education services.

For example, it has been held that parents do not need to exhaust administrative remedies under IDEA in a dispute involving discrimination under section 504 if the student is not receiving services under IDEA, even though the student may be disabled.[69]

## Hearing Rights

In addition to being represented by counsel, parties to a hearing have the right to present evidence, compel the attendance of witnesses, and cross-examine witnesses. Any information that is to be presented at a hearing must be disclosed to the other party at least five days prior to the hearing. In addition, the parties to a hearing have the right to obtain a verbatim record of the hearing and obtain written findings of fact and decisions.[70]

A district court in New Jersey held that an indigent parent who had proceeded *in forma pauperis* had the right to receive a written transcript of the administrative hearing at federal expense so that she could bring an appeal of the administrative decision.[71] The court indicated that a written transcript of the testimony and evidence presented at a lengthy and complex proceeding was an essential tool for the effective and efficient review of the administrative determination. However, the First Circuit Court of Appeals has held that the state could provide either a written transcript or an electronic record of the administrative hearings to indigent parents.[72]

IDEA stipulates that a hearing officer must render a final decision within 45 days of the request for a hearing.[73] Sometimes the parties to a hearing may request extensions or continuances. IDEA grants hearing officers the authority to grant such requests.[74] A district court in Texas ruled that parents who had requested an extension during a hearing did not waive their right to receive a final decision within 45 days but that the 45 day period would be extended for an amount of time equal to the length of the extension.[75]

IDEA states that a decision made in a hearing conducted under the act is final unless it is appealed.[76] It has been held that the finality requirement of IDEA precludes a hearing officer from taking any action that interferes with the rendering of a final decision. A district court in Delaware held that a hearing panel may not refer a case to some other body for review.[77] In this case a hearing panel had held that a student was entitled to a residential placement but did not specifically order such a placement. Instead the panel stated that a mechanism should be established to evaluate options. The court held that referring the case for further review did not comport with IDEA's finality requirements and undermined the concern for prompt resolution of placement decisions.

## COURT PROCEEDINGS

As was mentioned in the introduction to this chapter, IDEA provides for an appeal to the court systems of either the state or federal governments for any party involved in a special education dispute who is not satisfied with the final outcome of the administrative due process hearings. All actions in this regard would be civil actions and would proceed according to the rules of civil procedure established for the court's jurisdiction. Since an administrative proceedings record of the dispute would have been created, the courts generally do not conduct a trial *de novo;* that is, they do not repeat what has already occurred at the administrative level. Rather, the courts examine the administrative record and hear new or additional testimony when necessary but make an independent decision. Due to the importance Congress placed on the administrative process, courts are required to give due weight to those proceedings. A court will overturn the administrative decision only when it has determined that the decision was clearly erroneous.

### Burden of Proof

As in the administrative proceedings, courts must determine which party bears the burden of proof when the dispute reaches the court level. This issue has not been subject to unanimous thinking on the part of the courts, and thus, the burden of proof may be assigned differently in various jurisdictions.

Several courts have held that the party bringing the appeal to the court bears the burden of proof.[78] These courts generally stated the opinion that the administrative findings were entitled to some degree of deference, and therefore, the party seeking to overturn an administrative decision was required to show that it should be set aside.

Other courts have placed the burden of proof on the party challenging the IEP[79] or seeking to alter the current placement.[80] The courts that placed the burden of proof on the party seeking to overturn the IEP reasoned that IDEA creates a presumption in favor of the placement established by the IEP and thus the party attacking its terms should bear the burden of showing that it is inappropriate. Similarly, the courts that placed the burden on the party seeking to change the status quo did so after determining that Congress had placed an emphasis on maintaining the status quo when it passed IDEA.

A third line of reasoning places the burden of proof on the school district.[81] Courts following this line of reasoning have held that since the school district bears the ultimate responsibility for fashioning an appropriate education, it should bear the burden of proving that its proposal is appropriate. These courts also recognized the advantage school districts have as educational experts over parents in proceedings brought pursuant to IDEA. Recently, this line of reasoning has gained strength in lawsuits in which compliance with IDEA's least restrictive environment provision was the issue.[82]

Due to the fact that litigation may take more than one year, the IEP that is being challenged may have expired by the time a court renders a decision. In the meantime, subsequent IEPs have been developed and challenges to them may have been initiated. In that situation courts generally have held that the losing party in the dispute over the original IEP bears the burden of producing evidence and persuading the court of changing circumstances that would render the court's decision regarding the initial IEP inappropriate for the IEPs covering subsequent years.[83] In this situation the presumption is in favor of the placement ordered as a result of the first disputed IEP unless it can be shown that circumstances have changed.

The assignment of the burden of proof is important in terms of the school district's strategy when faced with litigation. When the burden is placed on the school district to show that its proposed IEP is appropriate, the school district is faced with a greater challenge than when a presumption is made in favor of that IEP.

## Deference Due School Authorities

Judges generally recognize that they are not experts on educational methodology. Combined with the warning provided by the U.S. Supreme Court that they should not substitute their judgment in educational matters for that of competent school authorities,[84] most judges prefer to defer to school officials on matters concerning appropriate methodology as long as all procedural requirements have been followed.

A district court in Indiana held that in determining whether an IEP was reasonably calculated to enable a student to receive educational benefits, the school district's assessment should be accorded substantial weight. The court noted that school district personnel had considerable experience teaching the student.[85]

The Fourth Circuit Court of Appeals held that the location where a particular service or method could feasibly be provided was an administrative determination that state and local school officials were far better qualified than the courts to make.[86] In this case the school board had offered a placement to a hearing-impaired student at a school located several miles from his home because an appropriate program was not available at the student's neighborhood school. The student's parents objected and demanded that an appropriate program be developed in the student's neighborhood school. After finding that the school district had complied with all of IDEA's procedures, the court approved its proposed IEP.

In a separate case that same court stated that neither a district court nor an appeals court should disturb an IEP simply because it disagreed with the content of the IEP.[87] The court further stated that courts should defer to educators as long as the IEP met IDEA's basic requirements. However, since school officials had not followed proper procedure in developing the IEP, the court held that the student had not been offered a free appropriate public education. In that particular situation the court held that no deference was due school officials.

The Eleventh Circuit Court of Appeals reversed a district court's decision after determining that the lower court had substituted its choice of educational methods for that of school officials.[88] The appeals court stated that the lower court had overstepped its authority in doing so.

## Deference Due Administrative Findings

The Supreme Court has stated that the fact that IDEA requires courts to receive the records of administrative due process hearings implies that due weight is to be given to those proceedings.[89] It is unclear exactly how much weight is due, however. The Court also stated that questions of methodology are for resolution by the states, which indicates that administrative findings should be deferred to on questions of methodology.

The First Circuit Court of Appeals stated that a trial court must make an independent ruling based on the preponderance of the evidence, but that the source of the evidence generally would be the administrative hearing record with some supplementation at trial.[90] The appeals court further indicated that the weight to be given to the administrative findings must be left to the discretion of the trial court; but considering the expertise of the administrative agency, the court must consider its findings carefully and endeavor to respond to the hearing officer's resolution of each material issue. In a separate decision, that same court stated that a trial court has not committed a legal error as long as it has not overlooked or misconstrued evidence and its overall decision is based on a supportable finding that the IEP was reasonably calculated to address the student's needs.[91]

A district court in California rejected the notion that courts had broad powers to overturn the decisions of hearing officers.[92] The court felt that IDEA's mandate for courts to base their decisions on the preponderance of the evidence standard was not an open invitation for them to substitute their views of sound educational policy for that of the school authorities they reviewed.

The Fourth Circuit Court of Appeals held that the court's decision is bounded by the administrative record and additional evidence but was independent by virtue of being based on the preponderance of the evidence before it.[93] The appeals court stated that courts have discretion to give the administrative findings proper weight, with the obligation to consider those findings carefully. However, the Fifth Circuit Court of Appeals has stated that a court is not required to defer to a hearing officer when its own review of the evidence indicates that the hearing officer erroneously assessed the facts or erroneously applied the law to the facts.[94]

The appeals court for the District of Columbia has stated that courts overturning the decision of a hearing officer must explain their basis for doing so.[95] The district court for that same jurisdiction ruled that a court may reverse a hearing officer's decision only when the court is satisfied that the school district has shown, by a preponderance of the evidence, that the hearing officer was wrong.[96] The district court in Massachusetts held that a hearing officer's decision must be accorded some deference; however, where that decision concerned an issue of law, it was not entitled to great deference.[97] Several other courts also have held that sufficient weight must be given to a hearing officer's decision.[98]

In a two-tiered administrative hearing scheme, deference is given to the final administrative decision.[99] Even if there is disagreement between the results of the local hearing and the state-level review decisions, deference is given to the final decision.[100] However, if the review procedure itself was flawed, then deference would be given to the initial hearing decision.[101] The Fourth Circuit Court of Appeals held that a reviewing officer should not have discredited a witness he had not seen or heard testify in the face of crediting by a hearing officer who heard the witness testify and, thus, no due weight should have been accorded the reviewing officer's decision.[102] However, on remand the district court considered the fact that all of the parents' witnesses had a record of testifying against the school district in determining the relative weight that should have been given the administrative findings.[103]

## Admission of Additional Evidence

IDEA states that courts shall hear additional evidence at the request of a party.[104] However, courts have placed limitations on the amount and kind of additional evidence they are willing to admit. Generally, evidence that could have been introduced in the administrative proceedings, but was not, is not accepted at the trial court level. However, evidence that is new or was not available at the time of the administrative hearing may be accepted. A question remains as to whether courts should admit evidence that results from events that occur after the disputed IEP was developed or after administrative hearings were concluded.

The First Circuit Court of Appeals held that a party seeking to admit additional evidence must provide some justification for doing so.[105] In this case the district court had refused to hear the testimony of witnesses for the parents who could have testified at the administrative level but whose testimony had deliberately been withheld by the parents' counsel. The appeals court ruled that the district court did not abuse its discretion by refusing to allow the witnesses to testify.

A party wishing to present additional evidence must make its intention to do so known clearly to the court. The Seventh Circuit Court of Appeals has stated that if neither party to a lawsuit makes known its intention to submit further evidence, a court is entitled to assume that the parties want the case decided on the basis of the administrative record.[106]

The Sixth Circuit Court of Appeals held that it was appropriate for a district court to have considered evidence that the hearing officer had failed to consider.[107] The court also stressed that the admission of this additional evidence did not undercut the administrative process. Similarly, the Fifth Circuit Court of Appeals held that a district court should give due weight to administrative findings but may take additional evidence and reach an independent decision based on the preponderance of the evidence.[108]

Due to the delay that often occurs between the time a placement decision is made and a court's review of that decision, additional evidence may be available to the court concerning how the student progressed in the disputed placement. It is not clear whether evidence that develops after a disputed placement has been made should be admitted. The Ninth Circuit Court of Appeals has held that a district court has the discretion to admit additional evidence concerning relevant events occurring after an administrative hearing.[109] Similarly, a district court in New York held that supplementing the record would bring the court up to date on the student's progress and give the court a complete picture of the student's academic standing.[110] That court felt that any relevant evidence that would assist the court in making a decision should be considered. However, the Third Circuit Court of Appeals has held that IEPs and placements should be judged from the perspective of the information that was available at the time the placement decision was made.[111] Although the Third Circuit Court recognized that events that occur after placement decisions are made may be relevant, it held that they cannot be substituted for the threshold determination of whether the IEP was reasonably calculated to confer an appropriate education. This decision indicates that courts should determine whether an IEP was appropriate at the time it was created.

## Mootness

Courts will not render a decision in a lawsuit unless it presents a live controversy. When a lawsuit does not present an actual controversy or the issues no longer exist, the case is said to be moot.[112] However, if the controversy that initiated the lawsuit is no longer alive, but is capable of repetition, a court will not declare the case moot. The U.S. Supreme Court has stated that courts may adjudicate ongoing controversies and has jurisdiction if there is a reasonable likelihood that the litigants will again suffer the deprivation of the rights that initiated the lawsuit.[113]

A district court in Indiana declared a case moot because the student involved had reached the maximum age to receive services under state law.[114] Since the student was no longer eligible for services, the court reasoned that she no longer had a claim under either state or federal law. The Fifth Circuit Court of Appeals declared a case moot after the school district made a commitment to provide the student with services.[115] Similarly, the district court in New Hampshire held that a case was moot where the student's circumstances had changed and the school district's position had changed and there was no reasonable expectation that the controversy would recur.[116] Once a student has been removed from the placement challenged in the lawsuit and has been placed in a new program the placement issue becomes moot.[117] Similarly, a lawsuit would become moot once the parties to it no longer had an interest in its outcome.[118]

The Supreme Court held that a lawsuit was not moot for a 20-year-old student who was still eligible to receive services under IDEA since there could be a reasonable expectation that he would once again be subjected to the deprivation of rights complained about in the litigation.[119] Other courts have held that lawsuits are not moot because the issues involved in them are capable of repetition (1) when the school year in question has ended,[120] (2) when the basic complaint still exists,[121] (3) when the IEP upon which the suit was brought is superseded by a new IEP,[122] and (4) when the student's parents enroll the student in a private school.[123] The appeals court for the District of Columbia Circuit even held that a lawsuit was not moot when the parents approved an IEP offered by the school district because the district's past failures to adhere to IDEA's requirements enhanced the probability that future violations would occur.[124]

## Confidentiality

IDEA includes specific language designed to protect the confidentiality of student records.[125] Courts frequently disguise the name of the student in the court records to protect the student's privacy and respect the confidentiality of the information admitted into evidence. The Eighth Circuit Court of Appeals, citing strong public policy favoring the protection of the privacy of minors where sensitive matters are concerned, held that court proceedings under IDEA may be closed to the public.[126] To safeguard student information and avoid stigmatizing the student, the court reasoned that it was appropriate to restrict access to the courtroom and case file. Similarly, the district court in Connecticut held that a parent's privacy rights were violated by a school district that released information pertaining to a due process hearing to a local newspaper.[127] The same principle would apply to information involved in a court proceeding.

## Exchange of Information

Contrary to the image portrayed in popular television shows depicting court battles, the counsel for both parties in an IDEA proceeding generally exchange information prior to the trial. Principles of fairness dictate that information that is crucial to one party's case cannot be withheld by the other party. The district court for the District of Columbia held that a school district can be required to provide parents with information concerning private schools, the qualifications of the teachers at those schools, and the disabilities of the students attending the schools, since this information was not privileged.[128] However, the court ruled that the school district was not required to provide information concerning due process hearings and lawsuits in which the district's placement decisions had been challenged as this information could be discovered by the parents' attorney through normal legal research.

## Res Judicata

Courts cannot hear a case or render a decision on a matter that has already been settled by a court of competent jurisdiction. The principle of res judicata, or a thing judged, indicates that a final judgment by a court of competent jurisdiction is conclusive and acts as an absolute bar to a subsequent action involving the same claim.[129] The Eleventh Circuit Court of Appeals, in a case that was appearing before the court for the second time, held that the district court's decision prior to the first appeal precluded further consideration of the issues under principles of res judicata.[131] The court had remanded the case after the first appeal[132] and on remand the district court indicated that its earlier order stood.

## Settlement Agreements

During the course of a dispute the parents and the school district frequently will negotiate a settlement agreement that effectively ends the controversy. A settlement agreement is sometimes reached as a result of a mediation process that occurs before administrative proceedings have begun. Settlement agreements also may be reached at any time during litigation. When a settlement agreement is negotiated during the course of litigation, the hearing officer or the court is then asked to approve the agreement to give it the full force of law. The hearing officer or court may void the agreement if it is deemed to be contrary to public policy or existing law.

The district court in New Jersey has held that a settlement agreement that was negotiated by the parents and school district during administrative proceedings did not bar action in the federal courts under IDEA.[132] The court stated that in spite of the settlement agreement the school district still had a duty under IDEA and state law to provide the student with a free appropriate public education. In a separate case that same court held that a settlement agreement reached through mediation formed a contract between the parties, but did not allow the school board to avoid its responsibilities under IDEA.[133] The court emphasized that there was a presumption that the services agreed to by the parties at the time the settlement agreement was entered met the student's special education needs and were in compliance with IDEA. However, the court stated that the parents did have the right to question the terms of the agreement if there was a change in circumstances.

The Eleventh Circuit Court of Appeals overturned a district court ruling that a settlement agreement was contrary to public policy due to its high cost.[134] The appeals court held that a settlement agreement may be voided as against public policy only if it directly contravened a state or federal statute or policy. Since the settlement in the case before it violated no statute or policy, the court held that it was not against public policy.

## STANDING TO SUE

In order to bring a lawsuit before the courts, the party bringing the suit must have a legitimate interest in the issues litigated. In order to sue, a party must be able to show a threatened injury or deprivation of rights secured by the legislation.

A district court in New York held that one school district lacked standing to sue another school district under IDEA.[135] The suit involved contracted services between two school districts for the placement of an autistic child. When the school district that operated the program the child was enrolled in determined that it could no longer provide the services, the child's home school district sued to require it to maintain the placement. The court ruled that one school district lacked standing to sue to prevent another school district from removing a student from one of its programs.

The Eleventh Circuit Court of Appeals held that school districts lacked standing to sue the state educational agency to compel it to provide special education services.[136] The court ruled that IDEA's procedures are set up to resolve disputes concerning a particular IEP and that nothing in the act indicates that a school district can sue the state to compel it to fulfill its statutory duties. However, a district court in Indiana held that local school districts had standing to sue the U.S. Department of Education concerning a policy letter issued by the Assistant Secretary for the Office of Special Education and Rehabilitative Services.[137] The court found that the school districts had stated a sufficient threatened injury regarding the interpretation of their obligations under IDEA that was not so speculative that it would defeat their standing to sue.

The Seventh Circuit Court of Appeals ruled that a nonprofit corporation that operated a licensed child care facility had standing to sue when it sought third party standing to advocate for the rights of students with disabilities who had been placed in its physical custody by either court order or state action.[138] The court held that the corporation had standing since the denial of the students' rights under IDEA would deprive it of money to which it otherwise would have been entitled. Furthermore, the court found that the corporation was a party aggrieved by the findings and decision of an administrative proceeding under IDEA.

Generally, parents of students with disabilities may sue on behalf of the students. The Second Circuit Court of Appeals held that the father of a student with disabilities had standing to sue regarding the methods by which hearing officers were selected.[139] The court held that parents have an enforceable right to impartial hearing officers and thus have standing to challenge how they are selected. Parents may lose their standing to sue if they no longer are the child's legal guardians. For example, the Fifth Circuit Court of Appeals held that under state law a child's managing conservator, not her father, had the authority to bring lawsuits on her behalf.[140]

In a lawsuit seeking reimbursement for the partial depletion of health insurance benefits that had been used to procure special education services, the Fourth Circuit Court of Appeals held that a student with disabilities had standing to sue.[141] The district court had held that the student lacked standing to sue since it had been her parents who suffered the injury. However, the appeals court reversed, holding that the use of her insurance benefits to pay for her special education diminished her resources because the policy capped the benefits available to her. In two separate cases a Pennsylvania district court held that an insurance company did not have standing to sue under IDEA.[142] The insurance company in each case had filed suit seeking to have the school district provide services that it had been paying for under health insurance policies. However, the court dismissed the lawsuits holding that only aggrieved parents or school districts had access to IDEA's due process mechanism.

IDEA states that any party aggrieved by the findings and decisions of administrative hearings may bring a lawsuit to the courts.[143] An aggrieved party generally is considered to be the losing party or a party who did not obtain the relief sought; the prevailing party in a hearing generally is not considered to be the aggrieved party. However, a district court in Delaware held that parents who had prevailed on the legal issues involved in a dispute, but had not obtained the relief they sought, were the aggrieved party and could appeal to the court.[144]

## STATUTE OF LIMITATIONS

IDEA does not specifically provide any statute of limitations for filing a lawsuit so one must be borrowed from analogous state law. Therefore, courts must turn to applicable state statutes to determine whether a given lawsuit is timely. Courts have imposed statutes of limitations as short as 30 days to as long as three years.

### Limitations Periods

Courts have held that a 30-day limitations period for the appeal of administrative decisions is applicable to IDEA lawsuits in Hawaii,[145] New Hampshire,[146] Indiana,[147] Massachusetts,[148] and the District of Columbia.[149] Several of these courts reasoned that a 30-day limitations period was consistent with the policies of IDEA in that it brought about a speedy resolution in a placement dispute and provided a resolution while a remedy was still available. Similarly, Connecticut has established a 45-day limitations period for state administrative appeals.[150]

However, other courts have indicated that a 30-day limitations period is not sufficient. A district court in Nebraska held that a 30-day period for judicial review of orders of the state commissioner of education would not fully effectuate the federal policies under IDEA, but failed to specifically designate a limitations period.[151] A district court in Illinois has determined that the 120-day limitations period for reviews of state administrative decisions regarding educational placements was applicable in a lawsuit over the appropriate placement for a student with disabilities.[152] Similarly, the Second Circuit Court of Appeals held that the four-month statute of limitations period for review of administrative decisions involving special education students under New York's state statutes was applicable to IDEA lawsuits.[153]

Several courts have held that the applicable statute of limitations in Virginia is the one-year period for personal actions.[154] Two-year limitations periods for tort claims in Texas[155] and for recovery of damages for injuries in Pennsylvania[156] were found to be applicable to IDEA claims. Each of these courts specifically rejected the contention that a 30-day period for review of administrative decisions was applicable, reasoning that 30 days was not a sufficient amount of time for preparing an appeal. Three-year limitations have been found to be applicable in Tennessee,[157] North Carolina,[158] and Michigan.[159]

The district court in New Jersey held that a lawsuit that was filed 71 days after an administrative hearing decision was rendered was not time-barred.[160] The court found that either a two-year or six-year statute of limitations could be borrowed from state law but did not need to decide which of the two was appropriate since the lawsuit was filed within the shorter time period. New Hampshire has passed legislation creating a 120-day statute of limitations for special education lawsuits.[161] However, the First Circuit Court of Appeals held that, in a lawsuit filed in New Hampshire seeking compensatory educational services, the most appropriate statute of limitations to borrow was the state's six-year general limitations period for personal actions.[162]

## Beginning of Limitations Period

Limitations periods generally would begin as soon as an unfavorable administrative decision is handed down. In two separate cases the district court in New Hampshire has held that the limitations period begins to run on the day the hearing decision is released, not the day the aggrieved party received it in the mail.[163] However, the Seventh Circuit Court of Appeals ruled that the statute of limitations for a lawsuit by a prevailing parent to recover attorney fees did not begin until the expiration of the time period the school district had to file an appeal of a hearing officer's decision.[164] The court held that the parent could not recover attorney fees until all administrative and judicial proceedings were finished and could not know that the school district would not appeal the administrative decision until the time to do so had passed. In lawsuits that did not necessarily involve an appeal of administrative decisions courts have held that the limitations period began to run on the day the student reached the age of majority,[165] reached the age in which eligibility for services ended,[166] or graduated.[167]

An Illinois decision indicates that a lawsuit filed beyond the statute of limitations would not be untimely if the parents were not aware of the limitations period and were not apprised of any deadline for filing an appeal of an administrative decision.[168] The court found that IDEA requires the state to fully inform parents of the procedural avenues available to them. Similarly, the federal district court in New Hampshire held that a lawsuit that was filed after the statute of limitations had expired was not time-barred since the hearing officer failed to inform the parents of the allotted time in which they could file an appeal.[169]

## Statute of Limitations Waivers

The Eleventh Circuit Court of Appeals held that since the school district had never raised the issue of a lawsuit being time-barred it waived its right to use the statute of limitations as an affirmative defense.[170] The First Circuit Court of Appeals held that a lawsuit that was filed after the limitations period had expired was not barred because the parents' delay in filing the lawsuit was not unreasonable.[171] During the time period in question the parents were attempting to resolve their differences with the school district. On remand the district court held that the lawsuit was not barred by the doctrine of laches[172] because the school district failed to show that witnesses were unavailable or had failed memories.

## ACTIONS UNDER OTHER STATUTES

Although IDEA is the major federal law governing special education in the United States, lawsuits may be filed alleging a deprivation of rights under other statutes as well. IDEA specifically stipulates that none of its provisions can be interpreted to restrict or limit the rights, procedures, and remedies available under the Constitution, title V of the Rehabilitation Act of 1973, or other federal statutes protecting the rights of students with disabilities.[173] However, the act further states that before an action can be filed under one of these other laws, all administrative remedies available under IDEA must be exhausted if relief is available under that law. The U.S. Supreme Court has indicated that IDEA provides the exclusive avenue for relief where denial of a free appropriate public education has been alleged.[174]

Generally, courts first turn to IDEA and will provide relief under one of these other laws only when relief is not available under IDEA. Such may be the case if access to the procedural safeguards of IDEA have been denied or the student does not qualify for special education services under one of the disability categories defined in IDEA, but has a disability that falls within the protections of the Rehabilitation Act.[175]

A majority of the lawsuits that have been filed seeking relief under a statute other than IDEA have been filed under the provisions of section 1983 of the Civil Rights Act of 1871.[176] Section 1983 can be used to enforce the rights secured by federal law or the Constitution. Several courts have held that section 1983 may be used to enforce administrative decisions[177] or to remedy a deprivation of due process or other rights secured by IDEA.[178] However, courts have made it clear that lawsuits filed under section 1983 must be predicated on more than a reallegation of claims made under IDEA,[179] that section 1983 lawsuits are not viable when adequate remedies exist under other laws,[180] and that section 1983 cannot be used to expand the rights a student has under IDEA.[181] Litigants must exhaust administrative remedies under IDEA prior to bringing a section 1983 lawsuit unless it would be futile to do so.[182]

Under section 1983 school officials who are acting under the color of state law may be held liable for their actions if those actions have the effect of depriving a student of rights secured by federal law. A district court in Indiana held that an attorney hired by a school district to represent it in special education litigation could be sued under section 1983.[183] The student's parents had alleged that the advice the attorney gave to the school district caused a deprivation of the student's federal rights.

Section 504 of the Rehabilitation Act of 1973 effectively prohibits discrimination against individuals with disabilities in any program receiving federal funds.[184] Lawsuits frequently are filed alleging discrimination under section 504 along with a deprivation of rights under IDEA. If the suit can be settled under IDEA's provisions, courts will not turn to section 504 for relief. A Pennsylvania case is illustrative.[185] The parents of a student with physical disabilities requested a due process hearing after the school district denied permission for the student's service dog to accompany him to his classes but stated that the dog could accompany him if he were transferred to a less restrictive placement. The hearing officer determined that the student could be educated in the less restrictive environment. Rather than appeal that decision, the parents filed a section

504 lawsuit. The court held that IDEA was the exclusive avenue through which a student with disabilities could assert an equal protection claim to a publicly financed special education and that section 504 did not provide a cause of action. However, if relief is not available under IDEA, a lawsuit may proceed under section 504.[186] If a school district is found to be in compliance with IDEA, generally it is held that such compliance establishes compliance with section 504.[187] Courts also have held that section 504 may not be used to expand the rights available under IDEA.[188] Additional section 504 cases will be discussed in Chapter 10.

In a lawsuit filed by the federal government under the Civil Rights of Institutionalized Persons Act (CRIPA),[189] alleging that residents of a state institution who were under the age of 22 were being denied a free appropriate public education, the district court held that the government was not required to exhaust administrative remedies prior to filing the suit. The court further held that a lawsuit could be filed under CRIPA alleging violations of IDEA and that CRIPA gave the attorney general standing to sue when the institutional conditions deprived residents of any rights, privileges, or immunities secured by the laws of the United States.

A district court in Oklahoma held that a rational jury could find that the actions of a teacher who had forced a student to clean her excrement from a bathroom floor were so demeaning and harmful to the student that they may have violated her substantive due process rights under the Fourteenth Amendment.[190] However, the court held that the student's procedural due process rights were not violated because her parents had been given the opportunity for an administrative hearing to contest the student's continued placement at the school but had chosen not to pursue that option.

## SUMMARY

One of the unique features of IDEA is that it contains an extensive mechanism for the resolution of disputes between parents and school districts concerning the provision of a free appropriate public education. This created a two-step process whereby the dispute is first brought to an administrative due process hearing and then to either the federal or state courts.

Prior to bringing the dispute to the court level, the parties involved must exhaust all available administrative remedies unless it clearly is not feasible to do so. Administrative proceedings are conducted in a quasi-judicial fashion with representation by counsel, cross-examining of witnesses, and decisions based on the preponderance of the evidence standard. Due process hearings are largely fact-finding endeavors; however, the hearing officer must apply the law to the factual situation to make a final determination.

If the dispute reaches the court level, the court will operate under the rules of civil procedure for its jurisdiction. However, judges will give the findings of the administrative process due consideration and will not substitute their views of what is proper educational methodology for that of the local and state authorities they review. The role of the court is to interpret the law in view of the facts before it and make a decision based on the preponderance of evidence. The disposition regarding the factual situation from the administrative hearings is accepted unless it clearly is erroneous. Although the court generally does not repeat what already has occurred at the administrative level, it may accept additional evidence.

Courts have been divided regarding the question of which party bears the burden of proof in the litigation. Some courts have held that the party challenging the IEP bears the burden, while others have held that the school district always bears the burden. In instances where the dispute reaches the trial court level, some courts have held that the party bringing the appeal bears the burden of showing that the administrative decision was incorrect. State law may dictate which party bears the burden of proof.[191]

In order to bring a lawsuit before a court a party must have standing to sue. In almost all situations a parent of a student with disabilities and the school district preparing the IEP would be the parties that have standing to sue. However, there are unique circumstances where other interested parties may be granted standing.

Unfortunately, IDEA does not stipulate any particular time frame under which an aggrieved party must file a lawsuit. Therefore, the statute of limitations for a given lawsuit would depend on state law. Courts in various states have held that the appropriate limitations period is anywhere from 30 days to three years.

Parents of students with disabilities frequently allege violations of the Constitution, other federal laws, or state law along with IDEA. Courts turn to IDEA first as an avenue for relief and will examine the additional allegations only when relief is not available under IDEA.

# ENDNOTES

1. 20 U.S.C. § 1400 et seq.
2. 20 U.S.C. § 1415(b)(2).
3. 20 U.S.C. § 1415(e)(2).
4. 20 U.S.C. § 1415(e)(3).

5. *Honig v. Doe,* 484 U.S. 305, 108 S. Ct. 592, 98 L. Ed.2d 686, 43 Ed.Law Rep. 857 (1988).
6. 20 U.S.C. § 1415(e)(2)(C).
7. *Board of Education of the Hendrick Hudson Central School District v. Rowley,* 458 U.S. 176, 102 S. Ct. 3034, 73 L. Ed.2d 690, 5 Ed.Law Rep. 34 (1982).
8. 20 U.S.C. § 1415(b)(1)(E).
9. 20 U.S.C. § 1415(b)(2).
10. *Id.*
11. 20 U.S.C. § 1415(c).
12. *Puffer v. Raynolds,* 761 F. Supp. 838, 67 Ed.Law Rep. 536 (D. Mass. 1988); *Burr v. Ambach,* 863 F.2d 1071, 50 Ed.Law Rep. 964 (2d Cir. 1988); *Antkowiak v. Ambach,* 838 F.2d 635, 44 Ed.Law Rep. 129 (2d Cir. 1988). In these cases the Massachusetts and New York schemes, whereby both the initial hearing and the review hearing were conducted by the respective state education department, were invalidated by the courts. In *Puffer* the court held that under IDEA the state was to have only one opportunity to adjudicate a special education dispute.
13. 20 U.S.C. § 1415(d)(1).
14. 20 U.S.C. § 1415(d)(2).
15. *Hiller v. Board of Education of the Brunswick Central School District,* 674 F. Supp. 73, 43 Ed.Law Rep. 560 (N.D.N.Y. 1987).
16. *Hacienda La Puente Unified School District of Los Angeles v. Honig,* 976 F.2d 487, 77 Ed.Law Rep. 1117 (9th Cir. 1992).
17. *Board of Education of Strongville City School District v. Theado,* 566 N.E.2d 667, 65 Ed.Law Rep. 880 (Ohio 1991).
18. 34 C.F.R. § 300.507.
19. 20 U.S.C. § 1415(b)(2).
20. *Leon v. State of Michigan Board of Education,* 807 F. Supp. 1278, 79 Ed.Law Rep. 878 (E.D. Mich. 1992).
21. *Jacky W. v. N.Y.C. Board of Education,* 848 F. Supp. 358, 90 Ed.Law Rep. 1046 (E.D.N.Y. 1994).
22. *Burr v. Ambach,* 863 F.2d 1071, 50 Ed.Law Rep. 964 (2d Cir. 1988); *Holmes v. Sobol,* 690 F. Supp. 154, 48 Ed.Law Rep. 524 (W.D.N.Y. 1988); *Antkowiak v. Ambach,* 838 F.2d 635, 44 Ed.Law Rep. 129 (2d Cir. 1988); *Louis M. v. Ambach,* 714 F. Supp. 1276, 54 Ed.Law Rep. 1157 (N.D.N.Y. 1989).
23. *Muth v. Central Bucks School District,* 839 F.2d 113, 44 Ed.Law Rep. 1037 (3d Cir. 1988); *aff'd on other grounds sub nom. Dellmuth v. Muth,* 491 U.S. 223, 109 S. Ct. 2397, 105 L. Ed.2d 181, 53 Ed.Law Rep. 792 (1989). *Also see Johnson v. Lancaster-Lebanon Intermediate Unit No. 13, Lancaster City School District,* 757 F. Supp. 606, 66 Ed.Law Rep. 227 (E.D. Pa. 1991).
24. *Grymes v. Madden,* 672 F.2d 321, 3 Ed.Law Rep. 238 (3d Cir. 1982).
25. *Kotowicz v. Mississippi State Board of Education,* 630 F. Supp. 925, 30 Ed.Law Rep. 813 (S.D. Miss. 1986).
26. *Board of Education of the Baldwin Union Free School District v. Commissioner of Education,* 610 N.Y.S.2d 426, 90 Ed.Law Rep. 752 (N.Y. Sup. Ct. 1994).

27. *See, for example, Kroot* v. *District of Columbia,* 800 F. Supp. 977, 78 Ed.Law Rep. 324 (D.D.C. 1992). Several courts also have held that the party seeking to change the status quo bears the burden of proof at a court trial. This is discussed later in this chapter in the section on *Court Proceedings.* It is reasonable to assume that these courts also would assign the burden of proof in administrative hearings to the party seeking to alter the status quo, absent state law to the contrary.

28. *See, for example, Lascari* v. *Board of Education of the Ramapo Indian Hills Regional High School District,* 560 A.2d 1180, 54 Ed.Law Rep. 1244 (N.J. 1989); *Davis* v. *District of Columbia Board of Education,* 530 F. Supp. 1209, 2 Ed.Law Rep. 1023 (D.D.C. 1982).

29. 20 U.S.C. § 1415(e)(4).

30. *Lester H.* v. *Gilhool,* 916 F.2d 865, 63 Ed.Law Rep. 458 (3d Cir. 1990).

31. *Cocores* v. *Portsmouth, New Hampshire School District,* 779 F. Supp. 203 (D.N.H. 1991).

32. Awards of tuition reimbursement and compensatory education services are discussed in greater detail in Chapter 8.

33. *Hiller* v. *Board of Education of the Brunswick Central School District,* 674 F. Supp. 73, 43 Ed.Law Rep. 560 (N.D.N.Y. 1987).

34. *L.P.* v. *Edison Board of Education,* 626 A.2d 473, 83 Ed.Law Rep. 1050 (N.J Super. Ct. 1993).

35. 20 U.S.C. § 1414(e)(2). *See Mrs. W.* v. *Tirozzi,* 832 F.2d 748, 42 Ed.Law Rep. 727 (2d Cir. 1987); *Honig* v. *Doe,* 484 U.S. 305, 108 S. Ct. 592, 98 L. Ed.2d 686, 43 Ed.Law Rep. 857 (1988); *Hoeft* v. *Tucson Unified School District,* 967 F.2d 1298, 76 Ed.Law Rep. 47 (9th Cir. 1992).

36. *T.S.* v. *Ridgefield Board of Education,* 808 F. Supp. 926, 80 Ed.Law Rep. 115 (D. Conn. 1992), *aff'd* 10 F.3d 87, 87 Ed.Law Rep. 386 (2d Cir. 1993).

37. *Edward B.* v. *Brunelle,* 662 F. Supp. 1025, 40 Ed.Law Rep. 771 (D.N.H. 1986); *Browning* v. *Evans,* 700 F. Supp. 978, 50 Ed.Law Rep. 1005 (S.D. Ind. 1988); *Secor* v. *Richmond School Joint District No. 2,* 689 F. Supp. 869, 48 Ed.Law Rep. 499 (E.D. Wis. 1988); *Christopher W.* v. *Portsmouth School Committee,* 877 F.2d 1089, 54 Ed.Law Rep. 797 (1st Cir. 1989); *Cox* v. *Jenkins,* 878 F.2d 414, 54 Ed.Law Rep. 1117 (D.C. Cir. 1989); *Doe* v. *Smith,* 879 F.2d 1340, 55 Ed.Law Rep. 50 (6th Cir. 1989); *Harper* v. *School Administrative District No. 37,* 727 F. Supp. 688, 58 Ed.Law Rep. 127 (D. Me. 1989); *Howell* v. *Waterford Public Schools,* 731 F. Supp. 1314, 59 Ed.Law Rep. 352 (E.D. Mich. 1990); *Waterman* v. *Marquette-Alger Independent School District,* 739 F. Supp. 361, 61 Ed.Law Rep. 561 (W.D. Mich. 1990); *Pink* v. *Mt. Diablo Unified School District,* 738 F. Supp. 345, 61 Ed.Law Rep. 120 (N.D. Cal. 1990); *Lawson* v. *Edwardsburg Public Schools,* 751 F. Supp. 1257, 64 Ed.Law Rep. 791 (W.D. Mich. 1990); *Gardener* v. *School Board of Caddo Parish,* 958 F.2d 108, 73 Ed.Law Rep. 439 (5th Cir. 1992); *Moss* v. *Smith,* 794 F. Supp. 11, 76 Ed.Law Rep. 764 (D.D.C. 1992); *Learning Disabilities Association of Maryland* v. *Board of Education of Baltimore County,* 837 F. Supp. 717, 87 Ed.Law Rep. 770 (D. Md. 1993); *Torrie* v. *Cwayna,* 841 F. Supp. 1434, 89 Ed.Law Rep. 89 (W.D. Mich. 1994); *Kelly K.* v. *Town of Framingham,* 36 Mass. App. Ct. 483, 633 N.E.2d 414, 91 Ed.Law Rep. 274 (Mass. App. Ct. 1994).

38. *Crocker v. Tennessee Secondary School Athletic Association,* 873 F.2d 933, 53 Ed.Law Rep. 440 (6th Cir. 1989); *Stauffer v. William Penn School District,* 829 F. Supp. 741, 85 Ed.Law Rep. 853 (E.D. Pa. 1993).
39. *Carey v. Maine School Administrative District #17,* 754 F. Supp. 906, 65 Ed.Law Rep. 725 (D. Me. 1990).
40. *Crocker v. Tennessee Secondary School Athletic Association,* 873 F.2d 933, 53 Ed.Law Rep. 440 (6th Cir. 1989).
41. *Texas Education Agency v. Stamos,* 817 S.W.2d 378, 70 Ed.Law Rep. 1020 (Tex. Ct. App. 1991).
42. *Hoeft v. Tucson Unified School District,* 967 F.2d 1298, 76 Ed.Law Rep. 47 (9th Cir. 1992).
43. *Jackson v. Fort Stanton Hospital and Training School,* 757 F. Supp. 1243, 66 Ed.Law Rep. 256 (D.N.M. 1990).
44. *Association for Retarded Citizens of Alabama, Inc. v. Teague,* 830 F.2d 158 (11th Cir. 1987); *Association for Community Living in Colorado v. Romer,* 992 F.2d 1040, 82 Ed.Law Rep. 764 (10th Cir. 1993).
45. *Association for Community Living in Colorado v. Romer,* 992 F.2d 1040, 82 Ed.Law Rep. 764 (10th Cir. 1993).
46. *Evans v. Evans,* 818 F. Supp. 1215, 82 Ed.Law Rep. 492 (N.D. Ind. 1993).
47. *Garro v. State of Connecticut,* 23 F.3d 734, 91 Ed.Law Rep. 478 (2d Cir. 1994).
48. *Stellato v. Board of Education of the Ellenville Central School District,* 842 F. Supp. 1512, 89 Ed.Law Rep. 459 (N.D.N.Y. 1994).
49. *Buffolino v. Board of Education of Sachem Central School District at Holbrook,* 729 F. Supp. 240, 58 Ed.Law Rep. 608 (E.D.N.Y. 1990); *Torrie v. Cwayna,* 841 F. Supp. 1434, 89 Ed.Law Rep. 89 (W.D. Mich. 1994).
50. *Hayes v. Unified School District No. 377,* 877 F.2d 809, 54 Ed.Law Rep. 450 (10th Cir. 1989).
51. *Norris v. Board of Education of Greenwood Community School Corporation,* 797 F. Supp. 1452, 77 Ed.Law Rep. 255 (S.D. Ind. 1992). See the section entitled "Actions under Other Statutes" later in this chapter for a related discussion.
52. *Begay v. Hodel,* 730 F. Supp. 1001, 58 Ed.Law Rep. 1128 (D. Ariz. 1990).
53. *Kerr Center Parents Association v. Charles,* 897 F.2d 1463, 59 Ed.Law Rep. 22 (9th Cir. 1990). *See also Louis M. v. Ambach,* 113 F.R.D. 133 (N.D.N.Y. 1986); *Robinson v. Pinderhughes,* 810 F.2d 1270, 37 Ed.Law Rep. 488 (4th Cir. 1987); *Doe v. Rockingham County School Board,* 658 F. Supp. 403, 39 Ed.Law Rep. 590 (W.D. Va. 1987).
54. *Heldman v. Sobol,* 962 F.2d 148, 74 Ed.Law Rep. 1042 (2d Cir. 1992).
55. *Straube v. Florida Union Free School District,* 778 F. Supp. 774, 71 Ed.Law Rep. 725 (S.D.N.Y. 1991).
56. *Vander Malle v. Ambach,* 667 F. Supp. 1015, 41 Ed.Law Rep. 913 (S.D.N.Y. 1987).
57. *Kerr Center Parents Association v. Charles,* 897 F.2d 1463, 59 Ed.Law Rep. 22 (9th Cir. 1990).
58. *Bray v. Hobart City School Corporation,* 818 F. Supp. 1226, 82 Ed.Law Rep. 503 (N.D. Ind. 1993).
59. *S-1 v. Turlington,* 646 F. Supp. 1564, 35 Ed.Law Rep. 1091 (S.D. Fla. 1986).

60. *Mathern v. Campbell County Children's Center,* 674 F. Supp. 816, 43 Ed.Law Rep. 699 (D. Wyo. 1987).
61. *J.G. v. Board of Education of the Rochester City School District,* 648 F. Supp. 1452, 36 Ed.Law Rep. 696 (W.D.N.Y. 1986), *aff'd* 830 F.2d 444, 42 Ed.Law Rep. 52 (2d Cir. 1987); *Esther C. v. Ambach,* 535 N.Y.S.2d 462 (N.Y. App. Div. 1988); *Sidney K. v. Ambach,* 535 N.Y.S.2d 468, 50 Ed.Law Rep. 1120 (N.Y. App. Div. 1988).
62. *Diamond v. McKenzie,* 602 F. Supp. 632, 23 Ed.Law Rep. 100 (D.D.C. 1985).
63. *J.G. v. Board of Education of Rochester City School District,* 648 F. Supp. 1452, 36 Ed.Law Rep. 696 (W.D.N.Y. 1986), *aff'd* 830 F.2d 444, 42 Ed.Law Rep. 52 (2d Cir. 1987).
64. *DeVries v. Spillane,* 853 F.2d 264, 48 Ed.Law Rep. 356 (4th Cir. 1988). *See also Holmes v. District of Columbia,* 680 F. Supp. 40, 45 Ed.Law Rep. 688 (D.D.C. 1988).
65. *Komninos v. Upper Saddle River Board of Education,* 13 F.3d 775, 88 Ed.Law Rep. 956 (3d Cir. 1994).
66. *Lester H. v. Gilhool,* 916 F.2d 865, 63 Ed.Law Rep. 458 (3d Cir. 1990).
67. *Frutiger v. Hamilton Central School District,* 928 F.2d 68, 66 Ed.Law Rep. 547 (2d Cir. 1991).
68. *United States v. State of Tennessee,* 798 F. Supp. 483, 77 Ed.Law Rep. 777 (W.D. Tenn. 1992).
69. *Doe v. Belleville Public School District No. 118,* 672 F. Supp. 342, 42 Ed.Law Rep. 1125 (S.D. Ill. 1987); *Robertson v. Granite City Community Unit School District No. 9,* 684 F. Supp. 1002, 46 Ed.Law Rep. 1147 (S.D. Ill. 1988).
70. 34 C.F.R. § 300.508.
71. *Militello v. Board of Education of the City of Union City,* 803 F. Supp. 974, 78 Ed.Law Rep. 745 (D.N.J. 1992).
72. *Edward B. v. Paul,* 814 F.2d 52 (1st Cir. 1987).
73. 34 C.F.R. § 300.512(a)(1).
74. 34 C.F.R. § 300.512(c).
75. *Andress v. Cleveland ISD,* 832 F. Supp. 1086, 86 Ed.Law Rep. 773 (E.D. Tex. 1993).
76. 20 U.S.C. § 1415(e)(1).
77. *Slack v. State of Delaware Department of Public Instruction,* 826 F. Supp. 115, 84 Ed.Law Rep. 944 (D. Del. 1993).
78. *Tracey T. v. McDaniel,* 610 F. Supp. 947, 26 Ed.Law Rep. 239 (N.D. Ga. 1985); *Puffer v. Raynolds,* 761 F. Supp. 838, 67 Ed.Law Rep. 536 (D. Mass. 1988); *Spielberg v. Henrico County Public Schools,* 853 F.2d 256, 48 Ed.Law Rep. 352 (4th Cir. 1988); *Kerkham v. McKenzie,* 862 F.2d 884, 50 Ed.Law Rep. 712 (D.C. Cir. 1988); *Hiller v. Board of Education of the Brunswick Central School District,* 743 F. Supp. 958, 62 Ed.Law Rep. 974 (N.D.N.Y. 1990); *Tice v. Botetourt County School Board,* 908 F.2d 1200, 61 Ed.Law Rep. 1207 (4th Cir. 1990); *Barnett v. Fairfax County School Board,* 927 F.2d 146, 66 Ed.Law Rep. 64 (4th Cir. 1991); *Board of Education of Community Consolidated School District v. Illinois State Board of Education,* 938 F.2d 712, 68 Ed.Law Rep. 987 (7th Cir. 1991); *Angevine v. Smith,* 959 F.2d 292, 73 Ed.Law Rep. 910 (D.C. Cir. 1992); *Remis v. New Jersey*

*Department of Human Services,* 815 F. Supp. 141, 81 Ed.Law Rep. 762 (D.N.J. 1993).

79. *Bales* v. *Clarke,* 523 F. Supp. 1366, 1 Ed.Law Rep. 218 (E.D. Va. 1981); *Tatro* v. *State of Texas,* 703 F.2d 823, 10 Ed.Law Rep. 73 (5th Cir. 1983), *aff'd on other grounds sub nom. Irving Independent School District* v. *Tatro,* 468 U.S. 883, 104 S. Ct. 3371, 82 L. Ed.2d 664, 18 Ed.Law Rep. 138 (1984); *Alamo Heights Independent School District* v. *State Board of Education,* 790 F.2d 1153, 32 Ed.Law Rep. 445 (5th Cir. 1986); *Doe* v. *Defendant I,* 898 F.2d 1186, 59 Ed.Law Rep. 619 (6th Cir. 1990); *Cordrey* v. *Euckert,* 917 F.2d 1460, 63 Ed.Law Rep. 798 (6th Cir. 1990); *Johnson* v. *Independent School District No. 4 of Tulsa County, OK,* 921 F.2d 1022, 64 Ed.Law Rep. 1027 (10th Cir. 1990); *Christopher M.* v. *Corpus Christi Independent School District,* 933 F.2d 1285, 67 Ed.Law Rep. 1048 (5th Cir. 1991).

80. *Doe* v. *Brookline School Committee,* 722 F.2d 910, 15 Ed.Law Rep. 72 (1st Cir. 1983); *Burger* v. *Murray County School District,* 612 F. Supp. 434, 26 Ed.Law Rep. 637 (N.D. Ga. 1984); *Swift* v. *Rapides Parish Public School System,* 812 F. Supp. 666, 81 Ed.Law Rep. 68 (W.D. La. 1993); *Bonnie Ann F.* v. *Calallen Independent School District,* 835 F. Supp. 340, 87 Ed.Law Rep. 95 (S.D. Tex. 1993).

81. *Lang* v. *Braintree School Committee,* 545 F. Supp. 1221, 6 Ed.Law Rep. 349 (D. Mass. 1982); *Oberti* v. *Board of Education of the Borough of Clementon School District,* 789 F. Supp. 1322, 75 Ed.Law Rep. 258 (D.N.J. 1992), 801 F. Supp. 1393 (D.N.J. 1992), *aff'd* 995 F.2d 1204, 83 Ed.Law Rep. 1009 (3d Cir. 1993); *Delaware County Intermediate Unit #25* v. *Martin K.,* 831 F. Supp. 1206, 86 Ed.Law Rep. 147 (E.D. Pa. 1993).

82. *Id. Oberti* v. *Board of Education of the Borough of Clementon School District; Mavis* v. *Sobol,* 839 F. Supp. 968, 88 Ed.Law Rep. 621 (N.D.N.Y. 1994).

83. *Town of Burlington* v. *Department of Education, Commonwealth of Massachusetts,* 736 F.2d 773, 18 Ed.Law Rep. 278 (1st Cir. 1984), *aff'd on other grounds sub nom. Burlington School Committee* v. *Department of Education of the Commonwealth of Massachusetts,* 471 U.S. 359, 105 S. Ct. 1996, 85 L. Ed.2d 385, 23 Ed.Law Rep. 1189 (1985); *Anderson* v. *District of Columbia,* 877 F.2d 1018, 54 Ed.Law Rep. 784 (D.C. Cir. 1989).

84. *Board of Education of the Hendrick Hudson Central School District* v. *Rowley,* 458 U.S. 176, 102 S. Ct. 3034, 73 L. Ed.2d 690, 5 Ed.Law Rep. 34 (1982).

85. *Timms* v. *Metropolitan School District,* EHLR 554:361 (S.D. Ind. 1982).

86. *Barnett* v. *Fairfax County School Board,* 927 F.2d 146, 66 Ed.Law Rep. 64 (4th Cir. 1991).

87. *Tice* v. *Botetourt County School Board,* 908 F.2d 1200, 61 Ed.Law Rep. 1207 (4th Cir. 1990).

88. *Todd D.* v. *Andrews,* 933 F.2d 1576, 67 Ed.Law Rep. 1065 (11th Cir. 1991).

89. *Board of Education of the Hendrick Hudson Central School District* v. *Rowley,* 458 U.S. 176, 102 S. Ct. 3034, 73 L. Ed.2d 690, 5 Ed.Law Rep. 34 (1982).

90. *Town of Burlington* v. *Department of Education, Commonwealth of Massachusetts,* 736 F.2d 773, 18 Ed.Law Rep. 278 (1st Cir. 1984), *aff'd on other grounds sub nom. Burlington School Committee* v. *Department of Education of the Commonwealth of Massachusetts,* 471 U.S. 359, 105 S. Ct. 1996, 85 L. Ed.2d 385, 23 Ed.Law Rep. 1189 (1985).

91. *Lenn* v. *Portland School Committee,* 998 F.2d 1083, 84 Ed.Law Rep. 685 (1st Cir. 1993).
92. *Bertolucci* v. *San Carlos Elementary School District,* 721 F. Supp. 1150, 56 Ed.Law Rep. 850 (N.D. Cal. 1989); *also see Woods* v. *New Jersey Department of Education,* 823 F. Supp. 254, 84 Ed.Law Rep. 165 (D.N.J. 1993).
93. *Burke County Board of Education* v. *Denton,* 895 F.2d 973, 58 Ed.Law Rep. 918 (4th Cir. 1990).
94. *Teague Independent School District* v. *Todd D.,* 999 F.2d 127, 84 Ed.Law Rep. 906 (5th Cir. 1993).
95. *Kerkham* v. *McKenzie,* 862 F.2d 884, 50 Ed.Law Rep. 712 (D.C. Cir. 1988).
96. *Block* v. *District of Columbia,* 748 F. Supp. 891, 63 Ed.Law Rep. 876 (D.D.C. 1990).
97. *Puffer* v. *Raynolds,* 761 F. Supp. 838, 67 Ed.Law Rep. 536 (D. Mass. 1988).
98. *Roncker* v. *Walter,* 700 F.2d 1058, 9 Ed.Law Rep. 827 (6th Cir. 1983); *Briggs* v. *Board of Education of Connecticut,* 882 F.2d 688, 55 Ed.Law Rep. 423 (2d Cir. 1989); *Kerkham* v. *Superintendent, District of Columbia Schools,* 931 F.2d 84, 67 Ed.Law Rep. 454 (D.C. Cir. 1991).
99. *Thomas* v. *Cincinnati Board of Education,* 918 F.2d 618, 64 Ed.Law Rep. 43 (6th Cir. 1990).
100. *Karl* v. *Board of Education of the Genesco Central School District,* 736 F.2d 873, 18 Ed.Law Rep. 310 (2d Cir. 1984).
101. *Puffer* v. *Raynolds,* 761 F. Supp. 838, 67 Ed.Law Rep. 536 (D. Mass. 1988).
102. *Doyle* v. *Arlington County School Board,* 953 F.2d 100, 72 Ed.Law Rep. 44 (4th Cir. 1991).
103. *Doyle* v. *Arlington County School Board,* 806 F. Supp. 1253, 79 Ed.Law Rep. 498 (E.D. Va. 1992).
104. 20 U.S.C. § 1415(e)(2).
105. *Roland M.* v. *Concord School Committee,* 910 F.2d 983, 62 Ed.Law Rep. 408 (1st Cir. 1990).
106. *Hunger* v. *Leininger,* 15 F.3d 664, 89 Ed.Law Rep. 421 (7th Cir. 1994).
107. *Metropolitan Government of Nashville and Davidson County* v. *Cook,* 915 F.2d 232, 63 Ed.Law Rep. 36 (6th Cir. 1990).
108. *Teague Independent School District* v. *Todd D.,* 999 F.2d 127, 84 Ed.Law Rep. 906 (5th Cir. 1993).
109. *Ojai Unified School District* v. *Jackson,* 4 F.3d 1467, 85 Ed.Law Rep. 724 (9th Cir. 1993).
110. *Mavis* v. *Sobol,* 839 F. Supp. 968, 88 Ed.Law Rep. 621 (N.D.N.Y. 1994).
111. *Fuhrmann* v. *East Hanover Board of Education,* 993 F.2d 1031, 83 Ed.Law Rep. 71 (3d Cir. 1993).
112. Black, H.C. (1979). *Black's Law Dictionary,* 5th Edition. St. Paul, MN: West Publishing Co.
113. *Honig* v. *Doe,* 484 U.S. 305, 108 S. Ct. 592, 98 L. Ed.2d 686, 43 Ed.Law Rep. 857 (1988).
114. *Merrifield* v. *Lake Central School Corporation,* 770 F. Supp. 468, 69 Ed.Law Rep. 801 (N.D. Ind. 1991); *also see McDowell* v. *Fort Bend Independent School District,* 737 F. Supp. 386, 60 Ed.Law Rep. 1145 (S.D. Tex. 1990).

115. *Lee v. Biloxi School District,* 963 F.2d 837, 75 Ed.Law Rep. 155 (5th Cir. 1992).
116. *Greene v. Harrisville School District,* 771 F. Supp. 1, 70 Ed.Law Rep. 469 (D.N.H. 1990).
117. *Robbins v. Maine School Administrative District No. 56,* 807 F. Supp. 11, 79 Ed.Law Rep. 799 (D. Me. 1992).
118. *Stellato v. Board of Education of the Ellenville Central School District,* 842 F. Supp. 1512, 89 Ed.Law Rep. 459 (N.D.N.Y. 1994).
119. *Honig v. Doe,* 484 U.S. 305, 108 S. Ct. 592, 98 L. Ed.2d 686, 43 Ed.Law Rep. 857 (1988).
120. *Jenkins v. Squillacote,* 935 F.2d 303, 68 Ed.Law Rep. 248 (D.C. Cir. 1991).
121. *Straube v. Florida Union Free School District,* 801 F. Supp. 1164, 78 Ed.Law Rep. 390 (S.D.N.Y. 1992).
122. *DeVries v. Spillane,* 853 F.2d 264, 48 Ed.Law Rep. 356 (4th Cir. 1988).
123. *Daniel R.R. v. State Board of Education,* 874 F.2d 1036, 53 Ed.Law Rep. 824 (5th Cir. 1989); *Heldman v. Sobol,* 962 F.2d 148, 74 Ed.Law Rep. 1042 (2d Cir. 1992).
124. *Abney v. District of Columbia,* 849 F.2d 1491, 47 Ed.Law Rep. 460 (D.C. Cir. 1988).
125. 20 U.S.C. § 1417(c).
126. *Webster Groves School District v. Pulitzer Publishing Co.,* 898 F.2d 1371, 59 Ed.Law Rep. 630 (8th Cir. 1990).
127. *Sean R. v. Board of Education of the Town of Woodbridge,* 794 F. Supp. 467, 76 Ed.Law Rep. 785 (D. Conn. 1992).
128. *Fagan v. District of Columbia,* 136 F.R.D. 5, 67 Ed.Law Rep. 679 (D.D.C. 1991).
129. Black, H. C. (1979). *Black's Law Dictionary, 5th Edition.* St. Paul, MN: West Publishing Co.
130. *Jenkins v. State of Florida,* 931 F.2d 1469, 67 Ed.Law Rep. 493 (11th Cir. 1991).
131. *Jenkins v. State of Florida,* 815 F.2d 629, 38 Ed.Law Rep. 909 (11th Cir. 1987).
132. *Woods v. New Jersey Department of Education,* 796 F. Supp. 767, 77 Ed.Law Rep. 126 (D.N.J. 1992).
133. *D.R. v. East Brunswick Board of Education,* 838 F. Supp. 184 (D.N.J. 1993).
134. *In re Smith,* 926 F.2d 1027, 65 Ed.Law Rep. 1105 (11th Cir. 1991).
135. *Board of Education of the Seneca Falls Central School District v. Board of Education of the Liverpool Central School District,* 728 F. Supp. 910, 58 Ed.Law Rep. 565 (W.D.N.Y. 1990).
136. *Andrews v. Ledbetter,* 880 F.2d 1287, 55 Ed.Law Rep. 95 (11th Cir. 1989).
137. *Metropolitan School District of Wayne Township v. Davila,* 770 F. Supp. 1331, 70 Ed.Law Rep. 446 (S.D. Ind. 1991), *rev'd and rem'd on other grounds* 969 F.2d 485, 76 Ed.Law Rep. 386 (7th Cir. 1992).
138. *Family & Children's Center, Inc. v. School City of Mishawaka,* 13 F.3d 1052, 88 Ed.Law Rep. 974 (7th Cir. 1994).
139. *Heldman v. Sobol,* 962 F.2d 148, 74 Ed.Law Rep. 1042 (2d Cir. 1992).
140. *Susan R.M. v. Northeast Independent School District,* 818 F.2d 455, 39 Ed.Law Rep. 525 (5th Cir. 1987).
141. *Shook v. Gaston County Board of Education,* 882 F.2d 119, 55 Ed.Law Rep. 403 (4th Cir. 1989).

142. *Allstate Insurance Co.* v. *Bethlehem Area School District,* 678 F. Supp. 1132, 45 Ed.Law Rep. 122 (E.D. Pa. 1987); *Gehman* v. *Prudential Property and Casualty Insurance Company,* 702 F. Supp. 1192, 51 Ed.Law Rep. 497 (E.D. Pa. 1989).

143. 20 U.S.C. § 1415 (e)(2).

144. *Slack* v. *State of Delaware Department of Public Instruction,* 826 F. Supp. 115, 84 Ed.Law Rep. 944 (D. Del. 1993).

145. *Department of Education, State of Hawaii* v. *Carl D.,* 695 F.2d 1154, 8 Ed.Law Rep. 253 (9th Cir. 1983).

146. *Bow School District* v. *Quentin W.,* 750 F. Supp. 546, 64 Ed.Law Rep. 370 (D.N.H. 1990); *Valerie J.* v. *Derry Cooperative School District,* 825 F. Supp. 434, 84 Ed.Law Rep. 702 (D.N.H. 1993). *Note:* New Hampshire has since amended its state special education law to create a limitations period of 120 days. However, the 30-day period is controlling in lawsuits that were filed before that legislation took effect. *See Hebert* v. *Manchester, N.H., School District,* 833 F. Supp. 80, 86 Ed.Law Rep. 786 (D.N.H. 1993).

147. *Elizabeth K.* v. *Warrick County School Corporation,* 795 F. Supp. 881, 76 Ed.Law Rep. 1033 (S.D. Ind. 1992).

148. *Gertel* v. *School Committee of Brookline School District,* 783 F. Supp. 701, 73 Ed.Law Rep. 81 (D. Mass. 1992); *Amann* v. *Town of Stow,* 991 F.2d 929, 82 Ed.Law Rep. 372 (1st Cir. 1993).

149. *Spiegler* v. *District of Columbia,* 866 F.2d 461, 51 Ed.Law Rep. 754 (D.C. Cir. 1989).

150. *Wills* v. *Ferrandino,* 830 F. Supp. 116, 85 Ed.Law Rep. 1091 (D. Conn. 1993).

151. *Monahan* v. *State of Nebraska,* 491 F. Supp. 1074 (D. Neb. 1980).

152. *Board of Education of the City of Chicago* v. *Wolinsky,* 842 F. Supp. 1080, 89 Ed.Law Rep. 133 (N.D. Ill. 1993).

153. *Adler* v. *Education Department of the State of New York,* 760 F.2d 454, 24 Ed.Law Rep. 726 (2d Cir. 1985). *Also see Vander Malle* v. *Ambach,* 667 F. Supp. 1015, 41 Ed.Law Rep. 913 (S.D.N.Y. 1987).

154. *Schimmel* v. *Spillane,* 819 F.2d 477, 39 Ed.Law Rep. 999 (4th Cir. 1987); *School Board of the County of York* v. *Nicely,* 408 S.E.2d 545, 69 Ed.Law Rep. 943 (Va. Ct. App. 1991); *Richards* v. *Fairfax County School Board,* 798 F. Supp. 338, 77 Ed.Law Rep. 764 (E.D. Va. 1992).

155. *Scokin* v. *State of Texas,* 723 F.2d 432, 15 Ed.Law Rep. 122 (5th Cir. 1984).

156. *Tokarcik* v. *Forest Hills School District,* 665 F.2d 443 (3d Cir. 1981).

157. *Janzen* v. *Knox County Board of Education,* 790 F.2d 484, 32 Ed.Law Rep. 92 (6th Cir. 1986).

158. *Shook* v. *Gaston County Board of Education,* 882 F.2d 119, 55 Ed.Law Rep. 403 (4th Cir. 1989).

159. *Lawson* v. *Edwardsburg Public Schools,* 751 F. Supp. 1257, 64 Ed.Law Rep. 791 (W.D. Mich. 1990).

160. *Bernardsville Board of Education* v. *J.H.,* 817 F. Supp. 14, 82 Ed.Law Rep. 392 (D.N.J. 1993).

161. *Hebert* v. *Manchester, N.H. School District,* 833 F. Supp. 80, 86 Ed.Law Rep. 786 (D.N.H. 1993).

162. *Murphy* v. *Timberlane Regional School District,* 22 F.3d 1186, 91 Ed.Law Rep. 62 (1st Cir. 1994).

163. *I.D.* v. *Westmoreland School District,* 788 F. Supp. 632, 74 Ed.Law Rep. 1107 (D.N.H. 1991); *G.D.* v. *Westmoreland School District,* 783 F. Supp. 1532, 73 Ed.Law Rep. 454 (D.N.H. 1992).

164. *McCartney C.* v. *Herrin Community Unit School District No. 4,* 21 F.3d 173, 90 Ed.Law Rep. 1010 (7th Cir. 1994).

165. *Shook* v. *Gaston County Board of Education,* 882 F.2d 119, 55 Ed.Law Rep. 403 (4th Cir. 1989).

166. *Hall* v. *Knott County Board of Education,* 941 F.2d 402, 69 Ed.Law Rep. 242 (6th Cir. 1991).

167. *Richards* v. *Fairfax County School Board,* 798 F. Supp. 338, 77 Ed.Law Rep. 764 (E.D. Va. 1992).

168. *Board of Education of the City of Chicago* v. *Wolinsky,* 842 F. Supp. 1080, 89 Ed.Law Rep. 133 (N.D. Ill. 1993).

169. *Hebert* v. *Manchester, N.H., School District,* 833 F. Supp. 80, 86 Ed.Law Rep. 786 (D.N.H. 1993).

170. *J.S.K.* v. *Hendry County School Board,* 941 F.2d 1563, 69 Ed.Law Rep. 689 (11th Cir. 1991).

171. *Murphy* v. *Timberlane Regional School District,* 973 F.2d 13, 77 Ed.Law Rep. 28 (1st Cir. 1992); *on rem'd* 819 F. Supp. 1127, 82 Ed.Law Rep. 798 (D. Mass. 1993); *aff'd* 22 F.3d 1186, 91 Ed.Law Rep. 62 (1st Cir. 1994).

172. The doctrine of laches refers to a situation where a party has failed, through neglect or omission, to assert a right. In conjunction with a lapse of time and other circumstances, that failure puts the other party at a disadvantage. A lawsuit may be time-barred due to the doctrine of laches.

173. 20 U.S.C. § 1415(f).

174. *Smith* v. *Robinson,* 468 U.S. 992, 104 S. Ct. 3457, 82 L. Ed.2d 746, 18 Ed.Law Rep. 148 (1984).

175. Rothstein, L. F. (1990). *Special Education Law.* White Plains, NY: Longman, Inc.

176. 42 U.S.C. § 1983.

177. *Robinson* v. *Pinderhughes,* 810 F.2d 1270, 37 Ed.Law Rep. 488 (4th Cir. 1987); *Reid* v. *Board of Education, Lincolnshire-Prairie View School District 103,* 765 F. Supp. 965, 68 Ed.Law Rep. 400 (N.D. Ill. 1990); *Grace B.* v. *Lexington School Committee,* 762 F. Supp. 416, 67 Ed.Law Rep. 660 (D. Mass. 1991).

178. *Manecke* v. *School Board of Pinellas County,* 553 F. Supp. 787, 8 Ed.Law Rep. 667 (M.D. Fla. 1982); *Digre* v. *Roseville Schools Independent School District No. 623,* 841 F.2d 245, 45 Ed.Law Rep. 523 (11th Cir. 1988); *Hiller* v. *Board of Education of the Brunswick Central School District,* 687 F. Supp. 735, 47 Ed.Law Rep. 951 (N.D.N.Y. 1988); *Mrs. W.* v. *Tirozzi,* 706 F. Supp. 164, 52 Ed.Law Rep. 126 (D. Conn. 1989); *Sean R.* v. *Board of Education of the Town of Woodbridge,* 794 F. Supp. 467, 76 Ed.Law Rep. 785 (D. Conn. 1992).

179. *Barnett* v. *Fairfax County School Board,* 721 F. Supp. 755, 56 Ed.Law Rep. 802 (E.D. Va. 1989).

180. *Fee* v. *Herndon,* 900 F.2d 804, 59 Ed.Law Rep. 1003 (5th Cir. 1990).

181. *Crocker* v. *Tennessee Secondary School Athletic Association,* 980 F.2d 382, 79 Ed.Law Rep. 389 (6th Cir. 1992).
182. *Quackenbush* v. *Johnson City School District,* 716 F.2d 141, 13 Ed.Law Rep. 262 (2d Cir. 1983); *Laura* v. *v. Providence School Board,* 680 F. Supp. 66, 45 Ed.Law Rep. 695 (D.R.I. 1988); *Lawson* v. *Edwardsburg Public Schools,* 751 F. Supp. 1257, 64 Ed.Law Rep. 791 (W.D. Mich. 1990).
183. *Bray* v. *Hobart City School Corporation,* 818 F. Supp. 1226, 82 Ed.Law Rep. 503 (N.D. Ind. 1993).
184. 29 U.S.C. § 794.
185. *Gaudiello* v. *Delaware County Intermediate Unit,* 796 F. Supp. 849, 77 Ed.Law Rep. 146 (E.D. Pa. 1992).
186. *University Interscholastic League* v. *Buchannan,* 848 S.W.2d 298, 81 Ed.Law Rep. 1145 (Tex. Ct. App. 1993).
187. *See, for example, Barnett* v. *Fairfax County School Board,* 721 F. Supp. 757, 56 Ed.Law Rep. 804 (E.D. Va. 1989), *aff'd* 927 F.2d 146, 66 Ed.Law Rep. 64 (4th Cir. 1991); *Doe* v. *Alabama State Department of Education,* 915 F.2d 651, 63 Ed.Law Rep. 40 (11th Cir. 1990); *Cordrey* v. *Euckert,* 917 F.2d 1460, 63 Ed.Law Rep. 798 (6th Cir. 1990).
188. *See, for example, Carey* v. *Maine School Administrative District #17,* 754 F. Supp. 906, 65 Ed.Law Rep. 725 (D. Me. 1990).
189. 42 U.S.C. § 1997 et seq.
190. *Gerks* v. *Deathe,* 832 F. Supp. 1450, 86 Ed.Law Rep. 780 (W.D. Okla. 1993).
191. For example, the District of Columbia Municipal Regulations place the burden of proof on the school district in all administrative hearings. 5 D.C.M.R. § 3022.16. *See Kroot* v. *District of Columbia,* 800 F. Supp. 977, 78 Ed.Law Rep. 324 (D.D.C. 1992).

# 5

# PLACEMENT DECISIONS

Under the Individuals with Disabilities Education Act (IDEA)[1] school districts are required to maintain a "continuum of alternative placements" to provide students with disabilities with the free appropriate public education called for in the act.[2] The continuum must range from placement within the general education classroom to a private residential facility and also must include homebound instruction and instruction in hospitals or institutions. However, all placements must be made in the least restrictive environment, and removal of a student with disabilities from the general education environment can occur only to the extent necessary to provide special education services.[3] All placements must be made at public expense and must meet state educational standards.[4] Although states must adopt policies and procedures that are consistent with federal law, they may provide greater benefits than those required by IDEA. If a state does establish higher standards, those higher standards can be enforced by the federal courts.[5]

## APPROPRIATE EDUCATIONAL PROGRAMS

Almost immediately after the passage of IDEA in 1975 school administrators, special educators, and parents began to speculate about what constituted an appropriate education. The language and legislative history of IDEA provided little guidance. The act's implementing regulations stated that an appropriate education consisted of special education and related services that were provided in conformity with an individualized education program (IEP).[6] Special education is further defined as "specially designed instruction, at no cost to the parents, to meet the unique needs of a child with a disability. . . ."[7] Since all of these terms and definitions were open to interpretation, it is not surprising that much of the early litigation concerned the meaning of the term *appropriate* as used in IDEA. Parents had fought long and hard for the rights contained in IDEA and would not accept a minimal level of services for their children.[8]

In the majority of these early decisions the courts held that an appropriate education was one that provided more than simple access to educational programs but fell somewhat short of the best that possibly could be provided.[9] The courts determined that although *appropriate* did not mean *best,* the educational program provided had to be one that was individually tailored to meet the student's specific needs.[10] Some courts further declared that even the existence of a better program did not automatically render a given program inappropriate.[11]

Courts have upheld the principle that when school district personnel develop an IEP for a student with disabilities, it must be developed to meet the needs of the student rather than those of the school district.[12] Although the courts have emphasized that placements must be suited to an individual student's unique needs, minor imperfections in an IEP have not been found to render an otherwise satisfactory program inappropriate.[13]

## U.S. Supreme Court Defines *Appropriate*

In 1980 litigation arose in the state of New York that eventually became the first case to be heard by the U.S. Supreme Court under IDEA. In 1982 in *Board of Education of the Hendrick Hudson Central School District* v. *Rowley*[14] the Court defined the term *appropriate* as used in the act.

The litigation involved the services to be provided to a student who was hearing impaired. She had minimal residual hearing but was an excellent lip-reader. She was placed in a regular kindergarten class on a trial basis when she entered the public schools. The school's staff took sign-language courses, and a teletype machine was installed to communicate with her parents who also were deaf. The student was provided with a sign-language interpreter; however, at the end of the trial period the interpreter reported that these services were not needed.

The dispute between the school system and the parents arose when an IEP for the first grade was proposed. That IEP called for regular class placement, an FM hearing aid to amplify the teacher's and other students' spoken words, one hour per day of instruction from a tutor for the deaf, and three hours per week of speech therapy. The student's parents agreed to the IEP but requested the addition of the sign-language interpreter. The school district denied their request.

The school district prevailed in administrative hearings, but the federal district and appeals courts held for the parents. These courts ruled that the proposed IEP was inappropriate because it did not provide the student with an opportunity to achieve her full potential commensurate with the opportunity provided to nondisabled students. The school district appealed.

The basic issue before the Supreme Court concerned the level of services that must be provided for an IEP, and consequently the student's educational placement, to be appropriate under IDEA. In a split decision the Court reversed the lower courts, holding that they had erred in determining that the level of services must be such that the potential of the student with disabilities must be maximized commensurate with the opportunity provided to nondisabled students.

The majority opinion stated that the requirements of IDEA to provide a free appropriate public education were satisfied when a school district provided "personalized instruction with sufficient support services to permit the child to benefit educationally from that instruction."[15] The Court further stated that the IEP must be formulated in accordance with the requirements of IDEA. Since the student involved in this litigation was performing better than average and was receiving personalized instruction that was reasonably calculated to meet her educational needs, the Court held that a sign-language interpreter was not required.

The Court found that several other provisions of IDEA are pertinent to determining whether a proposed IEP is appropriate. Specifically, the educational program must be provided in the least restrictive environment,[16] and related, or supportive, services that may be required to assist the child in benefiting from the special education program also must be provided.[17] Furthermore, all services are to be provided at public expense[18] and must meet state educational standards.[19]

## Initial Lower Court Reaction to *Rowley*

Most courts responded to the *Rowley* decision by holding that an IEP, and the educational program it called for, was appropriate if it resulted in some educational benefit to the student, even if that benefit was minimal. One court went so far as to state that it would not interfere in a situation where the school district was using a minimally acceptable approach that provided the student with an education that was of some benefit.[20] Most courts adopted the stance that once a school district showed that its proposed IEP was reasonably calculated to result in some educational benefit, regardless of how minimal that benefit was, the court was required to approve it.[21] These courts were not inclined to become entrenched in debates over the best methodology or even which of two competing placements would be better.[22] In the years immediately following the *Rowley* decision, the lower federal courts reasoned that all Congress intended was for IDEA to provide students with disabilities with access to educational programs.

Although the *Rowley* decision states that students with disabilities must be placed in an educational program that will confer some educational benefit, the First Circuit Court of Appeals held that a student with severe disabilities need not demonstrate an ability to benefit from a special education program to be eligible for services.[23] In holding that IDEA's mandates apply to students with severe disabilities, the court defined *education* in broad terms. According to the First Circuit ruling, education encompasses a wide spectrum of training including instruction in even the most basic life skills. According to this decision a school district cannot refuse to provide services to a student because it deems the student too disabled to derive any benefit from those services.

## Trivial Educational Benefit Is Not Sufficient

Approximately three years after the Supreme Court issued its *Rowley* decision, the lower courts began to expand their interpretation of the *some educational benefit* criteria. Whereas the initial court rulings indicated that minimal benefits met this standard, later decisions stated that IDEA required more. The Fourth Circuit Court of Appeals held that *Rowley* allowed the courts to make a case-by-case determination of the substantive standards needed to meet the criteria that an IEP must be reasonably calculated to enable the student to receive educational benefits.[24] The student in this case made only minimal progress that the court found to be insufficient in view of his intellectual potential. The court stated that Congress certainly did not intend for a school district to provide a program that produced only trivial academic advancement. In another case that same court held that a goal of four months' progress during an academic year was unlikely to allow the student to advance from grade to grade with passing marks and was thus not sufficient to provide the student with an appropriate education.[25]

The Third Circuit Court of Appeals held that to satisfy *Rowley*'s mandate that an IEP must confer educational benefit to be appropriate, required a plan likely to produce progress, not trivial educational advancement.[26] In a separate decision that same court held that IDEA calls for more than just trivial educational benefit and that Congress intended to provide students with disabilities with an education that would result in meaningful benefit.[27] Similarly, a district court in Georgia held that a proposed placement must confer some appreciable educational benefit on the student to be appropriate.[28]

Other similar decisions indicate that the courts expect more than just trivial academic gains. The Eleventh Circuit Court of Appeals stated that an appropriate education may be defined as one wherein the student makes measurable and adequate gains in the classroom.[29] A district court in New Hampshire held that an IEP calling for mainstreaming in several subjects was not appropriate for a 15-year-old student who read on a first grade level after receiving special education services since he entered school.[30] However, the Fifth Circuit Court of Appeals upheld a school district's IEP after determining that the student received significant benefit from his special education program as evidenced by passing grades and an increased ability to focus on tasks.[31]

## Best Available Option Is Not Required

In the *Rowley* decision the Supreme Court made it clear that school districts were not required to develop educational programs designed to maximize the potential of students with disabilities. The lower courts in the *Rowley* litigation had ruled that to be appropriate a program must provide the student with the opportunity to achieve her full potential commensurate with the opportunity provided to nondisabled students. However, that proposition was specifically rejected by the Supreme Court.

Several lower courts, using the *Rowley* rationale, have held that a school district is not required to maximize the potential of a student with disabilities but, rather, is required only to meet the some educational benefit criteria.[32] Even when faced with a choice between two competing programs, courts have not ordered school districts to provide the program that will give the student the best education or result in the greatest progress.[33] Again, once it has been determined that a school district has met its obligations under *Rowley* the courts have required no more. For example, a California district court declined the parents' invitation to pick between competing methodologies by ruling that their contention that a student made more progress in a private school program did not affect the appropriateness of the public school's offering.[34] Similarly, a district court in Virginia held that a school district's IEP offered a statutorily adequate degree of educational benefit and was thus appropriate even though there was evidence that a private school placement favored by the parents would provide greater benefit.[35]

## Effect of State Standards

The Supreme Court also held that a program must meet state educational standards to be appropriate. Under IDEA's scheme states may establish standards of appropriateness that are higher than the federal standard as interpreted in the *Rowley* opinion. The First Circuit Court of Appeals held that IDEA incorporates by reference state procedural and substantive standards that exceed federal level.[36] If state standards exceed federal standards the state standard operates to determine an appropriate education. Although the vast majority of states have statutes and regulations that define an appropriate education in a fashion similar to the federal standard, several states have established higher standards.

Courts in North Carolina,[37] New Jersey,[38] Massachusetts,[39] Michigan,[40] and California[41] have held that those states have higher standards of appropriateness. Courts in these states also ruled that the higher state standard becomes incorporated into the federal statute since one of the requirements of IDEA is that special education programs must meet "the standards of the state educational agency."[42] Many of these states have statutes that require school districts to provide programs that will maximize the potential of students with disabilities commensurate with the educational opportunities provided to nondisabled students. In these states the *Rowley* standard that a program need only provide some educational benefit to be appropriate does not apply.

## Indicators of Educational Benefit

In the *Rowley* decision the Supreme Court indicated that the program provided to a special education student placed in a general education classroom should enable the student to achieve passing marks and advance from grade to grade. However, several courts have held that promotion to the next grade by itself is not proof that a student has received an appropriate education. The Fourth Circuit Court of Appeals ruled that promotion alone, especially in conjunction with test scores that showed minimal progress, did not satisfy the *Rowley* standard of educational benefit.[43] In a later case that same court held that passing marks and annual grade promotions were important considerations under IDEA but that achieving each did not automatically mean that the student received an appropriate education.[44]

The fact that a student has graduated and received a high school diploma also does not mean that the student received an appropriate education. The Supreme Judicial Court of Massachusetts rescinded an award of a diploma to an 18-year-old student who was unable to adapt to a sheltered workshop or independent living following his graduation.[45] The court stated that awarding a diploma where evidence indicated that the student would not be able to earn one under normal requirements even by the age of 22 was substantively inappropriate.[46] Even when a student legitimately earns a high school diploma, it is not an indicator that the student received an appropriate education. In another Massachusetts case, the federal district court held that the fact that a student had earned a high school diploma did not mean that she had not required special education services; it simply meant that she succeeded despite the school district's failure to follow IDEA's mandates.[47] However, one court has held that completion of general graduation requirements with exceptional performance in mainstream classes indicated that a student had received an appropriate education.[48]

In determining whether a proposed IEP is appropriate, courts have held that past progress in the same or a similar program along with evidence that the progress should continue is an indicator that the program will confer educational benefit.[49] Likewise, the continuation of a program that had not resulted in educational benefit in the past would be inappropriate.[50] Similarly, regression after a particular service or program has been discontinued may be an indicator that the education provided after the discontinuation of the service was not meaningful.[51] Generally speaking, the progress a given student makes should be comparable with the progress made by other similarly situated students.[52] One court has held that progress should be measured in terms of the student's abilities as a child with disabilities.[53] However, lack of progress does not necessarily mean that the student's program is not appropriate. The courts recognize that some students are not motivated or that other factors, such as poor conduct, lack of motivation, failure to complete homework, and absenteeism, contribute to a student's lack of success.[54] To determine whether meaningful or significant progress has occurred, the courts may rely on objective data, such as test scores, and the opinions of experts in the field, such as psychologists and educational diagnosticians.

IEPs are prospective but a review of an IEP by a hearing officer or court can be retrospective. Since due process appeals and court action generally occur after the IEP in question was to have been implemented, those reviewing the IEP have the benefit of history in making decisions regarding the appropriateness of the IEP. How much weight the subsequent history should be given was the subject of much debate in a decision of the Third Circuit Court of Appeals.[55] Stating that a school district's action cannot be judged exclusively in hindsight, the two-member majority held that the court's determination should be based on whether the IEP was appropriate at the time it was developed, not on whether the child actually received benefit as a result of the placement. The court also noted that a student's gains could be attributed to other factors besides the educational program. However, one judge dissented, stating that evidence of what actually happened was material although it was not always dispositive.

## Individualization

A theme that runs throughout IDEA is that a placement must be suited to the student's unique needs. Although courts generally have held that the best possible placement is not required, it is evident that the IEP, and the placement it calls for, must be developed according to the educational needs of the student rather than according to the resources available to the school district.[56] For example, a district court in Pennsylvania stated that when determining whether a program is appropriate or not, consideration must be given to the student's individual requirements along with any potential harm a program may present.[57] Similarly, an Alabama court held that a proposed IEP that did not include individualized objectives and methods of evaluation and that did not address the student's unique needs and abilities was not appropriate.[58] Some school districts may use identical IEPs for all students in similar placement. This practice is not consistent with IDEA's individualization requirements. A state court in Pennsylvania invalidated an IEP that was not individualized but, rather, was written in a general fashion for all students attending the same class.[59]

In an interesting twist the Fifth Circuit Court of Appeals held that a full-day educational program was not required by a student with severe disabilities to receive an appropriate education. The court ruled that to presume that every student's school day should be the same length was contrary to IDEA's requirement that an IEP be individually tailored to meet the unique needs of the student.[60] Similarly, a district court in Alabama held that a full school day was not warranted for a 4-year-old student who was often asleep by the end of the school day.[61]

Courts will, however, look favorably on IEPs that present evidence that school district personnel considered the unique needs of the individual student for whom the IEP was written. For example, the First Circuit Court of Appeals approved a public school IEP ruling that it catered to the student's full range of academic and nonacademic needs through a variety of mechanisms.[62] The court also noted that the program proposed by the school district would be administered by a highly experienced and well-credentialed staff.

## Peer Groups

Some courts also have looked at the other students in a proposed instructional group or program when determining whether it would be appropriate for a given student. These courts have held that the element of peer interaction is an important consideration and that opportunities for appropriate peer interaction should be provided whenever possible.

One court declared that a residential facility whose current students were between the ages of 11 and 17 was not appropriate for a 10-year-old student who was severely emotionally disturbed.[63] The court found that the student required social interaction with other children of approximately the same developmental level. Since the student in question was below average in overall development, placement with students between the ages of 11 and 17 was deemed inappropriate. Similarly, another court held that a student who had imitative tendencies required placement in a program that offered an appropriate peer group.[64]

## Preconditions to Placement Not Allowed

A student's right to receive a free appropriate public education is absolute and may not be made contingent on his or her parents' consenting to preconditions as a placement requirement. One court has held that a school district could not require parents to medicate a student, or agree to remove him from class when he was unruly, before it would provide the student with an educational placement.[65] The court ruled that the student's right to a free appropriate public education could not be premised on the conditions that he be medicated without his parents' consent or that they take him home on days he disrupted the class.

## Parental Hostility to a Placement

Parental hostility to a proposed placement may be taken into consideration in determining whether or not that placement would be appropriate. In a very controversial case, the Seventh Circuit Court of Appeals held that an otherwise appropriate placement was rendered inappropriate by the parents' refusal to cooperate with the program's staff and their open hostility toward school district personnel.[66] The court stated that an IEP is designed to serve the educational interests of the child, and thus, the child's interests are paramount. The court held that a student with disabilities cannot be enrolled in a program that has been doomed to failure by the parents simply so the courts can discipline the parents. The guiding principle here is that the student cannot be punished for the parents' actions.

A school district should offer an educational placement it deems to be appropriate even if the parents indicate that it is unacceptable to them. The Ninth Circuit Court of Appeals has held that a school district cannot escape its obligation to formally offer an appropriate educational placement by arguing that the parents previously expressed an unwillingness to accept that placement.[67] During administrative hearings in which the parents sought approval for a private placement, the school district made that claim that it had an appropriate placement for the student even though the program in question had never been formally offered to the parents. The parents were awarded reimbursement for the costs of the private placement.

## Effect of Procedural Errors

The importance of following correct procedure in the development of an IEP cannot be overemphasized. The Supreme Court in *Rowley* held that to be appropriate, an IEP must be developed in accordance with the procedures outlined in IDEA. Those procedures were discussed in Chapter 3 and will not be repeated here.

All procedural errors are not fatal. However, procedural errors that interfere with or thwart parental participation in the IEP process may cause a court to hold that an otherwise appropriate IEP is inappropriate. Courts have held that the school district's failure to notify parents of their procedural rights under IDEA and state laws,[68] failure to adhere to the timelines set out in IDEA and state laws,[69] and failure to involve parents in the IEP process[70] will render an IEP inappropriate. Failure to develop an IEP in a timely fashion or conduct the required annual reviews also could result in a decision that the school district failed to provide an appropriate education.[71]

A guiding principle of IDEA is that the IEP determines the student's placement. Thus, courts would rule that an IEP is defective if the placement was determined first and the IEP was written to justify the placement.[72] Similarly, a placement that was made without first evaluating the student or developing an IEP would be invalidated.[73]

Courts, however, do not wish to exalt form over substance. They recognize the intricate nature of IDEA and realize that school officials may sometimes proceed in a manner that is technically incorrect but does not prejudice the IEP process. In these situations the courts will allow minor procedural flaws to stand.[74] For example, courts have allowed IEPs to stand when there were minor inadequacies in the notice provided to parents[75] or when the IEP itself did not contain all of the required elements but the missing information was known to all concerned.[76] Generally, courts will allow an IEP that is appropriate in spite of minor procedural errors to stand if those errors did not interfere with parental participation or prejudice the student in any way.[77] The First Circuit Court of Appeals summed it up best when it stated that before an IEP could be set aside there must be some rational basis to believe that procedural errors compromised the student's right to an appropriate education, seriously interfered with the parents' right to participate in the IEP process, or caused a deprivation of educational benefits.[78]

## LEAST RESTRICTIVE ENVIRONMENT

One of the major provisions of IDEA is that it requires school districts to educate students with disabilities in the least restrictive environment

(LRE). This provision applies across the continuum of placement alternatives. Specifically, IDEA requires states to establish procedures assuring that students with disabilities are educated to the maximum extent appropriate with students who do not have disabilities. Furthermore, the use of special classes and separate facilities or other removal from the general education environment may occur only when the nature or severity of the student's disability is such that instruction in general education classes cannot be achieved satisfactorily, even with supplementary aids and services. These provisions apply to students in private schools, institutions, or other care facilities as well as to students in public schools and facilities.[79] This section of the law frequently has been cited by courts in decisions regarding the provision of a free appropriate public education for students with disabilities.[80]

The terms *least restrictive environment* and *mainstreaming,* although distinct, are confused frequently. The terms should not be used interchangeably. Mainstreaming refers to the practice of placing students with disabilities in general education classes with appropriate instructional support. IDEA does not require mainstreaming in all cases, but requires that each student be educated in an environment that is the least restrictive possible and that removal from general education occurs only when absolutely necessary.

## Segregated Placements Not Prohibited

The U.S. Supreme Court, in the landmark *Rowley* decision, stated that to be appropriate, a special education program must be provided in the least restrictive environment. In several early cases courts weighed the benefits of mainstreaming against the benefits of providing greater or more specialized services in a segregated setting.[81] Generally, these courts held that the LRE mandate was secondary to the provision of an appropriate instructional program.[82] Since placement decisions are individualized it is difficult to provide general guidelines concerning how much mainstreaming is appropriate, if any. However, many of the court decisions issued in the years immediately following the enactment of IDEA in 1975 addressed the LRE mandate in terms of the degree to which a given student should be mainstreamed.[83]

Since the IDEA states that students with disabilities may be removed from the general education environment only to the extent necessary to provide needed special education services, the courts have had to determine if recommended services warranted removal from the general education environment or if they could be provided in a less restrictive setting. Many of the early courts ruled that the LRE requirement could not be used to preclude a placement in a segregated setting if such a setting was required to provide the appropriate education mandated by the federal law.[84] Similarly, placements in restrictive environments were approved by the courts when school districts showed that a satisfactory education could not be provided in a less restrictive setting, even with supplementary aids and services.[85]

## Mainstreaming versus Specialized Services

Some early courts, however, held that it was appropriate to sacrifice a degree of academic quality for the sake of socialization. In striking the balance between the benefits of mainstreaming and specialized educational services, these courts approved a trade-off in favor of mainstreaming only when it could be shown clearly that the student would benefit from the social aspects of mainstreaming.[86] One court indicated that mainstreaming should not be provided unless the mainstream program would teach the student the skills necessary to become integrated in the mainstream of life.[87] Ironically, the court found that a segregated program would provide the student with those skills.

Prior to 1989 the majority of court decisions on LRE held that mainstreaming was not required for all students with disabilities but was to be provided, where appropriate, to the maximum extent feasible. Recognizing the social benefits of mainstreaming, these courts held that students should not be mainstreamed solely for the sake of mainstreaming, but, rather, when there was benefit to be derived from it. In balancing the need for specialized services against the LRE provision of the IDEA, early courts tipped the scales in favor of specialized services.

## Placement in Neighborhood Schools

The LRE mandate does not require school districts to place students in their neighborhood schools in all situations. For reasons of economy most school districts centralize many special education services. The courts have upheld this practice consistently. For example, a centralized program for a hearing-impaired high school student was approved by a district court in Virginia and affirmed by the Fourth Circuit Court of Appeals.[88] The high school the student was required to attend was located several miles from his home. His parents objected to this arrangement and requested that a similar program be developed in the neighborhood school. Noting that the student was earning satisfactory grades, was participating in extracurricular activities, and was successfully mainstreamed, the court approved the centralized program. The court was cognizant of the limited resources available to school districts and felt that centralized programs better served the interests of all students. Similarly, the Eighth Circuit Court of Appeals approved a centralized program for a wheelchair-bound student.[89] The court held that the school district was not required to modify the student's neighborhood school to make it wheelchair accessible.

## Placement Should Be as Close to Home as Possible

If it is not feasible to place a student with disabilities in his or her neighborhood school, the placement should be as close to the student's home as possible.[90] This is particularly important when placements must be made outside the school district. A New Jersey case illustrates this point. The district court approved a mother's request to have her autistic child transferred from the facility she had been attending to one that was closer to her home.[91] The court found that the requested placement would provide an education that was comparable to the one the student had been receiving but would be located within her hometown.

## Emerging Trend toward Greater Mainstreaming

In recent years the LRE provision of IDEA has played a more prominent role in litigation concerned with the proper placement for students with disabilities. In many of these cases courts approved placements in segregated settings; however, ironically, the legal principles that have emerged from this recent litigation established a foundation for other courts to order placements in the general education setting. In several of the most recent cases the courts departed from previous case law and began to tip the scales in favor of inclusive programming for students with severe disabilities. These courts view the least restrictive environment provision as a mandatory requirement rather than a general goal of IDEA.[92]

In a decision that has been quoted frequently by other jurists, the Fifth Circuit Court of Appeals provided considerable guidance on the LRE issue. In *Daniel R.R. v. State Board of Education*[93] the court held that a substantially separate class was appropriate for a student with Down's syndrome who had been classified as mentally retarded. The student had been enrolled previously in a general education classroom for part of the school day; however, the court found that this arrangement was not successful because the student did not participate in class activities and failed to master the skills he was exposed to. The court was persuaded further by testimony indicating that the curriculum would have to be modified drastically to meet the student's instructional needs and that he required so much of the teacher's time that too much attention was diverted from the rest of the class.

The Fifth Circuit Court stated that students with severe disabilities may be removed from the general education environment when they cannot be satisfactorily educated in that setting. The court found that the school district's proposal for a substantially separate class placement did not violate the IDEA's LRE mandate. To assist lower courts with LRE decisions, the appeals court created a test for determining when a school district met its obligation to mainstream students with severe disabilities. Borrowing language from IDEA, the appeals court held that lower courts should determine first whether education in the general classroom with supplementary aids and services can be achieved satisfactorily. When it cannot, and special education must be provided, the appeals court instructed lower courts to determine whether the school district mainstreamed the student to the maximum extent appropriate. To find the answers to this two-part test, the Fifth Circuit advised lower courts to consider the student's ability to grasp the regular education curriculum, the nature and severity of the disability, the effect the student's presence would have on the functioning of the general education classroom, the student's overall experience in the mainstream, and the amount of exposure the special education student would have to nondisabled students.

The Fifth Circuit's two-part test has become the benchmark by which LRE cases in the past few years have been decided. It was a significant factor in most of the cases discussed in the following sections. In some of these cases courts approved placements in substantially separate programs; however, in others the courts have held that IDEA requires school districts to develop programs within the general education environment that will meet the needs of students with severe disabilities. The trend that has emerged from the most recent court decisions is toward greater mainstreaming.

### Decisions Approving Segregated Settings
In a 1989 case the Second Circuit Court of Appeals held that mainstreaming was not appropriate when the nature or severity of the student's disability was such that education in a typical classroom could not be achieved satisfactorily.[94] The controversy in this case involved the proper placement for a hearing-impaired student. School officials proposed a public preschool program for hearing-impaired students taught by a certified teacher of the hearing impaired. The parents preferred a private preschool program attended mostly by nondisabled students that was not taught by a certified teacher of the hearing impaired. The district court approved the parents' choice, holding that the program offered by the school district could be provided in a less restrictive setting and that any loss of effectiveness from a specialized placement was outweighed by the benefits of mainstreaming. The appeals court reversed, criticizing the lower court for substituting its judgment for that of school district experts who had determined that the segregated program was best for the student.

The appeals court found no evidence that would substantiate the claim that the student's needs could be met in a less restrictive environment.

A Nebraska district court held that a student with a profound hearing loss, unintelligible speech, severe language delays, visual impairments, and physical disabilities would not have meaningful communicative interaction with hearing individuals in a public school environment and, thus, should be educated in a state school for the hearing impaired rather than a public school class for the hearing impaired. The court reasoned that the student should not be mainstreamed since he would not receive any benefit from it.[95] A Pennsylvania district court also held that a hearing-impaired student who had deficiencies in oral communication could not be mainstreamed because he was unable to communicate with the hearing world.[96]

The Fourth Circuit Court of Appeals concluded that an autistic student who had depressed cognitive functioning, exhibited immature behavior, had difficulty with interpersonal communication and relationships, and required a predictable environment could not be educated satisfactorily in a general education setting, even with supplementary aids and services.[97] The Third Circuit Court of Appeals approved the placement of a student classified as educable mentally retarded and socially and emotionally disturbed in a class located in a segregated special education center over a less restrictive setting but ordered some mainstreaming in a public school.[98] The student had been placed previously in the less restrictive program on a part-time interim basis; however, testimony indicated that he made little academic progress in that program, was disruptive often, interfered with the operation of the class, and did not interact socially with the other students.

The Sixth Circuit Court of Appeals approved an IEP for a learning-disabled student that called for placement in a learning disabilities class with some mainstreaming.[99] The parents of the student preferred placement in a general education class with assistance from a learning disabilities specialist but, ironically, removed the student from the public school program and enrolled him in a private school when the dispute arose. The district court approved their action stating that the school district had not provided sufficient mainstreaming. However, the appeals court reversed, finding that the student had a greater opportunity to interact with nondisabled peers in the public school than in the private school but that he could not be fully mainstreamed without detriment to his own education and that of his classmates.

A district court in Alabama ordered a residential placement for a student who had exhibited aggressive and assaultive behavior in a public school program.[100] The court found that the student could not function academically in a school setting until his behavior was controlled. The school district had proposed homebound instruction or instruction in an isolated room located in an administration building. The court held that a residential facility was less restrictive since it provided the student contact with other students and would better facilitate his return to the general classroom setting.

A district court in Illinois approved the school district's recommended placement in a therapeutic day school for an emotionally disturbed student in spite of his father's preference for a mainstream setting after determining that the school district had made an effort to mainstream the student to the maximum extent possible.[101] The court found that the school district's effort to mainstream the student was unsuccessful, that the student did not benefit from mainstreaming, but that he would benefit from placement in a more structured program.

### Decisions Ordering Greater Mainstreaming

In the cases outlined in the previous sections, the courts have ordered school districts to mainstream students when evidence indicated that an appropriate educational program could be provided in a less restrictive environment or when the benefits to be gained from mainstreaming outweighed any loss of services resulting from movement to the less restrictive environment. However, the LRE mandate clearly was secondary to the provision of an appropriate education. As one court stated, mainstreaming was to be pursued as long as it was consistent with IDEA's primary goal of providing students with an appropriate education.[102] However, other courts have placed a greater emphasis on the LRE provision.

The Idaho Supreme Court approved a placement in a general education classroom in a parochial school over a special education classroom in the public schools for a student with multiple disabilities who had an assessed IQ of 37. The parochial school was willing to accept the student as long as a teacher's aide was provided. The school district refused to pay for the aide and offered a special education class placement. In a split decision, the court held that by accepting federal funds the school district was required to accept mainstreaming to the maximum extent appropriate. The court further stated that by arguing that its segregated program was appropriate, the school district ignored Congress' intent that mainstreaming was preferable to a segregated setting, no matter how appropriate that setting might be.[103]

A district court in Georgia emphasized mainstreaming over special education services and allowed a 9-year-old student with Down's syndrome to be mainstreamed in a general education kindergarten program for three years rather than the substantially separate special education class the school district had recommended.[104] The court found that the student had made some progress in the kindergarten class with supplemental aids and services and was not disruptive. The student was not ready for grade one, but the court felt she could be adequately educated in the kindergarten classroom. Recognizing that this placement might not be appropriate in the future, the court, in a footnote, stated: "The Court's decision is based on the evidence and law as it existed at the time of trial. What the court orders done this day may not be in the best interest of [the student]—that however is not the issue."[105]

The Eleventh Circuit Court of Appeals, citing the Fifth Circuit's test from *Daniel R.R.,* upheld that decision. The appeals court stated that before a school district could decide that a child should be educated outside the regular classroom it must determine that the child's education cannot be achieved satisfactorily with one or more supplemental aids or services. In making that determination the court held that school districts may compare the educational benefits the child will receive in a regular class with the benefits that will be received in a special education environment. Noting that academic achievement is not the only benefit of mainstreaming, the court added that school districts also could consider the nonacademic benefits the child will receive, the effect the student with disabilities will have on the classroom and the education of other children, and the cost of the supplemental aids and services. The court stated, however, that mainstreaming may not be appropriate if the child would make significantly more progress in a special education setting than in a general education classroom.[106]

In an Alabama case the district court held that a school district's IEP, calling for a special education class placement, was not appropriate since it did not offer the student a realistic prospect of returning to the general education environment. The court stated that supplementary aids and services must be used to allow a special education student to attend classes with nondisabled peers instead of being segregated in a special education classroom.[107]

### Inclusive Placements Ordered

In a case that may very well signal a new era of judicial activism in LRE cases, the federal district court in New Jersey held that a segregated special education class was not the least restrictive environment for a student with Down's syndrome.[108] The court, in *Oberti* v. *Board of Education of the Borough of Clementon School District,* held that school districts have an affirmative obligation to consider placing students with disabilities in general education classrooms with the use of supplementary aids and services before exploring other alternatives. Citing the Fifth Circuit's *Daniel R.R.* test, the court found that to meet IDEA's goals, school districts must maximize mainstreaming opportunities. According to the New

Jersey court the preference for mainstreaming can only be rebutted if the school district can show that the student's disabilities are so severe that he or she will receive little or no benefit from inclusion in the classroom, that he or she is so disruptive that the education of other students is impaired, or that the cost of providing supplementary services will have a negative effect on the provision of services to other students.

The court in *Oberti* held that IDEA requires school districts to supplement and realign their resources to move beyond the systems, structures, and practices that tend to unnecessarily segregate students with disabilities. The court recognized that including the student in this case in a general education classroom clearly would require a modification of the curriculum, but held that this alone was not a legitimate basis upon which to justify exclusion. Stating that inclusion is a right, not a privilege for a select few, the court placed ultimate responsibility on the school district to show that the student could not be educated in a general education setting with supplementary aids and services. Since the school district was unable to do this, the court ordered it to develop an inclusive educational plan for the student.

The Third Circuit Court of Appeals upheld the district court's ruling in *Oberti* but used a slightly different reasoning. The Third Circuit adopted the Fifth Circuit's *Daniel R.R.* two-part test but added that courts also should consider the benefits a student with disabilities would receive in a regular classroom as opposed to a segregated setting along with the possible negative effect the student's inclusion could have on the education of other students. The appeals court agreed that a fundamental value of the right of a student with disabilities to an education is the right to associate with nondisabled peers. The court emphasized that a full range of supplementary aids and services must be available to modify the regular classroom program to accommodate a student with disabilities and that the fact that a student may learn differently from his or her education in a regular classroom did not justify exclusion from that setting.

A district court in California stated that IDEA's presumption in favor of mainstreaming requires placement in a general education classroom if the student can receive a satisfactory education there, even if it is not the best academic setting for the student.[109] The court emphasized that a student can be placed in a special education class only if the student cannot receive a satisfactory education in the general education class with appropriate support services. That decision has been affirmed by the Ninth Circuit Court of Appeals, which held that the following four factors must be considered when determining the least restrictive environment: (1) the educational benefits of placement in a regular classroom, (2) the nonacademic benefits of such a placement, (3) the effect the student would have on the teacher and other students in the class, and (4) the costs of mainstreaming.

Lower courts have been cognizant of the decisions by the appeals courts regarding how the LRE provision should be interpreted. Many of these courts, after examining the evidence, have determined that school districts have not met the criteria established by the circuit courts for an appropriate level of mainstreaming.[110] However, the courts will order segregated placements if they determine that a school district has made a significant attempt to mainstream a child but failed in spite of its best efforts.[111]

## PLACEMENTS IN PRIVATE FACILITIES

IDEA requires school districts to offer a continuum of placement alternatives to meet the special education and related services needs of students with disabilities.[112] That continuum includes placements in private day schools or residential facilities, if necessary. Such placements often are necessary if the student's disabilities are severe or are of a type that cannot adequately be addressed by the school district's own programs. If a private placement is necessary, it must be made at public expense. When a placement is made in a residential facility to provide a student with special education and related services, it must be at no cost to the student's parents.[113] All necessary expenses, including nonmedical care and room and board, must be borne by the state or local school district.

### Effect of the *Rowley* Decision

Under the U.S. Supreme Court's decision in *Rowley* a school district would not be required to provide a placement in a private day or residential facility if it could provide an appropriate education in one of its own programs. A school district is under no obligation to provide a private school placement just because the student's parents desire one, even if the private placement would provide a better education than the public placement. Under *Rowley* school districts are not required to provide the best available program.

Shortly after the *Rowley* decision was announced, the district court in Massachusetts held that where a school district provided an education that was of some benefit and was utilizing an approach that was at least minimally acceptable, the court could not interfere.[114] Similarly, a district court in New York denied a parent's request for residential placement for a learning-disabled student after finding that the local school district could provide a program that was reasonably calculated to benefit the student educationally.[115] By the same token, a residential placement is not required if a private day program is appropriate.[116]

The Fourth Circuit Court of Appeals has held that once it has been determined that a public school program is appropriate, there is no duty to consider a private placement.[117] In this case the student's parents had argued that the public school program was inappropriate because the private school program was more appropriate. Other courts also have held that public school programs are sufficient even if it can be shown that a private school program would provide greater educational benefit.[118]

## Effect of Least Restrictive Environment Mandate

The LRE provision of IDEA is an important consideration in situations involving a possible private school placement. Since private schools generally cater to only a disabled population, students placed in these facilities have little opportunity to interact with students who are not disabled. As long as a placement within the local public schools meets the requirements of *Rowley* and all state standards, the courts generally will approve it over a more segregated private school placement. A district court in Virginia held that a program offered by the school district utilized an innovative, nontraditional, and hands-on approach that in the court's view was superior to the private school favored by the parents and was less restrictive.[119] Similarly, the First and Sixth Circuit Courts of Appeals have approved public school placements that addressed the student's disabilities and were less restrictive than the private school chosen by the parents.[120] The court noted that the school district's proposed IEP struck a balance between the goal of mainstreaming and Massachusetts' standard of appropriateness that called for maximum possible development of the student.

## Addition of Other Services in a Less Restrictive Environment

Sometimes students can be placed successfully in programs in less restrictive environments if additional aids and services are provided. For example, a district court in Texas, after considering IDEA's LRE provision, held that a residential placement was not necessary for a student with severe disabilities because she could be educated in a less restrictive environment if additional related services were provided.[121] The court ordered the school district to provide a year-round educational program with counseling and training services for the student's parents.

However, there are limits on the services a school district may be required to provide in order to educate a student in a less restrictive environment. Some court decisions indicate that costs may be a relevant factor in a court's decision. A decision of the Supreme Court of Kansas is illustrative. That court approved a residential placement for a visually impaired student after finding that the related services necessary to maintain him in a public school setting would cost $187,000 per year.[122] A district court in New Jersey, although it ordered a placement in a mainstreamed setting, indicated that costs can be a relevant factor in placement decisions.[123]

## When Public School Programs Are Not Available

School districts are not required to place students with disabilities in private facilities if a public school program is available that will provide an appropriate education. However, particularly in smaller districts, appropriate public school programs frequently are not available. Many school districts have banded together to form an intermediate school district, a collaborative arrangement to provide appropriate educational programs for students with low-incidence-type disabilities. Since many of these collaborative programs are located in a public school building, they are less restrictive than private facilities. However, even with the creation of intermediate school districts, public school placements are not always available.

In an early case a district court in Virginia ordered the school district to place a student with profound disabilities in a private residential school after it determined that the district had failed to provide an appropriate education and was incapable of developing one in a public school setting.[124] Evidence at the trial indicated that the student had made little progress in the public school program. Similarly, a district court in Rhode Island ordered a residential placement for two students with learning disabilities and emotional disturbance after determining that the severity of their disabilities required a highly individualized, highly structured, and closely monitored program that, in the court's opinion, could not be provided within the public schools.[125] That decision was affirmed by the appeals court.

A district court in New York stated that when education within the regular school system is not effective, a private school placement must be considered.[126] The federal district court in Massachusetts ordered placement in a private day school after finding that a student with learning disabilities had not made sufficient progress in a public school program.[127] The court found that the student required an environment that provided careful monitoring, intensive instruction, small groups of only learning-disabled students, minimum distractions, and individual attention. Since the school district had not provided, and appeared to be unable to provide, that environment, the court ordered a private school placement. In another case the Supreme Court of Nebraska ordered a private day school placement after determining that the student required a 12-month program and that the school district could provide only a 9-month program.[128]

Many states have established a system of state-operated (or county-operated) facilities for students with particular types of disabilities. For example, many of these state schools serve populations that are visually impaired, hearing impaired, or multiply disabled. These facilities often offer residential placements. However, even state-operated programs are not always found to be sufficient. In one case the Sixth Circuit Court of Appeals held that a state school that provided educational and psychiatric services on a residential basis was not appropriate as it did not provide all of the elements required by the student.[129] The court found that the student needed long-term treatment in a secure, locked facility. Placement in an out-of-state residential facility that could provide those services was ordered. Similarly, a district court in Hawaii ordered a residential placement for a student who was deaf, blind, and moderately retarded, after determining that the state-operated school for the deaf and blind the student had been attending had not provided a structured extended educational program that emphasized independent living skills.[130] The state-operated program was held to be insufficient and a residential placement was ordered.

## When Twenty-Four-Hour Care and Instruction Are Needed

Residential placements frequently are ordered when the court determines that the student's unique educational needs require constant care and supervision or instruction on a full-time basis. For some students, total immersion in a mode of instruction is required. Generally, only a residential setting can provide the consistency that is needed between the educational and home environments. Since most school districts do not operate residential programs, private placements must be obtained when the student's needs require such services.

Residential placements most often are required when students suffer from severe or multiple disabilities. In one of the earliest cases decided under IDEA the district court for the District of Columbia held that 24-hour-a-day care was required for a student with Down's syndrome who had a mental age of 18 months, was not toilet trained, and could not speak.[131] The court found that the student had regressed because of inadequate follow-up in the home. Similarly, a residential placement was ordered by a district court in Virginia after it determined that a student with multiple disabilities needed a 24-hour total immersion setting in order to remediate a language disorder.[132]

Residential placements often are required for students with behavior disorders. A district court in Texas ordered a residential placement for a student who had been diagnosed as being mentally retarded and schizophrenic after determining that she needed a constant structured environment, a 24-hour-per-day behavior modification program, and an intensive language program.[133] In a similar case a district court in Tennessee ordered a residential placement for a student with mental retardation and emotional disturbance after determining that a 24-hour behavior modification program was required.[134]

Courts often order residential placement for students who are emotionally disturbed. The district court for the District of Columbia was persuaded by testimony indicating that a student with learning disabilities and emotional disturbance required a 24-hour structured program and ordered a residential placement.[135] Similarly, an Alabama district court ordered a residential placement for a student with emotional problems after determining that he required consistent and systematic round-the-clock behavioral training.[136]

Residential placements frequently are required for students with autism due to the unique characteristics of that disability. The Supreme Court of Nebraska ordered a residential placement for an autistic student when testimony indicated that the student required a 24-hour management program.[137] A Texas district court also found that an autistic student required extensive training and monitoring on a 24-hour a day basis.[138] Similarly, a district court in Oregon ordered a residential placement after finding that a student required a 24-hour, seven-day-a-week, consistent environment in order to learn.[139] The court determined that daily living skills such as dressing, eating, and toileting could be taught and reinforced only with the consistency of a residential setting.

A residential placement also may be ordered when it is determined that consistency between the school and home environments is needed when dealing with the student. Such was the case in a Third Circuit Court of Appeals decision in which it was determined that the student's unique combination of disabilities required that he receive a greater degree of consistency of programming than most students with disabilities.[140] The student was profoundly retarded and had cerebral palsy. He could not walk, dress himself, or eat unaided. In addition, he was not toilet trained, did not speak, and had a history of emotional difficulties. In a separate case that same court found that a student with multiple disabilities required a constant, consistent, professionally administered behavior modification program and ordered a residential placement.[141] The First Circuit Court of Appeals also found that a student with severe retardation who could not dress, eat, or otherwise care for himself required a residential placement as he needed consistent instruction and reinforcement on a round-the-clock basis.[142]

## For Students Who Are Dangerous

Courts have ordered residential placements for students who are considered to be dangerous or who may have exhibited violent behavior. As in many of the cases cited here, students who exhibit aggressive, disruptive, or dangerous behavior may require a specialized treatment approach that must be consistently applied in the home and school environments. These students frequently may require services other than purely educational services that can be best provided in a residential setting.

As will be explained in greater detail in Chapter 7, special education students who exhibit behavior that is dangerous to themselves or other students cannot be excluded from the educational process. Often placement in a private facility is the only viable alternative when it is no longer feasible for the student to remain in a public school setting due to behavioral issues.

A state appellate court in Illinois approved a residential placement unilaterally made by the mother of a student who was emotionally disturbed after the student's behavior had become violent.[143] The student's grades and behavior had deteriorated while he had attended a public school program for severely emotionally disturbed students. The court found that the student's needs were so profound, complex, and unique that the public schools could not appropriately meet them. Similarly, a residential placement was approved by a federal district court in North Carolina for a student who had been diagnosed as having a schizoid personality and who had exhibited behavior and learning problems throughout his schooling.[144] Again, in this situation the student's behavior had deteriorated in previous public and private day school programs.

The Sixth Circuit Court of Appeals ordered placement in a private residential facility for an 18-year-old student who had a history of psychiatric hospitalizations after finding that the student required a secure, locked facility that specialized in long-term treatment.[145] The court found that a state-operated residential school that provided educational and psychiatric services was not appropriate as it specialized in short-term treatment and did not want the student due to his oppositional behavior.

## When Emotional Support Is Needed

Residential placements may be required when the student's home environment is not supportive or conducive to the student's making educational progress. For example, a state court in California ordered a residential placement for a student with academic and behavior problems after determining that the student's home would not provide him with the emotional support necessary to compensate for his learning difficulties.[146] The student had a family history that was chaotic and marked with conflict, and the court found that the student's emotional needs adversely affected his learning. A residential placement was deemed necessary as it appeared that the student needed to be removed from his home environment to make satisfactory progress.

The district court in New Jersey ordered a residential placement for a student who had exhibited behavioral problems and difficulty learning after determining that such a placement was necessary for learning.[147] The court had determined that the student's emotional problems could not be severed from the learning process. Similarly, the Eleventh Circuit Court of Appeals found that a student who suffered from a number of physical and emotional disabilities required an integrated program of educational and supportive services that could be provided only in a residential setting.[148]

## Placement for Other than Educational Reasons

Very often students with disabilities need a residential placement for reasons that are not educational in nature. For example, residential placements may be required for social, emotional, or medical reasons. In some of the cases cited in the previous section, residential placements were ordered after the court determined that the student's home did not provide an environment that was conducive to educational progress. Whether or not a school district is responsible for the full costs of a residential placement that is made for other than educational reasons depends on the extent to which those other causes affect attainment of the educational objectives of the student's IEP. Frequently, school districts and other agencies "cost share" residential placements that are made for primarily noneducational reasons.

In an early District of Columbia case the court ordered the school district to provide a residential placement after determining that the student's educational, emotional, social, and medical needs were so intimately intertwined that it was impossible to treat them separately.[149] The student had been diagnosed as being epileptic, emotionally disturbed, and learning disabled and required a residential placement that provided special education, medical supervision, and psychological support. The court held that it was impossible to determine which of the student's needs was dominant and assign financial responsibility to the appropriate agencies. Similarly, the district court in Connecticut found that it could not separate a student's emotional needs from his educational needs and ordered the school district to pay the full costs of a residential placement.[150]

The First Circuit Court of Appeals approved a residential placement for a student who had never lived with his parents but who had been raised and educated in a residential facility at his parents' expense prior to the implementation of IDEA.[151] The school district had proposed a public school placement and had argued that the parents' unwillingness to have the student live at home was not relevant to whether or not its proposed placement was appropriate. The appeals court disagreed, finding that forcing the student into an unreceptive or even hostile home environment would have a negative effect on his educational development.

However, in another District of Columbia case the court held that the school district was not responsible for the residential component costs of a program for a student who was enrolled in a private psychiatric hospital and school.[152] The court found that the primary reason for the student's placement in the psychiatric facility was medical and had little to do with special education. A Delaware district court found that a student with multiple disabilities did not require a residential placement in spite of having emotional problems because those problems did not interfere with her achievement.[153] Her parents had placed her in a residential facility after she began to exhibit behavioral problems in reaction to a stressful home environment; however, the court found that she was achieving academically up to expectations for her capacity.

Students do not always act the same way in school as they do at home. A decision by a district court in Louisiana indicates that school districts are not responsible for problems a student may have in the home as long as those problems do not spill over into the classroom.[154] The parents had requested a residential placement after the student's behavior at home had become severe. However, school personnel testified that he was not violent at school and was progressing academically. The court, noting that IDEA does not require a school district to maximize a student's potential, held that a public school placement was appropriate and that the school district was not required to remedy the problems the student had in the home.[155]

## Medical versus Educational

Questions often arise concerning whether a residential placement is being made for medical reasons rather than educational reasons. These questions arise most often in the context of placements in psychiatric facilities. Under IDEA school districts are not required to pay a student's medical expenses, except for medical expenses that are for diagnostic or evaluative purposes.[156] Psychiatric facilities often are characterized as hospitals, and psychiatrists are medical doctors. Also, students with physical disabilities frequently are placed in facilities that offer a number of services of a medical nature. As some of the cases cited here indicate, it is often impossible to separate out the various services provided by a rehabilitation facility and assign the costs accordingly. Whether a program taken as a whole is considered to be medical or educational depends on the extent and purpose of the provided medical services.

A state appellate court in Tennessee held that the parents of a student who had been placed in a private psychiatric facility were not entitled to be reimbursed for the costs of that placement.[157] The court characterized the services rendered by a psychiatrist as medical services and found that the decision to place the student in the psychiatric facility was a medical, not an educational, decision. The district court for the District of Columbia arrived at a similar conclusion in holding that a residential placement for psychiatric reasons was primarily a medical placement.[158]

The Ninth Circuit Court of Appeals held that a placement in a residential school and psychiatric hospital was appropriate under IDEA.[159] The court found that the facility was primarily a boarding school with the capacity to provide medical services and that the placement was ordered by the district court for educational, not medical, reasons. The court was persuaded by the fact that the facility in question was a state-accredited educational institution.

A district court in Tennessee approved a placement in a residential facility for brain-injured victims after determining that the limited medical services provided to the student were for diagnostic and evaluative purposes.[160] The court stated that the rehabilitative program qualified as special education and related services under IDEA and that the limited medical services the student received could not be used to characterize the program as a medical program. The medical services were provided to monitor and adjust the student's medication.

## Placements Must Be at No Cost to Parents

IDEA mandates that students with disabilities are to be provided with a free appropriate public education. Therefore, if a private day or residential school placement is necessary for educational reasons, that placement must be made at no cost to the student's parents. A state or school district may cost share the placement with other agencies but may not assign any financial responsibility to the parents. Policies that require the parents to pay a portion of the costs of residential placements have been struck down by the courts.

An early class action lawsuit challenged a Connecticut state policy that required the parents of students with disabilities to contribute to the costs of residential placements. The district court approved a settlement agreement between the parties that stipulated that the placements would be at no cost to the parents, including nonmedical care and room and board.[161] An Illinois state law that provided that responsible relatives of recipients of the Department of Mental Health and Developmental Disabilities' services were to be assessed a portion of the costs of services rendered according to their income was struck down by a federal district court.[162] The court found that the state law conflicted with IDEA and could not stand under the supremacy of federal law clause of the U.S. Constitution.

A district court in California invalidated that state's practice of requiring the parents of students with disabilities to turn over guardianship of the students to the Department of Social Services for them to receive a residential placement.[163] The court held that students with disabilities were entitled to have their residential placements paid for by the school districts and that their parents could not be required to surrender guardianship as a prerequisite for receipt of services.

A district court in New York held that the state is responsible for the costs of residential placements when medical, social, or emotional problems that require the placement are intertwined with the educational problem.[164] In this case the student had been placed in a psychiatric hospital that provided therapeutic and educational services. The state agreed to pay the educational tuition costs of the placement but required the parents to assign their health insurance benefits to the psychiatric hospital. Similarly, a court in Tennessee held that a student's social security funds could not be used to fund the residential component costs of a residential placement that was necessary for educational reasons.[165]

In a case with an interesting twist, the Ninth Circuit Court of Appeals held that a school district was required to pay for room and board at the home of a student's grandparents so that he could attend a private school nearby.[166] A hearing officer had determined that the student required a private school placement. The only facility that could meet the student's needs was a good distance from his home but had no openings in its residential program. However, the student's grandparents lived near the facility, and he was able to stay with them. The hearing officer approved that arrangement but ordered the school district to pay all associated costs. The courts upheld that decision.

## Placement Must Be Made Immediately

IDEA's regulations require school districts to implement an IEP as soon as possible following the meetings held to develop it.[167] Various states have adopted different regulations regarding residential placement. Since some states provide some, if not all, of the funding for residential placements, state agencies sometimes become involved in residential placement decisions.

Parents in two Indiana cases contested that state's residential placement procedures. In the first case the court held that the long delay (up to 200 days) that frequently occurred between IEP meetings and placements in that state violated IDEA and was illegal under the supremacy clause of the U.S. Constitution.[168] Stating that it is expected that an IEP will be implemented immediately, the court held that state officials must either hold meetings prior to the IEP meeting or attend the IEP meeting if the state wished to become involved in the process. In the second case the court ruled that the state's residential placement application review procedures allowed the state to circumvent IDEA's due process procedures by permitting the state to review a hearing officer's residential placement determination even if no appeal had been filed.[169] The court held that this procedure created an extra step in the process that delayed implementation of IEPs.

## Return to a Public School Placement

Once placed, a student with disabilities does not necessarily need to remain in a private day or residential program indefinitely. Under IDEA all placements must be reviewed at least annually.[170] Since one of the major mandates of IDEA is to have students with disabilities educated in the least restrictive environment, students should be returned to a less restrictive placement as soon as it is feasible to do so.

The Second Circuit Court of Appeals held that the state has an obligation to maintain a residential placement until an appropriate alternative placement can be found.[171] In this situation the student had been placed in a facility that lost its state approval as a residential school. The court ruled that once a placement is made by an evaluation team, it must be maintained until either an appropriate alternative is found or the student no longer requires the placement. A district court in Pennsylvania ordered a school district to maintain a private school placement for a hearing-impaired student after weighing the benefits of a return to the public schools against the risks the change presented.[172] The court noted that the student was making progress and that it was important for momentum to be maintained.

A district court in New York held that a private school did not have to be found to be inappropriate for a student to be transferred from it to a public school program.[173] The court found the public school program to be less restrictive, yet appropriate. Since the student had made marked improvement in the areas covered by his IEP, the court felt that he should be educated in a less restrictive environment. Similarly, the Fourth Circuit

Court of Appeals found that a residential program was no longer required for a student to receive an appropriate education and approved a day program proposed by the school district.[174]

## EXTENDED SCHOOL YEAR PROGRAMS

IDEA and its regulations do not directly mandate the provision of special education and related services that extend beyond the traditional school year. However, if extended school year programming is required in order for the student with disabilities to receive an appropriate education, school districts must make the necessary provisions. The vast majority of students with disabilities does not require services during traditional school vacations; however, some students with severe disabilities do require these services. The statutes and regulations are silent as to the circumstances in which a school district must provide extended school year programming; however, the courts have not been silent on this issue.

In the 1990 amendments to IDEA, Congress authorized the Secretary of Education to create grants to develop and operate model extended school year (ESY) programs for students with severe disabilities.[175] Priority for awarding these grants is to be given to programs that increase the likelihood that students with severe disabilities will be educated with their nondisabled peers.[176]

## Must Be an Available Option

In some of the first cases to come before the courts in which parents sought ESY programming, courts in three circuits established that programming beyond the traditional school year must be an available option. A district court in Georgia held that state practices that effectively limited educational programming to 180 days per year violated the federal statutes.[177] The court found that the state's plan did not require local school districts to provide for educational services beyond the traditional school year and had never ordered a local school district to consider ESY services. The court concluded that both state and local educational agencies had policies and procedures that prohibited consideration of ESY programs. Since IDEA requires the full consideration of the unique needs of each child, the court reasoned that any policy that prohibited or inhibited such full consideration violated IDEA. The Court of Appeals affirmed. The Fifth Circuit Court of Appeals also held that IDEA did not tolerate policies or practices that imposed a rigid pattern on the education of students with disabilities but, rather, favored the development of IEPs based on an individual evaluation.[178] The court ruled that categorical limitations on the length of special education programs were not consistent with IDEA. Similarly, a district court in Missouri held that any policy that refused to consider ESY programming violated IDEA.[179] That decision also was affirmed on appeal.

## Must Be Provided at No Cost

When ESY programs are required, they must be provided at no cost to the student's parents. Two state courts have held that when students are placed in residential programs on a year-round basis, the tuition expenses must be borne by the school district.[180] The reasoning of these courts was that if a student's needs required placement in a residential facility that covered a full 12 months, the mandate that students be provided with a free appropriate public education dictated that such a placement be at no cost to the child's parents. Not all ESY programs are provided in a residential setting, but the principle that they must be provided at no cost would apply.

## Required to Prevent Substantial Regression

Numerous courts established the principle that ESY programming is required when it is needed to prevent substantial regression and if the time required for the student to recoup lost skills would substantially impede progress toward the objectives of the IEP. That principle first surfaced in a Pennsylvania case in which the district court found that some students with severe disabilities suffered substantial regression during breaks in programming and that the time required to regain lost skills also was substantial.[181] The court concluded that these students would not receive an appropriate education if they were not provided with a program in excess of the traditional 180-day school year. Similarly, a district court in Texas found that a student who required an ESY program to prevent serious regression was entitled to receive one under IDEA.[182]

The regression/recoupment standard, as it has become known, has been refined further by several subsequent court cases. The Fifth Circuit Court of Appeals held that an ESY program is required if the benefits accrued during the school year would be significantly jeopardized in the absence of a summer program.[183] The Sixth Circuit Court of Appeals ruled that regression in the past does not need to be shown to justify the need for ESY programs.[184] The court held that the need for ESY programming could be established by expert opinion based on a professional individual evaluation. However, past regression certainly would substantiate the need for an ESY program.[185] The regression a student suffers does not necessarily need to be academic regression to qualify for an ESY program.[186] Emotional regression, regression in communication skills, or regression in physical skills have all been held to be sufficient reasons for summer programs. ESY programs do not need to be strictly academic either. Summer enrichment and recreation programs also have been required.[187]

## Additional Factors

Although the regression/recoupment standard has received almost universal adoption by the courts in ESY cases, some courts have looked at additional factors in determining whether students should be given ESY programming. The district court in Hawaii held that the state's education department was to consider the following factors in determining whether an ESY program was necessary: nature of the disability, areas of learning crucial to the goals of self-sufficiency and independence, extent of regression caused by an interruption in education, and rate of recoupment.[188] Similarly, the Tenth Circuit Court of Appeals held that the following factors must be considered: degree of impairment, amount of regression, recoupment time, rate of progress, availability of other resources, and the student's skill level.[189]

## Not Required if Regression Is Minimal

The regression/recoupment standard does not require that ESY programs must be provided in every instance where a student with disabilities experiences regression. The courts recognize that regression during the summer vacation is normal for all students. ESY programs are required only if the rate of regression and/or the recoupment time is excessive.

A district court in Wisconsin declined to order the school department to provide a summer school program after it determined that the student's regression during the summer months was no greater than that of a nondisabled student.[190] The court found that the student would suffer no irreparable loss of progress without summer school. Similarly, a district court in Virginia held that year-round schooling was not required unless it could be shown that an irreparable loss of progress would take place during the summer recess.[191] The Sixth Circuit Court of Appeals added that if a child benefits meaningfully from an IEP for a traditional school year, an ESY program would not be required unless those benefits would be significantly jeopardized without it.[192]

## SUMMARY

IDEA mandates that students with disabilities are to be given a free appropriate public education in the least restrictive environment; however, the term *appropriate* is not defined by either the statute or its implementing regulations. The U.S. Supreme Court has defined an appropriate education as one that is developed in conformance with IDEA's procedures and is reasonably calculated to provide educational benefits to the student.

Courts have held that each case must be decided on its individual merits since every child is a unique individual with unique abilities and needs. Given this fact, it is impossible to formulate a definition of appropriate that will fit all cases. The courts have given some guidance, but ultimately, what is appropriate must be decided on a case-by-case basis.

After the Supreme Court issued its definition of appropriate, most lower courts applied that definition strictly to cases before them and held that any program that provided some, albeit minimal, educational benefit was appropriate. However, recently courts have determined that some educational benefit means more than just trivial benefit. These courts have held that the educational benefit conferred must be meaningful. Given the individualization requirement of IDEA, school districts must first determine what a student can reasonably be expected to achieve and then design an IEP that will permit the student to progress accordingly.

State standards also are a factor in determining what is appropriate. Several states have established standards of appropriateness that are higher than the federal level. In those states the higher state standard must be met. Generally, the higher state standard calls for an educational program that will allow the student to reach his or her maximum feasible potential.

The LRE provision was designed to end the practice of segregating special education students by either educating them in special facilities or relegating them to classes in remote areas of the school building. In making placement decisions, courts have been required to balance the equities between an appropriate level of specialized services and an appropriate level of mainstreaming. In performing this balancing act in the early days of IDEA, most courts have tipped the scales in favor of the specialized services, even when they were provided in segregated settings. However, recent court decisions indicate that a trend has developed whereby courts are ordering placements in more inclusive settings. In this regard the courts have recognized that academic benefit is not the sole criterion for determining whether a given placement is appropriate. However, some courts have stated that a special education setting is preferred if the student would make considerably more progress in that setting than in the general educational environment.

The current position in most jurisdictions is to order inclusive settings if a satisfactory education can be achieved in the regular classroom with the addition of supplemental aids and services. In this respect the courts recognize that the nonacademic benefits a student will gain may justify an inclusive setting even if academic progress does not come as quickly as it would in a segregated setting. Courts also have held that the effort to educate students with disabilities in the general education environment must be genuine. School districts may not place a student in a mainstreamed setting without the proper support services and later use the student's failure in that environment as justification for a segregated setting. However, courts will approve placements in segregated settings if the school district is able to show that it made a good faith effort to mainstream the student but that effort was not successful.

Under IDEA school districts must offer a continuum of placement alternatives to meet the needs of students with disabilities. That continuum includes placements in private day and residential schools. Generally, a private school placement is required when the school district does not have an appropriate placement option in a public school setting. Under the Supreme Court's interpretation of an appropriate program, school districts need not turn to private facilities if an appropriate program can be provided in the public schools, even if the private facility could offer a better program. To meet the needs of students with low-incidence-type disabilities, many school districts have banded together to form collaboratives or intermediate school districts. Even with the formation of these intermediate school districts, many students with disabilities still require placement in private day or residential schools.

Despite IDEA's LRE provision, residential school placements may be required in some instances. Generally, such placements are required when the student needs 24-hour-per-day programming or consistency between the home and school environments. When residential placements are required, they must be made at no cost to the student's parents. School districts frequently cost share such placements with other agencies, particularly when the residential placement is required for reasons that are not strictly educational.

The needs of some students with disabilities also may require year-round programming. Courts have held that ESY programs must be provided when the regression the student suffers during a break in programming, combined with the time required to recoup lost skills, interferes with the attainment of the goals and objectives of the student's IEP. Again, the Supreme Court's definition of *appropriate* indicates that a summer program is not required if the student's school year program would confer educational benefit without it.

## ENDNOTES

1. 20 U.S.C. § 1400 et seq.
2. 34 C.F.R. § 300.551.
3. 34 C.F.R. § 300.550.

4. 20 U.S.C. § 1401(a)(18).

5. *See, for example, David D. v. Dartmouth School Committee,* 775 F.2d 411, 28 Ed.Law Rep. 70 (1st Cir. 1985).

6. 34 C.F.R. § 300.8.

7. 34 C.F.R. § 300.17.

8. Osborne, A. G. (1992). Legal standards for an appropriate education in the post-*Rowley* era. *Exceptional Children, 58,* 488–494.

9. O'Hara, J. (1985). Determinants of an appropriate education under 94-142. *Education Law Reporter, 27,* 1037–1045.

10. *Springdale School District v. Grace,* 656 F.2d 300 (8th Cir. 1981), *vac'd and rem'd* 102 S. Ct. 3504 (1982), *on remand* 693 F.2d 41, 7 Ed.Law Rep. 509 (8th Cir. 1982); *Rettig v. Kent City School District,* 539 F. Supp. 768, 4 Ed.Law Rep. 1083 (N.D. Ohio 1981), *aff'd in part, vac'd and rem'd in part* 720 F.2d 463, 14 Ed.Law Rep. 445 (6th Cir. 1983), *on remand* (unpublished opinion 1/26/84), *rev'd* 788 F.2d 328, 31 Ed.Law Rep. 759 (6th Cir. 1986); *Norris v. Massachusetts Department of Education,* 529 F. Supp. 759, 2 Ed.Law Rep. 659 (D. Mass. 1981).

11. *Buchholtz v. Iowa Department of Public Instruction,* 315 N.W.2d 789, 2 Ed.Law Rep. 848 (Iowa 1982); *Age v. Bullitt County Public Schools,* 673 F.2d 141, 3 Ed.Law Rep. 303 (6th Cir. 1982).

12. *Campbell v. Talladega County Board of Education,* 518 F. Supp. 47 (N.D. Ala. 1981); *Gladys J. v. Pearland Independent School District,* 520 F. Supp. 869 (S.D. Tex. 1981); *Laura M. v. Special School District,* EHLR 552:152 (D. Minn. 1980); *Anderson v. Thompson,* 495 F. Supp. 1256 (E.D. Wis. 1980).

13. *Bales v. Clarke,* 523 F. Supp. 1366, 1 Ed.Law Rep. 218 (E.D. Va. 1981).

14. 458 U.S. 176, 102 S. Ct. 3034, 73 L. Ed.2d 690, 5 Ed.Law Rep. 34 (1982).

15. 102 S. Ct. 3034, 3049 (1982).

16. 20 U.S.C. § 1412(5)(B).

17. 20 U.S.C. § 1401(a)(17).

18. 20 U.S.C. § 1401(a)(18)(A).

19. 20 U.S.C. § 1401(a)(18)(B).

20. *Lang v. Braintree School Committee,* 545 F. Supp. 1221, 6 Ed.Law Rep. 349 (D. Mass. 1982).

21. *See, for example, Doe v. Lawson,* 579 F. Supp. 1314, 16 Ed.Law Rep. 498 (D. Mass. 1984); *Karl v. Board of Education of Genesco Central School District,* 736 F.2d 873, 18 Ed.Law Rep. 310 (2d Cir. 1984); *Manual R. v. Ambach,* 635 F. Supp. 791, 33 Ed.Law Rep. 203 (E.D.N.Y. 1986).

22. In *Rowley* the Supreme Court cautioned judges not to substitute their views of proper educational methodology for that of competent school officials. Most jurists, recognizing that they are not experts in the field of education, defer to school officials on matters of methodology. Most courts also have held that parents do not have the right to require a school district to utilize a specific methodology. *See, for example, Visco v. School District of Pittsburgh,* 684 F. Supp. 1310, 47 Ed.Law Rep. 142 (W.D. Pa. 1988); *Lachman v. Illinois State Board of Education,* 852 F.2d 290, 48 Ed.Law Rep. 105 (7th Cir. 1988); *Bertolucci v. San Carlos Elementary School District,* 721 F. Supp. 1150, 56 Ed.Law Rep. 850 (N.D. Cal. 1989).

23. *Timothy W. v. Rochester, NH School District,* 875 F.2d 954, 54 Ed.Law Rep. 74 (1st Cir. 1989).

24. *Hall* v. *Vance County Board of Education,* 774 F.2d 629, 27 Ed.Law Rep. 1107 (4th Cir. 1985).
25. *Carter* v. *Florence County School District Four,* 950 F.2d 156, 71 Ed.Law Rep. 633 (4th Cir. 1991), *aff'd on other grounds sub nom. Florence County School District Four* v. *Carter,* ___ U.S. ___, 114 S. Ct. 361, 126 L. Ed. 2d 284, 86 Ed.Law Rep. 41 (1993).
26. *Board of Education of East Windsor Regional School District* v. *Diamond,* 808 F.2d 987, 36 Ed.Law Rep. 1136 (3d Cir. 1986).
27. *Polk* v. *Central Susquehanna Intermediate Unit 16,* 853 F.2d 171, 48 Ed.Law Rep. 336 (3d Cir. 1988).
28. *Chris C.* v. *Gwinnet County School District,* 780 F. Supp. 804, 72 Ed.Law Rep. 146 (N.D. Ga. 1991).
29. *J.S.K.* v. *Hendry County School Board,* 941 F.2d 1563, 69 Ed.Law Rep. 689 (11th Cir. 1991).
30. *Manchester School District* v. *Christopher B.,* 807 F. Supp. 860, 79 Ed.Law Rep. 865 (D.N.H. 1992).
31. *Teague Independent School District* v. *Todd D.,* 999 F.2d 127, 84 Ed.Law Rep. 906 (5th Cir. 1993).
32. *See, for example, Frank* v. *Grover,* EHLR 554:148 (Wis. Cir. Ct. 1982); *Lang* v. *Braintree School Committee,* 545 F. Supp. 1221, 6 Ed.Law Rep. 349 (D. Mass. 1982); *J.S.K.* v. *Hendry County School Board,* 941 F.2d 1563, 69 Ed.Law Rep. 689 (11th Cir. 1991).
33. *See, for example, Timms* v. *Metropolitan School District,* 718 F.2d 212, 13 Ed.Law Rep. 951 (7th Cir. 1983), *amended* 722 F.2d 1310, 15 Ed.Law Rep. 102 (7th Cir. 1983); *Hessler* v. *State Board of Education of Maryland,* 700 F.2d 134, 9 Ed.Law Rep. 499 (4th Cir. 1983); *Karl* v. *Board of Education of Genesco Central School District,* 736 F.2d 873, 18 Ed.Law Rep. 310 (2d Cir. 1984); *Granite School District* v. *Shannon M.,* 787 F. Supp. 1020, 74 Ed.Law Rep. 496 (D. Utah 1992); *Angevine* v. *Smith,* 959 F.2d 292, 73 Ed.Law Rep. 910 (D.C. Cir. 1992); *Swift* v. *Rapides Parish Public School System,* 812 F. Supp. 666, 81 Ed.Law Rep. 68 (W.D. La. 1993).
34. *Bertolucci* v. *San Carlos Elementary School District,* 721 F. Supp. 1150, 56 Ed.Law Rep. 850 (N.D. Cal. 1989).
35. *Lewis* v. *School Board of Loudoun County,* 808 F. Supp. 523, 80 Ed.Law Rep. 108 (E.D. Va. 1992).
36. *Town of Burlington* v. *Department of Education, Commonwealth of Massachusetts,* 736 F.2d 773, 18 Ed.Law Rep. 278 (1st Cir. 1984) *aff'd on other grounds sub nom. Burlington School Committee* v. *Department of Education of the Commonwealth of Massachusetts,* 471 U.S. 359, 105 S. Ct. 1996, 85 L. Ed.2d 385, 23 Ed.Law Rep. 1189 (1985).
37. *Harrell* v. *Wilson County Schools,* 293 S.E.2d 687, 5 Ed.Law Rep. 658 (N.C. Ct. App. 1982); *Burke County Board of Education* v. *Denton,* 895 F.2d 973, 58 Ed.Law Rep. 918 (4th Cir. 1990).
38. *Geis* v. *Board of Education of Parsippany-Troy Hills,* 774 F.2d 575, 27 Ed.Law Rep. 1093 (3d Cir. 1985).

39. *David D. v. Dartmouth School Committee,* 775 F.2d 411, 28 Ed.Law Rep. 70 (1st Cir. 1985); *Roland M. v. Concord School Committee,* 910 F.2d 983, 62 Ed.Law Rep. 408 (1st Cir. 1990).
40. *Nelson v. Southfield Public School,* 384 N.W.2d 423, 31 Ed.Law Rep. 567 (Mich. Ct. App. 1986); *Barwacz v. Michigan Department of Education,* 681 F. Supp. 427, 46 Ed.Law Rep. 98 (W.D. Mich. 1988).
41. *Pink v. Mt. Diablo Unified School District,* 738 F. Supp. 345, 61 Ed.Law Rep. 120 (N.D. Cal. 1990).
42. 20 U.S.C. § 1401(a)(18)(B).
43. *Hall v. Vance County Board of Education,* 774 F.2d 629, 27 Ed.Law Rep. 1107 (4th Cir. 1985).
44. *In re Conklin,* 946 F.2d 306, 70 Ed.Law Rep. 351 (4th Cir. 1991).
45. *Stock v. Massachusetts Hospital School,* 467 N.E.2d 448, 19 Ed.Law Rep. 637 (Mass. 1984).
46. Osborne, A. G. (1985). Graduation as a change in placement under the EHCA: *Stock v. Massachusetts Hospital School. Education Law Reporter, 27,* 1159–1164.
47. *Puffer v. Raynolds,* 761 F. Supp. 838, 67 Ed.Law Rep. 536 (D. Mass. 1988).
48. *Chuhran v. Walled Lake Consolidated Schools,* 839 F. Supp. 465, 88 Ed.Law Rep. 588 (E.D. Mich. 1993).
49. *See, for example, School Board of Campbell County v. Beasley,* 380 S.E.2d 884, 54 Ed.Law Rep. 1363 (Va. 1989); *Petersen v. Hastings Public Schools,* 831 F. Supp. 742, 86 Ed.Law Rep. 122 (D. Neb. 1993); *Bonnie Ann F. v. Calallen Independent School District,* 835 F. Supp. 340, 87 Ed.Law Rep. 95 (S.D. Tex. 1993).
50. *Straube v. Florida Union Free School District,* 801 F. Supp. 1164, 78 Ed.Law Rep. 390 (S.D.N.Y. 1992); *Manchester School District v. Christopher B.,* 807 F. Supp. 860, 79 Ed.Law Rep. 865 (D.N.H. 1992); *Ojai Unified School District v. Jackson,* 4 F.3d 1467, 85 Ed.Law Rep. 724 (9th Cir. 1993).
51. *Johnson v. Lancaster-Lebanon Intermediate Unit 13, Lancaster City School District,* 757 F. Supp. 606, 66 Ed.Law Rep. 227 (E.D. Pa. 1991).
52. *School Board of Campbell County v. Beasley,* 380 S.E.2d 884, 54 Ed.Law Rep. 1363 (Va. 1989).
53. *Mavis v. Sobol,* 839 F. Supp. 968, 88 Ed.Law Rep. 621 (N.D.N.Y. 1994).
54. *Hiller v. Board of Education of the Brunswick Central School District,* 743 F. Supp. 958, 62 Ed.Law Rep. 974 (N.D.N.Y. 1990); *McDowell v. Fort Bend Independent School District,* 737 F. Supp. 386, 60 Ed.Law Rep. 1145 (S.D. Tex. 1990); *School Board of Campbell County v. Beasley,* 380 S.E.2d 884, 54 Ed.Law Rep. 1363 (Va. 1989); *Hampton School District v. Dobrowolski,* 976 F.2d 48, 77 Ed.Law Rep. 1109 (1st Cir. 1992).
55. *Fuhrmann v. East Hanover Board of Education,* 993 F.2d 1031, 83 Ed.Law Rep. 71 (3d Cir. 1993).
56. *Norris v. Massachusetts Department of Education,* 529 F. Supp. 759, 2 Ed.Law Rep. 659 (D. Mass. 1981).
57. *Visco v. School District of Pittsburgh,* 684 F. Supp. 1310, 47 Ed.Law Rep. 142 (W.D. Pa. 1988).
58. *Chris D. v. Montgomery County Board of Education,* 753 F. Supp. 922, 65 Ed.Law Rep. 355 (M.D. Ala. 1990).

59. *Big Beaver Falls Area School District* v. *Jackson,* 615 A.2d 910, 78 Ed.Law Rep. 888 (Pa. Commw. Ct. 1992).
60. *Christopher M.* v. *Corpus Christi Independent School District,* 933 F.2d 1285, 67 Ed.Law Rep. 1048 (5th Cir. 1991).
61. *Myles S.* v. *Montgomery County Board of Education,* 824 F. Supp. 1549, 84 Ed.Law Rep. 264 (M.D. Ala. 1993).
62. *Lenn* v. *Portland School Committee,* 998 F.2d 1083, 84 Ed.Law Rep. 685 (1st Cir. 1993). *Also see Brougham* v. *Town of Yarmouth,* 823 F. Supp. 9, 84 Ed.Law Rep. 155 (D. Me. 1993); *Doe* v. *Board of Education of Tullahoma City Schools,* 9 F.3d 455, 87 Ed.Law Rep. 354 (6th Cir. 1993).
63. *Hines* v. *Pitt County Board of Education,* 497 F. Supp. 403 (E.D.N.C. 1980).
64. *County School Board of Loudoun County* v. *Lower,* EHLR 555:130 (E.D. Va. 1983).
65. *Valerie J.* v. *Derry Cooperative School District,* 771 F. Supp. 483, 69 Ed.Law Rep. 1067 (D.N.H. 1991).
66. *Board of Education of Community Consolidated School District No. 21, Cook County, Illinois* v. *Illinois State Board of Education,* 938 F.2d 712, 68 Ed.Law Rep. 987 (7th Cir. 1991).
67. *Union School District* v. *Smith,* 15 F.3d 1519, 89 Ed.Law Rep. 449 (9th Cir. 1994).
68. *Hall* v. *Vance County Board of Education,* 774 F.2d 629, 27 Ed.Law Rep. 1107 (4th Cir. 1985).
69. *Tice* v. *Botetourt County School Board,* 908 F.2d 1200, 61 Ed.Law Rep. 1207 (4th Cir. 1990).
70. *Board of Education of the County of Cabell* v. *Dienelt,* 843 F.2d 813, 46 Ed.Law Rep. 64 (4th Cir. 1988); *W.G. and B.G.* v. *Board of Trustees of Target Range School District No. 23, Missoula, Montana,* 789 F. Supp. 1070, 75 Ed.Law Rep. 254, *aff'd* 960 F.2d 1479 (9th Cir. 1992); *Big Beaver Falls Area School District* v. *Jackson,* 615 A.2d 910, 78 Ed.Law Rep. 888 (Pa. Commw. Ct. 1992).
71. *Delaware County Intermediate Unit #25* v. *Martin K.,* 831 F. Supp. 1206, 86 Ed.Law Rep. 147 (E.D. Pa. 1993).
72. *See, for example, Spielberg* v. *Henrico County Public Schools,* 853 F.2d 256, 48 Ed.Law Rep. 352 (4th Cir. 1988).
73. *See, for example, P.J.* v. *State of Connecticut Board of Education,* 788 F. Supp. 673, 74 Ed.Law Rep. 1117 (D. Conn. 1992).
74. Osborne, A. (1993). Parental rights under the IDEA. *Education Law Reporter, 80,* 771–777.
75. *Scituate* v. *Robert B.,* 620 F. Supp. 1224, 28 Ed.Law Rep. 793 (D.R.I. 1985), *aff'd without published opinion,* 795 F.2d 77 (1st Cir. 1986); *Doe* v. *Alabama State Department of Education,* 915 F.2d 651, 63 Ed.Law Rep. 40 (11th Cir. 1990).
76. *Doe* v. *Defendant I,* 898 F.2d 1186, 59 Ed.Law Rep. 619 (6th Cir. 1990).
77. *Hiller* v. *Board of Education of Brunswick Central School District,* 743 F. Supp. 958, 62 Ed.Law Rep. 974 (N.D.N.Y. 1990); *Livingston* v. *DeSoto County School District,* 782 F. Supp. 1173, 72 Ed.Law Rep. 790 (N.D. Miss. 1992); *Myles S.* v. *Montgomery County Board of Education,* 824 F. Supp. 1549, 84 Ed.Law Rep. 264 (M.D. Ala. 1993).
78. *Roland M.* v. *Concord School Committee,* 910 F.2d 983, 62 Ed.Law Rep. 408 (1st Cir. 1990).

79. 20 U.S.C. § 1412(5)(B).
80. Dubow, S. (1989). Into the turbulent mainstream—A legal perspective on the weight to be given to the least restrictive environment in placement decisions for deaf children. *Journal of Law and Education, 18,* 215–228.
81. *See, for example, Bonadonna v. Cooperman,* 619 F. Supp. 401, 28 Ed.Law Rep. 430 (D.N.J. 1985).
82. *Johnston v. Ann Arbor Public Schools,* 569 F. Supp. 1502, 13 Ed.Law Rep. 680 (E.D. Mich. 1983).
83. Julnes, R. & Brown, S. (1991). Least restrictive environment: The legal mandate and practice implications. *Law and Education Desk Notes, 1,* 1–45.
84. *Matthews v. Campbell,* EHLR 551:264 (E.D. Va. 1979); *Board of Education of East Windsor Regional School District v. Diamond,* 808 F.2d 987, 36 Ed.Law Rep. 1136 (3d Cir. 1986); *St. Louis Developmental Disabilities Center v. Mallory,* 591 F. Supp. 1416, 20 Ed.Law Rep. 133 (W.D. Mo. 1984).
85. *Johnston v. Ann Arbor Public School,* 569 F. Supp. 1502, 13 Ed.Law Rep. 680 (E.D. Mich. 1983); *Wilson v. Marana Unified School District,* 735 F.2d 1178, 18 Ed.Law Rep. 197 (9th Cir. 1984); *Lachman v. Illinois State Board of Education,* 852 F.2d 290, 48 Ed.Law Rep. 105 (7th Cir. 1988).
86. *Roncker v. Walter,* 700 F.2d 1058, 9 Ed.Law Rep. 827 (6th Cir. 1983); *Bonadonna v. Cooperman,* 619 F. Supp. 401, 28 Ed.Law Rep. 430 (D.N.J. 1985).
87. *Visco v. School District of Pittsburgh,* 684 F. Supp. 1310, 47 Ed.Law Rep. 142 (W.D. Pa. 1988).
88. *Barnett v. Fairfax County School Board,* 721 F. Supp. 757, 56 Ed.Law Rep. 804 (E.D. Va. 1989), *aff'd* 927 F.2d 146, 66 Ed.Law Rep. 64 (4th Cir. 1991).
89. *Schuldt v. Mankato Independent School District No. 77,* 937 F.2d 1357, 68 Ed.Law Rep. 968 (8th Cir. 1991).
90. 34 C.F.R. § 300.552(a)(3).
91. *Remis v. New Jersey Department of Human Services,* 815 F. Supp. 141, 81 Ed.Law Rep. 762 (D.N.J. 1993).
92. *See, for example, Doyle v. Arlington County School Board,* 806 F. Supp. 1253, 79 Ed.Law Rep. 498 (E.D. Va. 1992).
93. 874 F.2d 1036, 53 Ed.Law Rep. 824 (5th Cir. 1989).
94. *Briggs v. Board of Education of Connecticut,* 882 F.2d 688, 55 Ed.Law Rep. 423 (2d Cir. 1989).
95. *French v. Omaha Public Schools,* 766 F. Supp. 765, 68 Ed.Law Rep. 638 (D. Neb. 1991).
96. *Johnson v. Lancaster-Lebanon Intermediate Unit 13, Lancaster City School District,* 757 F. Supp. 606, 66 Ed.Law Rep. 227 (E.D. Pa. 1991).
97. *DeVries v. Fairfax County School Board,* 882 F.2d 876, 55 Ed.Law Rep. 442 (4th Cir. 1989).
98. *Liscio v. Woodland Hills School District,* 734 F. Supp. 689, 60 Ed.Law Rep. 47 (W.D. Pa. 1989), *aff'd* 902 F.2d 1561, 60 Ed.Law Rep. 1083 (3d Cir. 1990).
99. *Gillette v. Fairland Board of Education,* 932 F.2d 551, 67 Ed.Law Rep. 510 (6th Cir. 1991).
100. *Chris D. v. Montgomery County Board of Education,* 753 F. Supp. 1524, 62 Ed.Law Rep. 1001 (M.D. Ala. 1990).

101. *MR v. Lincolnwood Board of Education, District 74,* 843 F. Supp. 1236, 89 Ed.Law Rep. 834 (N.D. Ill. 1994).
102. *Carter v. Florence County School District Four,* 950 F.2d 156, 71 Ed.Law Rep. 633 (4th Cir. 1991), *aff'd on other grounds sub nom. Florence County School District Four v. Carter,* ___ U.S. ___, 114 S. Ct. 361, 126 L. Ed.2d 284, 86 Ed.Law Rep. 41 (1993).
103. *Thornock v. Boise Independent School District,* 767 P.2d 1241, 52 Ed.Law Rep. 272 (Idaho 1988).
104. *Greer v. Rome City School District,* 762 F. Supp. 936, 67 Ed.Law Rep. 666 (N.D. Ga. 1990), *aff'd* 950 F.2d 688, 71 Ed.Law Rep. 647 (11th Cir. 1991), *withdrawn* 956 F.2d 1025, 73 Ed.Law Rep. 34 (11th Cir. 1992), *reinstated* 967 F.2d 470, 76 Ed.Law Rep. 26 (11th Cir. 1992).
105. *Id.* 762 F. Supp. 936, 947 n. 10.
106. *Id.* 950 F.2d 688, 71 Ed.Law Rep. 647 (11th Cir. 1991).
107. *Chris D. v. Montgomery County Board of Education,* 753 F. Supp. 922, 65 Ed.Law Rep. 355 (M.D. Ala. 1990).
108. *Oberti v. Board of Education of the Borough of Clementon School District,* 789 F. Supp. 1322, 75 Ed.Law Rep. 258 (D.N.J. 1992), 801 F. Supp. 1393 (D.N.J. 1992), *aff'd* 995 F.2d 1204, 83 Ed.Law Rep. 1009 (3d Cir. 1993).
109. *Board of Education, Sacramento City Unified School District v. Holland,* 786 F. Supp. 874, 73 Ed.Law Rep. 969 (E.D. Cal. 1992), *aff'd sub nom. Sacramento City Unified School District, Board of Education v. Rachel H.,* 14 F.3d 1398, 89 Ed.Law Rep. 57 (9th Cir. 1994). *Also see Mavis v. Sobol,* 839 F. Supp. 968, 88 Ed.Law Rep. 621 (N.D.N.Y. 1994).
110. *See, for example, Mavis v. Sobol,* 839 F. Supp. 968, 88 Ed.Law Rep. 621 (N.D.N.Y. 1994); *Board of Education of the Baldwin Union Free School District v. Commissioner of Education,* 610 N.Y.S.2d 426, 90 Ed.Law Rep. 752 (N.Y. Sup. Ct. 1994).
111. *See, for example, MR v. Lincolnwood Board of Education, District 74,* 843 F. Supp. 1236, 89 Ed.Law Rep. 834 (N.D. Ill. 1994).
112. 34 C.F.R. § 300.551(a).
113. 34 C.F.R. § 300.302.
114. *Lang v. Braintree School Committee,* 545 F. Supp. 1221, 6 Ed.Law Rep. 349 (D. Mass. 1982).
115. *Riley v. Ambach,* EHLR 554:180 (E.D.N.Y. 1982).
116. *Hall v. Freeman,* 700 F. Supp. 1106, 50 Ed.Law Rep. 1007 (D. Ga. 1987).
117. *Hessler v. State Board of Education of Maryland,* 700 F.2d 134, 9 Ed.Law Rep. 499 (4th Cir. 1983).
118. *See, for example, Martin v. School Board of Prince George County,* 348 S.E.2d 857, 35 Ed.Law Rep. 302 (Va. Ct. App. 1986); *Kerkam v. Superintendent, D.C. Public Schools,* 931 F.2d 84, 67 Ed.Law Rep. 454 (D.C. Cir. 1991).
119. *Doyle v. Arlington County School Board,* 806 F. Supp. 1253, 79 Ed.Law Rep. 498 (E.D. Va. 1992), *on remand from* 953 F.2d 100, 72 Ed.Law Rep. 44 (4th Cir. 1991).
120. *Amann v. Stow School System,* 982 F.2d 644, 80 Ed.Law Rep. 42 (1st Cir. 1992); *Doe v. Board of Education of Tullahoma City Schools,* 9 F.3d 455, 87 Ed.Law Rep. 354 (6th Cir. 1993).

121. *Stacey G. v. Pasadena Independent School District,* 547 F. Supp. 61, 6 Ed.Law Rep. 663 (S.D. Tex. 1982), *partially vac'd and rem'd* 695 F.2d 949, 8 Ed.Law Rep. 237 (5th Cir. 1983).
122. *Bailey v. Unified School District,* 664 P.2d 1379, 12 Ed.Law Rep. 131 (Kan. 1983).
123. *Oberti v. Board of Education of the Borough of Clementon School District,* 801 F. Supp. 1393 (D.N.J. 1992), *aff'd* 995 F.2d 1204, 83 Ed.Law Rep. 1009 (3d Cir. 1993).
124. *Matthews v. Campbell,* EHLR 551:264 (E.D. Va. 1979).
125. *Colin K. v. Schmidt,* 536 F. Supp. 1375, 4 Ed.Law Rep. 128 (D.R.I. 1982); *aff'd* 715 F.2d 1, 13 Ed.Law Rep. 221 (1st Cir. 1983).
126. *Straube v. Florida Union Free School District,* 801 F. Supp. 1164, 78 Ed.Law Rep. 390 (S.D.N.Y. 1992).
127. *Norris v. Massachusetts Department of Education,* 529 F. Supp. 759, 2 Ed.Law Rep. 659 (D. Mass. 1981).
128. *Williams v. Gering Public Schools,* 463 N.W.2d 799, 64 Ed.Law Rep. 901 (Neb. 1990).
129. *Clevenger v. Oak Ridge School Board,* 744 F.2d 514, 20 Ed.Law Rep. 404 (6th Cir. 1984).
130. *Department of Education v. Mr. and Mrs. S.,* 632 F. Supp. 1268, 32 Ed.Law Rep. 137 (D. Haw. 1986).
131. *Ladson v. Board of Education of the District of Columbia,* EHLR 551:188 (D.D.C. 1979).
132. *DeWalt v. Burkholder,* EHLR 551:550 (E.D. Va. 1980).
133. *Gladys J. v. Pearland Independent School District,* 520 F. Supp. 869 (S.D. Tex. 1981).
134. *Brown v. Wilson County School Board,* 747 F. Supp. 436, 63 Ed.Law Rep. 525 (M.D. Tenn. 1990).
135. *Diamond v. McKenzie,* 602 F. Supp. 632, 23 Ed.Law Rep. 100 (D.D.C. 1985).
136. *Chris D. v. Montgomery County Board of Education,* 743 F. Supp. 1524, 62 Ed.Law Rep. 1001 (M.D. Ala. 1990).
137. *Adams Central School District v. Deist,* 334 N.W.2d 775, 11 Ed.Law Rep. 1020 (Neb. 1983), *modified* 338 N.W.2d 591, 13 Ed.Law Rep. 846 (Neb. 1983). *Also see Cremeans v. Fairland Local School District Board of Education,* 633 N.E.2d 570, 91 Ed.Law Rep. 280 (Ohio App. Ct. 1993).
138. *Garland Independent School District v. Wilks,* 657 F. Supp. 1163, 39 Ed.Law Rep. 92 (N.D. Tex. 1987). *Also see Drew P. v. Clarke County School District,* 676 F. Supp. 1559, 44 Ed.Law Rep. 250 (M.D. Ga. 1987), *aff'd* 877 F.2d 927, 54 Ed.Law Rep. 456 (11th Cir. 1989).
139. *Ash v. Lake Oswego School District,* 766 F. Supp. 852, 68 Ed.Law Rep. 683 (D. Or. 1991), *aff'd* 980 F.2d 585, 79 Ed.Law Rep. 408 (9th Cir. 1992).
140. *Kruelle v. Biggs,* 489 F. Supp. 169 (D. Del. 1980,) *aff'd sub nom. Kruelle v. New Castle,* 642 F.2d 687 (3d Cir. 1981).
141. *Board of Education of East Windsor Regional School District v. Diamond,* 808 F.2d 987, 36 Ed.Law Rep. 1136 (3d Cir. 1986).
142. *Abrahamson v. Hershman,* 701 F.2d 223, 9 Ed.Law Rep. 837 (1st Cir. 1983).
143. *Walker v. Cronin,* 438 N.E.2d 582, 5 Ed.Law Rep. 1224 (Ill. App. Ct. 1982).

144. *Hines v. Pitt County Board of Education,* 497 F. Supp. 403 (E.D.N.C. 1980).
145. *Clevenger v. Oak Ridge School Board,* 744 F.2d 514, 20 Ed.Law Rep. 404 (6th Cir. 1984).
146. *San Francisco Unified School District v. State of California,* 131 Cal. App.3d 54, 182 Cal. Rptr. 525, 3 Ed.Law Rep. 1057 (Cal. Ct. App. 1982).
147. *B.G. v. Cranford Board of Education,* 702 F. Supp. 1140, 51 Ed.Law Rep. 470 (D.N.J. 1988).
148. *Jefferson County Board of Education v. Breen,* 853 F.2d 853, 48 Ed.Law Rep. 382 (11th Cir. 1988).
149. *North v. District of Columbia Board of Education,* 471 F. Supp. 136 (D.D.C. 1979).
150. *Erdman v. State of Connecticut,* EHLR 552:218 (D. Conn. 1980). *Also see Woods v. New Jersey Department of Education,* 796 F. Supp. 767, 77 Ed.Law Rep. 126 (D.N.J. 1992) *and Vander Malle v. Ambach,* 667 F. Supp. 1015, 41 Ed.Law Rep. 913 (S.D.N.Y. 1987).
151. *Doe v. Anrig,* 692 F.2d 800 (1st Cir. 1982), *on rem'd* 561 F. Supp. 121, 10 Ed.Law Rep. 1038 (D. Mass. 1983).
152. *McKenzie v. Jefferson,* EHLR 554:338 (D.D.C. 1983).
153. *Ahern v. Keene,* 593 F. Supp. 902, 20 Ed.Law Rep. 555 (D. Del. 1984). *Also see Metropolitan Government of Nashville and Davidson County v. Tennessee Department of Education,* 771 S.W.2d 427, 54 Ed.Law Rep. 1001 (Tenn. Ct. App. 1989).
154. *Swift v. Rapides Parish Public School System,* 812 F. Supp. 666, 81 Ed.Law Rep. 68 (W.D. La. 1993).
155. A different result may be obtained in a state that does require maximization of potential. *See David D. v. Dartmouth School Committee,* 775 F.2d 411, 28 Ed.Law Rep. 70 (1st Cir. 1985) where a residential placement was ordered under the state's higher standard of appropriateness when it was found that the student experienced problems outside of school that were not manifested in school.
156. 20 U.S.C. § 1401(a)(17). See Chapter 6 for additional information.
157. *Metropolitan Government of Nashville and Davidson County v. Tennessee Department of Education,* 771 S.W.2d 427, 54 Ed.Law Rep. 1001 (Tenn. Ct. App. 1989).
158. *McKenzie v. Jefferson,* EHLR 554:338 (D.D.C. 1983).
159. *Taylor v. Honig,* 910 F.2d 627, 62 Ed.Law Rep. 78 (9th Cir. 1990).
160. *Brown v. Wilson County School Board,* 747 F. Supp. 436, 63 Ed.Law Rep. 525 (M.D. Tenn. 1990).
161. *Michael P. v. Maloney,* 551:155 (D. Conn. 1979).
162. *Parks v. Pavkovic,* 557 F. Supp. 1280, 9 Ed.Law Rep. 1237 (N.D. Ill.), *aff'd* 753 F.2d 1397, 22 Ed.Law Rep. 1128 (7th Cir. 1985). For previous litigation *see* 536 F. Supp. 296, 4 Ed.Law Rep. 66 (N.D. Ill. 1982).
163. *Christopher T. v. San Francisco Unified School District,* 553 F. Supp. 1107, 8 Ed.Law Rep. 951 (N.D. Cal. 1982).
164. *Vander Malle v. Ambach,* 667 F. Supp. 1015, 41 Ed.Law Rep. 913 (S.D.N.Y.).
165. *McClain v. Smith,* 793 F. Supp. 756, 76 Ed.Law Rep. 408 (E.D. Tenn. 1989); 793 F. Supp. 761, 76 Ed.Law Rep. 413 (E.D. Tenn. 1990).
166. *Ojai Unified School District v. Jackson,* 4 F.3d 1467, 85 Ed.Law Rep. 724 (9th Cir. 1993).

167. 34 C.F.R. § 300.342(b)(2).
168. *Evans* v. *Evans*, 818 F. Supp. 1215, 82 Ed.Law Rep. 492 (N.D. Ind. 1993).
169. *Bray* v. *Hobart City School Corporation*, 818 F. Supp. 1226, 82 Ed.Law Rep. 503 (N.D. Ind. 1993).
170. 34 C.F.R. § 300.343(d) and 34 C.F.R. § 300.552(a)(1). *See Drew P.* v. *Clarke County School District*, 877 F.2d 927, 54 Ed.Law Rep. 456 (11th Cir. 1989) where the appeals court held that the district court did not abuse its discretion by ordering a school district to maintain a residential placement until the student was 21 since the district court stated that it would not interfere if the school district could demonstrate in the future that the student no longer required the residential placement. *But see Manchester School District* v. *Christopher B.*, 807 F. Supp. 860, 79 Ed.Law Rep. 865 (D.N.H. 1992) where the court held that a hearing officer erred in ordering a private school placement for more than one year.
171. *Vander Malle* v. *Ambach*, 673 F.2d 49, 3 Ed.Law Rep. 293 (2d Cir. 1982).
172. *Grkman* v. *Scanlon*, 528 F. Supp. 1032, 2 Ed.Law Rep. 90 (W.D. Pa. 1981).
173. *Zvi D.* v. *Ambach*, 520 F. Supp. 196 (E.D.N.Y. 1981), *aff'd* 694 F.2d 904, 8 Ed.Law Rep. 10 (2d Cir. 1982).
174. *Matthews* v. *Davis*, 742 F.2d 825, 19 Ed.Law Rep. 935 (4th Cir. 1984).
175. 20 U.S.C. § 1424(b).
176. 20 U.S.C. § 1424(e).
177. *Georgia Association of Retarded Citizens* v. *McDaniel*, 511 F. Supp. 1263 (N.D. Ga. 1981), *aff'd* 716 F.2d 1565, 13 Ed.Law Rep. 609 (11th Cir. 1983), *vac'd and rem'd* 104 S. Ct. 3581, 19 Ed.Law Rep. 25 (1984), *mod'd* 740 F.2d 902, 19 Ed.Law Rep. 117 (11th Cir. 1984).
178. *Crawford* v. *Pittman*, 708 F.2d 1028, 11 Ed.Law Rep. 815 (5th Cir. 1983).
179. *Yaris* v. *Special School District, St. Louis County*, 558 F. Supp. 545, 9 Ed.Law Rep. 1314 (E.D. Mo. 1983), *aff'd* 728 F.2d 1055, 16 Ed.Law Rep. 757 (8th Cir. 1984).
180. *In re Scott K.*, 400 N.Y.S. 289 (N.Y. Fam. Ct. 1977); *Mahoney* v. *Administrative School District No. 1*, 601 P.2d 826 (Or. Ct. App. 1979).
181. *Armstrong* v. *Kline*, 476 F. Supp. 583 (E.D. Pa. 1979), *rem'd sub nom. Battle* v. *Commonwealth of Pennsylvania*, 629 F.2d 269 (3d Cir. 1980), *on rem'd* 513 F. Supp. 425 (E.D. Pa. 1981).
182. *Stacey G.* v. *Pasadena Independent School District*, 547 F. Supp. 61, 6 Ed.Law Rep. 663 (S.D. Tex. 1982), *partially vac'd and rem'd* 695 F.2d 949, 8 Ed.Law Rep. 237 (5th Cir. 1983).
183. *Alamo Heights Independent School District* v. *State Board of Education*, 790 F.2d 1153, 32 Ed.Law Rep. 445 (5th Cir. 1986).
184. *Cordrey* v. *Euckert*, 917 F.2d 1460, 63 Ed.Law Rep. 798 (6th Cir. 1990). *Also see Rettig* v. *Kent City School District*, 539 F. Supp. 768, 4 Ed.Law Rep. 1083 (N.D. Ohio 1981), *aff'd in part, vac'd and rem'd in part* 720 F.2d 463, 14 Ed.Law Rep. 445 (6th Cir. 1983), *on rem'd* (unpublished opinion 1/26/84), *rev'd* 788 F.2d 328, 31 Ed.Law Rep. 759 (6th Cir. 1986) [court held that the determination for an ESY program should be made on the basis of a multifaceted evaluation].

185. *Williams* v. *Gering Public Schools,* 463 N.W.2d 799, 64 Ed.Law Rep. 901 (Neb. 1990); *Johnson* v. *Lancaster-Lebanon Intermediate Unit 13, Lancaster City School District,* 757 F. Supp. 606, 66 Ed.Law Rep. 227 (E.D. Pa. 1991).
186. *Bucks County Public Schools* v. *Commonwealth of Pennsylvania,* 529 A.2d 1201, 41 Ed.Law Rep. 251 (Pa. Commw. Ct. 1987); *Holmes* v. *Sobol,* 690 F. Supp. 154, 48 Ed.Law Rep. 524 (W.D.N.Y. 1988); *Johnson* v. *Lancaster-Lebanon Intermediate Unit 13, Lancaster City School District,* 757 F. Supp. 606, 66 Ed.Law Rep. 227 (E.D. Pa. 1991); *Cremeans* v. *Fairland Local School District Board of Education,* 633 N.E.2d 570, 91 Ed.Law Rep. 280 (Ohio App. Ct. 1993).
187. *Birmingham and Lamphere School District* v. *Superintendent of Public Instruction,* 328 N.W.2d 59, 8 Ed.Law Rep. 467 (Mich. Ct. App. 1982).
188. *Lee* v. *Thompson,* EHLR 554:429 (D. Haw. 1983).
189. *Johnson* v. *Independent School District No. 4 of Bixby, Tulsa County, Oklahoma,* 921 F.2d 1022, 64 Ed.Law Rep. 1027 (10th Cir. 1990).
190. *Anderson* v. *Thompson,* 495 F. Supp. 1256 (E.D. Wis. 1980), aff'd 658 F.2d 1205 (7th Cir. 1981).
191. *Bales* v. *Clarke,* 523 F. Supp. 1366, 1 Ed.Law Rep. 218 (E.D. Va. 1981).
192. *Cordrey* v. *Euckert,* 917 F.2d 1460, 63 Ed.Law Rep. 798 (6th Cir. 1990).

# 6

# PROVISION
# OF RELATED SERVICES

Under the Individuals with Disabilities Education Act (IDEA)[1] school districts are required to provide related, or supportive, services to students with disabilities if such services are needed to assist the students in benefitting from their special education programs.[2] IDEA specifically delineates developmental, supportive, or corrective services such as transportation, speech pathology, audiology, psychological services, physical therapy, occupational therapy, recreation (including therapeutic recreation), social work services, counseling services (including rehabilitation counseling), medical services (for diagnostic or evaluative purposes only), and early identification and assessment as related services.[3]

The only limit placed on what could be a related service is that medical services are exempted unless they are specifically for diagnostic or evaluative purposes. A comment in IDEA's regulations indicates that the list of related services is not exhaustive and could include other services that may be required to assist a student with disabilities to benefit from special education.[4] The comment suggests that services such as artistic and cultural programs or art, music, and dance therapy could be related services. The comment further suggests that related services may be provided by persons of varying professional backgrounds with a variety of occupational titles.

Related services need be provided only to students who are receiving special education services. Under IDEA's definitions, a child is disabled only if the child requires special education services. A comment attached to the definition of special education indicates that since related services are to be provided when necessary for a child to benefit from special education, there is no requirement to provide related services when the child is not receiving special education.[5]

Much litigation has occurred concerning whether or not certain services needed by a student with disabilities constituted related services under IDEA. Although each of the categories of related services listed in IDEA is defined in the regulations, the precise parameters of some categories have been disputed. Also, since the list is not exhaustive, lawsuits have been brought seeking services that are not specifically listed in the act. Much of the litigation has been over whether certain health-related services fell within the medical exclusion.

## COUNSELING, PSYCHOLOGICAL, AND SOCIAL WORK SERVICES

IDEA's regulations define counseling as a service that is provided by a qualified social worker, psychologist, guidance counselor, or other qualified person.[6] The definition of psychological services includes psychological counseling[7] and the definition of social work services includes group and individual counseling.[8] However, the term *psychotherapy* is not used or defined in the regulations.

One of the controversies that has developed over the medical exclusion clause of the related services mandate concerns the provision of psychotherapy. Counseling, psychological, and social work services clearly would be required related services when needed for a student with disabilities to benefit from special education. Although psychotherapy can be classified as a psychological service, in some instances it may fit within the medical exclusion. This depends on individual state laws governing psychotherapy. The laws of some states stipulate that only psychiatrists can provide psychotherapy whereas, in other states, clinical psychologists are allowed to provide psychotherapy. Since a psychiatrist is a licensed physician, psychotherapy would be an exempted medical service in those states that restrict its provision to psychiatrists.

It is important to note that the distinguishing criteria regarding whether psychotherapy is a related service or an exempted medical service is how it is defined by state law, not by who actually provides the service. In Illinois, state law allows nonpsychiatric professionals to provide psychotherapy. A district court in that state held that a school district was responsible for the costs of psychotherapy even though, in the case at bar, the psychotherapy was actually provided by a psychiatrist.[9] The court held that the criterion that services that must be performed by a physician were exempted did not mean that services that could be provided by a non-physician, but were in actuality provided by a physician, were excluded. However, in such an instance, the school district would be required to pay for the services only to the extent of the costs of their being performed by a nonphysician.

Since students with emotional difficulties may not be able to benefit from their special education programs until their emotional problems are addressed, counseling, psychotherapy, or social work services may be required as related services. Although IDEA does not mention, let alone define, the word *psychotherapy*, it can be a related service. The Supreme Court of Montana turned to the dictionary to find a definition of the term.[10] The court found that, according to Webster, psychotherapy is a psychological service and thus ruled that it is a related service. A district court in New Jersey also categorized psychotherapy as a counseling or psychological service and held that it was a required related service.[11]

Federal district courts in Illinois and Massachusetts have held that psychotherapy is a required related service because it can be necessary for some children to benefit from their educational programs.[12] The Illinois court found that although psychotherapy was related to mental health, it also may be required before a child could derive any benefit from education. Similarly, the New Jersey federal district court held that psychotherapy was an essential service that allowed an emotionally disturbed student to benefit from his educational program.[13]

Counseling generally is not considered to be a medical service and thus may be a required related service. For example, the district court in Connecticut held that psychological and counseling services that were required by a student with disabilities to benefit from the special education program were not embraced within the exempted medical services clause.[14] The court found that the therapy services offered as part of a residential placement were essential to render the student educable and thus were required related services.[15]

An important element in the requirement to provide related services is that they must be necessary for the student to benefit from special education services. Thus, the Fourth Circuit Court of Appeals held that counseling services were not required for a student who had made great improvement under an IEP that did not include counseling.[16]

If the therapeutic services can be classified as psychiatric services, however, courts will declare that they fall within the medical exception. The district court for the District of Columbia held that the school district was not responsible for payment of the residential component costs of a placement in a psychiatric hospital and school.[17] The court found that the primary reasons for the student's placement were medical, not educational. Similarly, a district court in Illinois found that psychiatric services are medical since psychiatrists are licensed physicians and held that they were not related services.[18] Several other courts also have held that psychiatric facilities are medical facilities and that school districts are not required to pay for the services rendered at these facilities.[19]

Psychiatric services could be required as related services if they are for diagnostic or evaluative purposes. A Tennessee district court held that the limited medical services a student received in a residential rehabilitation facility could not be used to characterize the entire program as medical.[20] The medical services were provided to monitor and adjust the child's medication, and the court ruled that they were for diagnostic and evaluative purposes and, thus, were related services. Similarly, an evaluation by a neurologist has been held to be a related service.[21] Although the students in these cases were not receiving psychiatric treatment, the same principle would apply to psychiatric services that are diagnostic or evaluative.

Whether a placement in a facility that provides psychiatric services is primarily for medical or educational reasons may determine what costs the school district is responsible for. Two cases decided months apart by the Ninth Circuit Court of Appeals are illustrative. In the first case[22] the student was admitted to an acute care psychiatric hospital when the residential school she had been attending could no longer control her behavior. Her parents sought payment of the costs of that placement from the school district. However, the court compared the placement to one for a student suffering from a physical illness and declared that it had been made for medical reasons. The court held that room and board costs were medically related, not educationally related, since the hospital did not provide educational services. In the second case[23] the student was placed in a residential school and psychiatric hospital after he had assaulted a family member. In this instance the court found the residential facility to be a boarding school that had the capacity to offer medical services that may be necessary. The court held that the placement was made for primarily educational reasons and was appropriate under IDEA.

## SCHOOL HEALTH SERVICES

School health services are defined as services performed by a qualified school nurse or other qualified person.[24] Again, controversy has developed over the provision of health-related services in the schools because of the medical exclusion clause. Since a number of medical procedures can be performed by a registered nurse, questions have arisen as to whether certain nursing services fall within the definition of school health services or are exempted medical services.

The U.S. Supreme Court, in *Irving Independent School District* v. *Tatro,* held that catheterization was a required related service for a student who could not voluntarily empty her bladder due to spina bifida.[25] She had to be catheterized every three to four hours. The Court found that services that allow a student to remain in class during the school day, such as catheterization, are no less related to the effort to educate than services that allow the student to reach, enter, or exit the school. The catheterization procedure could be performed by a school nurse or trained health aide, and the Court ruled that Congress did not intend to exclude these services as medical services.

The Court also provided clarification as to when related services must be provided to students with disabilities. The Court stated that in the absence of a disability that requires special education, the need for related services does not create an obligation under IDEA and that only those services that are necessary to aid a student in benefitting from special education must be provided. The Court further emphasized that a life-support service would not be a related service if it did not need to be provided during school hours.

The district court in Hawaii held that a school district was required to provide a student who had cystic fibrosis with health services attendant to a tracheotomy tube.[26] The tube became dislodged occasionally and needed to be reinserted, and mucus needed to be suctioned from her lungs periodically. Again, these procedures could be performed by a school nurse or trained layperson, and the court held that they were required related services. In another case a district court in Michigan ruled that the school district was required to provide an aide on a school bus to attend to a medically fragile student.[27] The court held that the provision of an aide or other health professional did not constitute an exempted medical service.

These cases indicate that services that may be provided by the school nurse, a health aide, or even a trained layperson fall within IDEA's mandated related services provision. However, the fragile medical conditions of some students require the presence of a full-time nurse. Courts have held that extensive nursing services are more akin to medical services and that school districts are not required to provide them.[28] In one case a New York district court held that a school district was not required to provide constant nursing care to a physically disabled child.[29] The student's condition required that a person trained to monitor her health be available at all times. The availability of a school nurse, who would have other duties, was not sufficient. The court noted the extensive nursing services fell somewhere in between school health services and medical services but more closely resembled medical services. Similarly, a district court in Pennsylvania held that constant nursing services resembled private duty nursing as opposed to school nursing services and were thus more in the nature of medical services.[30] However, one court held that a school district was required to provide the services of either a full-time nurse or a respiratory care professional for a student who suffered from a rare condition that caused difficulty breathing.[31] Although the court found that the costs of such services were clearly medical in nature, it held that they were not so burdensome that they should fall within the medical exclusion.

## DIAGNOSTIC AND EVALUATIVE SERVICES

Proper diagnosis and evaluation of students suspected of having a disability is an important component of the special education process. Medical evaluations can be part of that process. IDEA makes it clear that medical services can be related services when used for that purpose.[32]

In an interesting case from Tennessee the district court held that a school district was responsible for payment of a neurological and psychological evaluation ordered by the student's pediatrician.[33] School district personnel had requested an evaluation by the pediatrician for a student who had a seizure disorder, visual difficulties, and learning disabilities, whose behavior and school performance had deteriorated. The pediatrician referred the student to a neurologist who subsequently referred him to a psychologist. A dispute arose over who was responsible for paying for the neurological and psychological evaluations. The court held that the student's needs were intertwined and that these evaluations were necessary for him to benefit from his special education. The court further held that the parents could be required to use their health insurance to pay for the evaluations if it did not incur a cost to them. Their policy placed a lifetime cap on psychological services that would be reduced by the amount of the evaluation bill; thus, the court held that the school district was responsible for payment. Since no such cap existed for neurological services, the court held that the parents were required to use their insurance for that evaluation.

The phrase *diagnostic and evaluative services* does not refer just to assessments that may be conducted as part of an initial evaluation. A ruling by a district court in Tennessee indicates that ongoing monitoring of a student's condition could fall within the realm of diagnostic and evaluative services.[34] The court held that medical services that were provided to monitor and adjust a student's medication were medical services for diagnostic and evaluation purposes and thus were the responsibility of the school district.

## SUBSTANCE ABUSE TREATMENT

School districts would not be required to provide substance abuse programs under the related services mandate if those programs follow a medical model. The district court in New Jersey held that a substance abuse program does not fall within the domain of related services that must be provided under IDEA even though it would benefit learning.[35] In this case a special education student who attended a private school was expelled from that school for possession of drugs. His parents were informed that he could return to school if he attended a substance abuse program. The school district refused to pay for the program and the parents filed suit. The court found that the program was medical as it consisted of psychiatric counseling, physical examinations, and administration of medication.

A substance abuse program that is not primarily medical could be a required related service. Since counseling, psychological, and social work services are required related services, any substance abuse program that primarily utilized one of those services could be a required related service.

## HABILITATION SERVICES

The Fourth Circuit Court of Appeals held that in-home habilitation services do not fall within the federal definitions of special education and related services.[36] The parents had requested the services, which were primarily designed to help control the student's behavior at home, when the student returned to the family home after attending a residential program. The court also noted that the student had made educational progress without the requested services.

## PHYSICAL, OCCUPATIONAL, AND SPEECH THERAPY

Occupational therapy refers to services that improve, develop, or restore functions impaired or lost through illness, injury, or deprivation.[37] Physical therapy is defined in IDEA's regulations simply as the services provided by a qualified physical therapist.[38] Speech pathology includes the identification, diagnosis, and appraisal of speech or language impairments and the provision of appropriate services for the habilitation or prevention of communication impairments.[39]

A New York district court ordered a school district to provide a student with occupational therapy over the summer months after it found that the student would regress in the areas of upper body strength and ambulation skills.[40] The court also found that the student's ability to perform classroom work and function in the classroom would be adversely affected without the summer therapy. The district court for the District of Columbia held that a proposed placement for a student with multiple disabilities was not appropriate as it did not provide for an integrated occupational therapy program as called for in the student's IEP.[41] The court found that the student would not benefit from her special education program without this service.

The Third Circuit Court of Appeals stated that for some children physical therapy is an important facilitator of classroom learning.[42] Stating that IDEA calls for an education that provides meaningful benefit, the court found that physical therapy is an essential prerequisite for learning for some students with severe disabilities.

Since an inability to communicate effectively could interfere with a student's learning, speech and language therapy, when needed, generally would be considered a related service. Although there has been no major litigation involving the need for speech or language therapy, it is safe to say that courts would require its provision. Most school districts provide extensive speech and language therapy services, and in some states it is considered to be a special education service rather than a related service.

## ALTERATIONS TO THE PHYSICAL PLANT

School districts may be required to make alterations to the physical plant to allow a student with disabilities to participate fully in and benefit from the educational program. Most of these alterations allow access to the building. However, a Texas case illustrates the fact that modifications may be required to allow a student to remain in the classroom. A federal district court ordered a school district to provide an air-conditioned classroom for a student who, due to brain injuries suffered in an accident, could not regulate his body temperature.[43] The student required a temperature-controlled environment at all times due to his inability to regulate his body temperature. The school district had provided the student with an air-conditioned Plexiglas cubicle. Although the student was achieving satisfactorily, he was restricted in his ability to socialize and participate in group activities. The court found use of the cubicle to be a violation of the least restrictive environment (LRE) mandate because it caused the student to miss out on class participation and group interaction that were important to his education.

School districts are not required to make alterations to every school building within the district to make them accessible to students with disabilities. A decision by the Eighth Circuit Court of Appeals indicates that a school district would be in compliance as long as they could offer a student a placement in an accessible school that is reasonably close to the student's home.[44] In this case a lawsuit was filed on behalf of a student who used a wheelchair, seeking to require the school district to modify the student's neighborhood school to make it accessible. Three other schools in the district were accessible, and the school district offered the student a placement in one of those schools. The court upheld that arrangement.

## RECREATION AND ENRICHMENT PROGRAMS

Recreation and therapeutic recreation are specifically listed as related services in IDEA. The definition of recreation indicates that it includes assessment of leisure function, recreation programs in schools and community agencies, and leisure education, along with therapeutic recreation.[45] IDEA's regulations also state that school districts are to provide nonacademic and extracurricular services and activities to the extent necessary to afford students with disabilities an equal opportunity for participation.[46] Nonacademic and extracurricular services and activities may include athletics, recreational activities, special interest groups or clubs, employment, and many of the services listed as related services. These activities must be provided in the mainstream to the maximum extent appropriate.[47]

If participation in a school district's general extracurricular program is not appropriate, under these regulations special extracurricular programs may need to be developed for students with disabilities. Students who meet the eligibility requirements for participation in the general extracurricular program cannot be denied access to it under section 504 of the Rehabilitation Act.[48] Reasonable accommodations may need to be provided to allow students with disabilities to participate in the general extracurricular program. For example, eligibility rules that would prevent students with disabilities from participating because of their disabilities may need to be waived.[49]

The exact requirements of the extracurricular activities regulation are unclear. The Sixth Circuit Court of Appeals ruled that this regulation was in conflict with the U.S. Supreme Court's *Rowley*[50] decision.[51] The court found the regulation to require strict equality of opportunity, whereas it interpreted *Rowley* as not absolutely requiring that every service that is available to nondisabled students be provided to students with disabilities. However, the regulation has not been removed or altered in subsequent revisions of the regulations. In the case before it, the appeals court found that the student in question would receive no significant benefit from participation in extracurricular activities and that the student would benefit from his special education program without extracurricular activities. The court ruled that under *Rowley* a school district was not required to provide every service that might be beneficial. Under the Sixth Circuit's ruling it would be necessary to provide extracurricular activities only when the student would not benefit from special education without them.

A state court in Michigan ordered a school district to provide a summer enrichment program to an autistic student.[52] Testimony at the trial indicated that the student needed a program that included outdoor activities. The court held that the requested program fell within the parameters of special education and related services since physical education was included in the definition of special education and recreation was a related service.

## PARENT TRAINING AND COUNSELING

Parent training and counseling, as defined in IDEA's regulations, means assisting parents in understanding the special needs of the student and providing them with information about child development.[53] Frequently, courts have ordered residential placements for students who required consistency and support that was not available in the home environment.[54] Less restrictive placements would be appropriate if the parents could be trained to deal with the student appropriately in the home using similar techniques to those used at school. However, avoidance of a residential placement is not the sole criterion for providing parent training and counseling.

A district court in Texas held that an appropriate placement could be provided within a public school setting for a student who had severe disabilities if training and counseling were provided to her parents.[55] In doing so, a residential placement could be averted according to the court's findings. The court found that the student needed a highly structured educational program and that this program needed to be maintained year-round. In order to maintain that structure after school hours, the court ordered the school district to provide the student's parents with training in behavioral techniques. Counseling to help relieve the stress of the burdensome demands placed on them by her disability also was to be provided.

An Alabama district court ordered a school district to provide parent training and counseling to the parents of a student who exhibited academic and behavioral problems.[56] In finding that the student's overall IEP was not appropriate, the court held that school officials had ignored a crucial component of a behavioral control program by failing to counsel and instruct the parents in how to reinforce at home the training the student received at school.

## TRANSPORTATION

It is easy to see why transportation is an important related service: the student cannot benefit from an educational program if the student can't get to the program. Special transportation arrangements need to be provided if the student is unable to access the standard transportation provisions. The term *transportation* encompasses travel to and from school, between schools, and around school buildings. Specialized equipment, such as adapted busses, lifts, and ramps, are required if needed to provide the transportation.[57]

A ruling by the district court in Rhode Island indicates that the term *transportation* includes transportation from the student's house to the vehicle.[58] In this case the student had been denied assistance in getting from his house to the school bus. Since he was unable to get to the vehicle without assistance, his father transported him to school for a time. When the father was unable to transport him to school, the student was unable to attend classes. The situation was finally resolved, but the court awarded the parents compensation for their efforts in transporting him to school after holding that transportation clearly was the responsibility of the school district.

Students who are placed in private schools by the school district are entitled to transportation;[59] however, if they are placed in the private school by their parents, the school district is not required to provide transportation.[60] If a student attends a residential school, the student is entitled to transportation between the home and school for usual vacation periods. A Florida state court ruled that a student was not entitled to additional trips home for therapeutic purposes even though improved family relations was a goal of the student's IEP.[61]

The Third Circuit Court of Appeals held that a minor change in a student's transportation plan did not constitute a change in placement under IDEA.[62] The court realized that transportation could have an effect on a student's learning but found that a change that added 10 minutes to the student's return trip home would not impact the student's learning. Transportation arrangements must be reasonable, however. A district court in Virginia ordered a school district to develop a better arrangement for a student whose transportation took more than 30 minutes even though she lived only 6 miles from school.[63]

In this day and age many students do not return home after school but go to a caretaker. The Fifth Circuit Court of Appeals has held that students with disabilities are entitled to transportation to caretakers even if those caretakers reside out of the district's attendance boundaries.[64] The court ruled that the parents' request for transportation to the caretaker was reasonable and would not place any burden on the school district. A state court in Florida, however, held that a school district was not required to transport a student to a geographically distant facility when the student had been enrolled in that facility at her parents' request and an appropriate education could have been provided at a closer facility.[65]

In addition to providing specialized equipment, if needed, to transport a student safely, school districts also may be required to provide aides on the transportation vehicle. A district court in Michigan ordered the school district to provide a trained aide to attend to a medically fragile student during transport.[66] The court held that under IDEA students with disabilities were entitled to transportation and incidents thereto.

## LODGING

Many students with disabilities require a placement in a residential school or facility in order to receive an appropriate education. In some cases the residential placement is required because the student needs instructional services on a round-the-clock basis in order to receive an appropriate education.[67] However, in other situations the student does not necessarily require 24-hour-per-day instruction but must remain at the school on a residential basis because it is the only facility that can provide an appropriate education and is not within commuting distance of the student's home. In that situation, the room and board portion of the residential placement must still be borne by the school district as it would be considered a related service. IDEA's regulations state that if a residential program "is necessary to provide special education and related services to a child with a disability, the program, including non-medical care and room and board, must be at no cost to the parents of the child."[68] This regulation would apply whether the residential portion of the placement was needed for educational reasons or access reasons.

School districts also may be required to provide lodging to a student with disabilities off the campus of the school if appropriate arrangements cannot be made for the student to live at the school and the school is located too far from the student's home for the student to commute.[69] This could occur if the school the student attends either does not offer a residential component or does not have any room for the student in its residential program but has an opening in its day program.

## ASSISTIVE TECHNOLOGY

In 1990 IDEA was amended to include definitions of assistive technology devices and services. An assistive technology device is any item or piece of equipment that is used to increase, maintain, or improve the functional capabilities of individuals with disabilities.[70] These devices may include commercially available, modified, or customized equipment. An assistive technology service is designed to assist an individual in the selection, acquisition, or use of an assistive technology device.[71] It includes an evaluation of the individual's needs, provision of the assistive technology device, training in its use, coordination of other services with assistive technology, and maintenance and repair of the device.

Assistive technology may be provided as special education services, related services, or supplementary aids and services. Assistive technology will be required when it is necessary for a child to receive an appropriate education under the *Rowley* standard.[72] Assistive technology may allow many students with disabilities to benefit from education in less restrictive settings.[73]

## RELATED SERVICES AT PRIVATE SCHOOLS

IDEA states that provisions must be made for private school students to participate in programs of special education and related services.[74] The regulations further stipulate that school districts must provide special education and related services designed to meet the needs of students who are placed in private schools by their parents. Naturally, a school district must provide related services to a student it places in a private school just as it would if the student had remained in the public schools. Whether a school district is required to provide related services to students enrolled in private schools by their parents, and where those services must be provided, depends on the particular circumstances of the situation.

School districts are required to make related services available to the student, but that does not mean that the services must be made available at the private school. The Ninth Circuit Court of Appeals affirmed a district court ruling that a school district was not responsible for providing related services at a student's private school where it had offered an appropriate education in the public schools and the parents had opted to enroll the student in a private school.[75] In this situation the private school was

located out of state. Similarly, a district court in Alabama held that a
school district was not required to provide related services to a student
on-site at a private school.[76]

A school district would not be required to transport a student to a
private school if the student's disability did not require special transportation or if it had offered an appropriate program in the public schools
but the parents opted for a private school instead. The Sixth Circuit Court
of Appeals held that a hearing-impaired student who did not require
special transportation was not entitled to transportation as a related
service.[77] The district court had denied the request for transportation but
used a different reasoning. The district court decision, which was affirmed
by the appeals court, was based on the rationale that the school district
was not required to provide transportation since it had offered an appropriate program.[78] However, the appeals court ruling was based on the fact
that the student's disability did not require transportation to begin with.

The situation of parochial schools is somewhat different. The first
amendment to the Constitution, as interpreted by the U.S. Supreme Court
in a number of cases,[79] prevents a school district from providing certain
services on-site to parochial school students.[80] However, in *Zobrest* v.
*Catalina Foothills School District,* the U.S. Supreme Court has held that it is
not unconstitutional to provide a sign-language interpreter to a parochial
school student.[81] However, the Court did not specifically state that a school
district must provide such a service. In this case the school district had
offered the student an appropriate education within the public schools
but the student's parents had opted to enroll him in the parochial school.
The situation regarding the provision of a sign-language interpreter is
somewhat different than other related services in that it is impossible to
provide sign-language interpretation off-site.[82] Services that can be provided off-site should be provided off-site to avoid any constitutional
conflict. However, the school district may be required to provide transportation between the parochial school and the site where the services will
be provided.[83]

## SUMMARY

In addition to special education, school districts also must provide students with disabilities with related services when such services would be
necessary for them to benefit from their special education programs. The
only limitation that has been placed on what may be considered a related
service is that medical services are exempted unless they are for diagnostic
or evaluative purposes.

The exempted medical services clause has figured in much of the litigation. Courts have been asked to draw the line between exempted medical services and health services that should be provided by the schools. If the service must be provided by a licensed physician, it is exempted. If it can be provided by a school nurse, health aide, or other trained layperson, the courts have required schools to provide the service. The courts also have found that constant nursing services more closely resemble exempted medical services and generally have not required school districts to provide full-time nurses to students with disabilities. However, one court ordered a school district to provide either a full-time nurse or a respiratory care professional after determining that the costs of providing such a service would not be overly burdensome.

The Supreme Court has held that related services need only be provided to students who are receiving special education. Thus, a student who has a disability that does not require special education services would not be entitled to receive related services. This is because related services are designed to assist the student in receiving benefit from special education. If there is no special education, there is no legal requirement for related services. The Court also has indicated that related services of a life-support nature, such as catheterization, need be provided only if they are necessary during the school day.

Many students require psychotherapy or counseling to address emotional concerns. If the resolution of these emotional concerns is a prerequisite to learning, the school district would be required to provide psychotherapy or counseling as a related service. However, in some states that allow only psychiatrists to provide psychotherapy, this would be an exempted medical service.

There is no dispute that school districts are required to provide special transportation if the student is not able to access the standard mode of transportation. It has been held that transportation includes travel between the buildings and the vehicle. Transportation arrangements must be reasonable. Excessively long bus rides have been held to be not reasonable. While transportation to and from a residential facility is required, a school district does not have to pay for therapeutic trips home.

Courts also have required school districts to provide training to parents so that there is consistency between the techniques used in school and at home. In addition, courts have ordered school districts to provide parents with counseling to help them deal with the stress of having a child with a disability.

School districts must provide private school students with related services; however, it is not necessary to provide those services at the private school. If a school district has offered the parents a free appropriate public education within the public schools, it has met its obligation under IDEA. If the parents choose to enroll the student in a private school, the school district is not obligated to provide related services on-site. If the private school happens to be a parochial school, the first amendment to the U.S. Constitution would add additional restrictions to the provision of on-site services.

# ENDNOTES

1. 20 U.S.C. § 1401 et seq.
2. 20 U.S.C. § 1401(a)(17).
3. Id.
4. 34 C.F.R. § 300.16 Note.
5. 34 C.F.R. § 300.17 Note 1.
6. 34 C.F.R. § 300.16(b)(2).
7. 34 C.F.R. § 300.16(b)(8).
8. 34 C.F.R. § 300.16(b)(12).
9. *Max M. v. Thompson,* 566 F. Supp. 1330, 12 Ed.Law Rep. 761 (N.D. Ill. 1983), 585 F. Supp. 317, 17 Ed.Law Rep. 1114 (N.D. Ill. 1984), 592 F. Supp. 1437, 20 Ed.Law Rep. 489 (N.D. Ill. 1984), 592 F. Supp. 1450, 20 Ed.Law Rep. 502 (N.D. Ill. 1984), 629 F. Supp. 1504, 31 Ed.Law Rep. 437 (N.D. Ill. 1986).
10. *In re the A Family,* 602 P.2d 157 (Mont. 1979).
11. *T.G. and P.G. v. Board of Education of Piscataway,* 576 F. Supp. 420, 15 Ed.Law Rep. 722 (D.N.J. 1983).
12. *Gary B. v. Cronin,* 542 F. Supp. 102, 5 Ed.Law Rep. 755 (N.D. Ill. 1980); *Doe v. Anrig,* 651 F. Supp. 424, 37 Ed.Law Rep. 511 (D. Mass. 1987).
13. *T.G. and P.G. v. Board of Education of Piscataway,* 576 F. Supp. 420, 15 Ed.Law Rep. 722 (D.N.J. 1983).
14. *Papacoda v. State of Connecticut,* 528 F. Supp. 68, 2 Ed.Law Rep. 59 (D. Conn. 1981).
15. *Also see North v. District of Columbia Board of Education,* 471 F. Supp. 136 (D.D.C. 1979); *Erdman v. State of Connecticut,* EHLR 552:218 (D. Conn. 1980). In these cases the courts found that the various needs of the students were so inter-twined that they could not be separated and that all of the needs had to be dealt with in an integrated fashion. Therapeutic services were required as part of the total program.
16. *Tice v. Botetourt County School Board,* 908 F.2d 1200, 61 Ed.Law Rep. 1207 (4th Cir. 1990).
17. *McKenzie v. Jefferson,* EHLR 554:338 (D.D.C. 1983).
18. *Darlene L. v. Illinois Board of Education,* 568 F. Supp. 1340, 13 Ed.Law Rep. 282 (N.D. Ill. 1983).
19. *Doe v. Anrig,* 651 F. Supp. 424, 37 Ed.Law Rep. 511 (D. Mass. 1987); *Metropolitan Government of Nashville and Davidson County v. Tennessee Department of Education,* 771 S.W.2d 427, 54 Ed.Law Rep. 1001 (Tenn. Ct. App. 1989); *Clovis Unified School District v. California,* 903 F.2d 635, 60 Ed.Law Rep. 728 (9th Cir. 1990);

*Tice* v. *Botetourt County School Board,* 908 F.2d 1200, 61 Ed.Law Rep. 1207 (4th Cir. 1990).

20. *Brown* v. *Wilson County School Board,* 747 F. Supp. 436, 63 Ed.Law Rep. 525 (M.D. Tenn. 1990).
21. *Seals* v. *Loftis,* 614 F. Supp. 302, 27 Ed.Law Rep. 111 (E.D. Tenn. 1985).
22. *Clovis Unified School District* v. *California Office of Administrative Hearings,* 903 F.2d 635, 60 Ed.Law Rep. 728 (9th Cir. 1990).
23. *Taylor* v. *Honig,* 910 F.2d 627, 62 Ed.Law Rep. 78 (9th Cir. 1990).
24. 34 C.F.R. § 300.16(b)(11).
25. *Irving Independent School District* v. *Tatro,* 468 U.S. 883, 104 S. Ct. 3371, 82 L. Ed.2d 664, 18 Ed.Law Rep. 138 (1984). *Also see Tokarcik* v. *Forest Hills School District,* 665 F.2d 443 (3d Cir. 1981).
26. *Department of Education, State of Hawaii* v. *Katherine D.,* 531 F. Supp. 517, 2 Ed.Law Rep. 1057 (D. Haw. 1982), *aff'd* 727 F.2d 809, 16 Ed.Law Rep. 378 (9th Cir. 1983).
27. *Macomb County Intermediate School District* v. *Joshua S.,* 715 F. Supp. 824, 54 Ed.Law Rep. 1189 (E.D. Mich. 1989).
28. Osborne, A. G. (1988). Extensive Nursing Services Are Not Required Under the EHCA. *Education Law Reporter, 45,* 935–940.
29. *Detsel* v. *Board of Education of Auburn Enlarged City School District,* 637 F. Supp. 1022, 33 Ed.Law Rep. 726 (N.D.N.Y. 1986), *aff'd* 820 F.2d 587, 40 Ed.Law Rep. 79 (2d Cir. 1987).
30. *Bevin H.* v. *Wright,* 666 F. Supp. 71, 41 Ed.Law Rep. 535 (W.D. Pa. 1987). *Also see Granite School District* v. *Shannon M.,* 787 F. Supp. 1020, 74 Ed.Law Rep. 496 (D. Utah 1992); *Ellison* v. *Board of Education of the Three Villages Central School District,* 597 N.Y.S.2d 483, 82 Ed.Law Rep. 1147 (N.Y. App. Div. 1993).
31. *Neely* v. *Rutherford County Schools,* 851 F. Supp. 888, 91 Ed.Law Rep. 973 (M.D. Tenn. 1994).
32. 34 C.F.R. § 300.16(b)(4).
33. *Seals* v. *Loftis,* 614 F. Supp. 302, 27 Ed.Law Rep. 111 (E.D. Tenn. 1985).
34. *Brown* v. *Wilson County School Board,* 747 F. Supp. 436, 63 Ed.Law Rep. 525 (M.D. Tenn. 1990).
35. *Field* v. *Haddonfield Board of Education,* 769 F. Supp. 1313, 69 Ed.Law Rep. 724 (D.N.J. 1991).
36. *Burke County Board of Education* v. *Denton,* 895 F.2d 973, 58 Ed.Law Rep. 918 (4th Cir. 1990).
37. 34 C.F.R. § 300.16(b)(5).
38. 34 C.F.R. § 300.16(b)(7).
39. 34 C.F.R. § 300.16(b)(13).
40. *Holmes* v. *Sobol,* 690 F. Supp. 154, 48 Ed.Law Rep. 524 (W.D.N.Y. 1988).
41. *Kattan* v. *District of Columbia,* 691 F. Supp. 1539, 48 Ed.Law Rep. 1218 (D.D.C. 1988).
42. *Polk* v. *Central Susquehanna Intermediate Unit 16,* 853 F.2d 171, 48 Ed.Law Rep. 336 (3d Cir. 1988).
43. *Espino* v. *Besteiro,* 520 F. Supp. 905 (S.D. Tex. 1981).

44. *Schuldt v. Mankato Independent School District No. 77*, 937 F.2d 1357, 68 Ed.Law Rep. 968 (8th Cir. 1991).
45. 34 C.F.R. § 300.16(b)(9).
46. 34 C.F.R. § 300.306.
47. 34 C.F.R. § 300.553.
48. 29 U.S.C. § 794.
49. *See, for example, Crocker v. Tennessee Secondary School Athletic Association*, 735 F. Supp. 753, 60 Ed.Law Rep. 502 (M.D. Tenn. 1990), *aff'd sub nom. Metropolitan Government of Nashville and Davidson County v. Crocker*, 908 F.2d 973, 61 Ed.Law Rep. 1187 (6th Cir. 1990) [transfer rule must be waived where student transferred in order to receive special education services]; *Texas Education Agency v. Stamos*, 817 S.W.2d 378, 70 Ed.Law Rep. 1020 (Tex. Ct. App. 1991) [no pass, no play rule as applied to special education students challenged]; *University Interscholastic League v. Buchanan*, 848 S.W.2d 298, 81 Ed.Law Rep. 1145 (Tex. Ct. App. 1993) [age limitation rule must be waived where students repeated grades due to their learning disabilities].
50. *Board of Education of the Hendrick Hudson Central School District v. Rowley*, 458 U.S. 176, 102 S. Ct. 3034, 73 L. Ed.2d 690, 5 Ed.Law Rep. 34 (1982). See Chapter 5 for a complete analysis of this decision.
51. *Rettig v. Kent City School District*, 788 F.2d 328, 31 Ed.Law Rep. 759 (6th Cir. 1986).
52. *Birmingham and Lamphere School Districts v. Superintendent of Public Instruction*, 328 N.W.2d 59, 8 Ed.Law Rep. 467 (Mich. Ct. App. 1982).
53. 34 C.F.R. § 300.16(b)(6).
54. See Chapter 5 for a complete discussion of instances where residential placements are required.
55. *Stacey G. v. Pasadena*, 547 F. Supp. 61, 6 Ed.Law Rep. 663 (S.D. Tex. 1982), *vac'd and rem'd on other grounds* 695 F.2d 949, 8 Ed.Law Rep. 237 (5th Cir. 1983).
56. *Chris D. v. Montgomery County Board of Education*, 753 F. Supp. 922, 65 Ed.Law Rep. 355 (M.D. Ala. 1990).
57. 34 C.F.R. § 300.16(b)(14).
58. *Hurry v. Jones*, 560 F. Supp. 500, 10 Ed.Law Rep. 528 (D.R.I. 1983), *aff'd in part, rev'd in part* 734 F.2d 879, 17 Ed.Law Rep. 774 (1st Cir. 1984).
59. 20 U.S.C. § 1413(a)(4)(B)(i). *Also see Union School District v. Smith*, 15 F.3d 1519, 89 Ed.Law Rep. 449 (9th Cir. 1994).
60. *Work v. McKenzie*, 661 F. Supp. 225, 40 Ed.Law Rep. 233 (D.D.C. 1987); *A.A. v. Cooperman*, 526 A.2d 1103, 39 Ed.Law Rep. 1157 (N.J. Super. Ct. App. Div. 1987); *McNair v. Cardimone*, 676 F. Supp. 1361, 44 Ed.Law Rep. 236 (S.D. Ohio 1987) *aff'd sub nom. McNair v. Oak Hills Local School District*, 872 F.2d 153, 52 Ed.Law Rep. 950 (6th Cir. 1989). The related services that must be provided to private school students are discussed in a later section of this chapter.
61. *Cohen v. School Board of Dade County*, 450 So.2d 1238, 17 Ed.Law Rep. 1290 (Fla. Ct. App. 1984).
62. *DeLeon v. Susquehanna Community School District*, 747 F.2d 149, 21 Ed.Law Rep. 24 (3d Cir. 1984). See Chapter 3 for a discussion of IDEA's change in placement requirements.

63. *Pinkerton* v. *Moye,* 509 F. Supp. 107 (W.D. Va. 1981).
64. *Alamo Heights Independent School District* v. *State Board of Education,* 790 F.2d 1153, 32 Ed.Law Rep. 445 (5th Cir. 1986).
65. *School Board of Pinellas County* v. *Smith,* 537 So.2d 168, 51 Ed.Law Rep. 680 (Fla. Ct. App. 1989).
66. *Macomb County Intermediate School District* v. *Joshua S.,* 715 F. Supp. 824, 54 Ed.Law Rep. 1189 (E.D. Mich. 1989).
67. See Chapter 5 for a complete discussion of residential placements.
68. 34 C.F.R. § 300.302.
69. *Ojai Unified School District* v. *Jackson,* 4 F.3d 1467, 85 Ed.Law Rep. 724 (9th Cir. 1993); *Union School District* v. *Smith,* 15 F.3d 1519, 89 Ed.Law Rep. 449 (9th Cir. 1994).
70. 20 U.S.C. § 1401(a)(25).
71. 20 U.S.C. § 1401(a)(26).
72. Julnes, R. and Brown S. (1993). The Legal Mandate to Provide Assistive Technology in Special Education Programming. *Education Law Reporter, 82,* 737–748.
73. *Id.*
74. 20 U.S.C. § 1413(a)(4)(A).
75. *Dreher* v. *Amphitheater Unified School District,* 797 F. Supp. 753, 77 Ed.Law Rep. 211 (D. Ariz. 1992), *aff'd* 22 F.3d 228, 91 Ed.Law Rep. 32 (9th Cir. 1994).
76. *Tribble* v. *Montgomery County Board of Education,* 798 F. Supp. 668, 77 Ed.Law Rep. 784 (M.D. Ala. 1992).
77. *McNair* v. *Oak Hills Local School District,* 872 F.2d 153, 52 Ed.Law Rep. 950 (6th Cir. 1989). *Also see A.A.* v. *Cooperman,* 526 A.2d 1103, 39 Ed.Law Rep. 1157 (N.J. Super. Ct. App. Div. 1987).
78. *McNair* v. *Cardimone,* 676 F. Supp. 1361, 44 Ed.Law Rep. 236 (S.D. Ohio 1987). *Also see Work* v. *McKenzie,* 661 F. Supp. 225, 40 Ed.Law Rep. 233 (D.D.C. 1987).
79. See Chapter 2 for a discussion of the effect of the first amendment on a parochial school student's entitlement to receive special education services.
80. *See, for example, Aguilar* v. *Felton,* 473 U.S. 402, 105 S. Ct. 3232, 87 L. Ed.2d 290, 25 Ed.Law Rep. 1022 (1985) where the U.S. Supreme Court held that it was unconstitutional to provide Chapter I remedial services on the premises of a parochial school.
81. *Zobrest* v. *Catalina Foothills School District,* ___ U.S. ___, 113 S. Ct. 2462, 125 L. Ed.2d 1, 83 Ed.Law Rep. 930 (1993). See Chapter 2 for an expanded discussion of this case.
82. For a discussion of the circumstances leading up to and the issues involved in the *Zobrest* decision, *see* Osborne, A. G. (1993). Special Education and Related Services for Parochial School Students. *Education Law Reporter, 81,* 1–9; *and* Osborne, A. G. (1994). Providing Special Education and Related Services to Parochial School Students in the Wake of *Zobrest. Education Law Reporter, 87,* 329–339.
83. *Felter* v. *Cape Girardeau School District,* 810 F. Supp. 1062, 80 Ed.Law Rep. 595 (E.D. Mo. 1993).

# 7

# DISCIPLINARY SANCTIONS

Unfortunately students in today's schools are not always perfectly well-behaved. From time to time school administrators must take disciplinary action. Some of these disciplinary actions result in a loss of privileges for the student but do not result in a loss of educational opportunity. Sometimes more severe sanctions that do result in a loss of educational privileges are necessary. Suspensions and expulsions have been used by school officials as disciplinary sanctions for many years. Generally a suspension is defined as a short-term exclusion and an expulsion as a long-term exclusion from school. For practical purposes a suspension longer than 10 days is treated as an expulsion.

The U.S. Supreme Court, in *Goss* v. *Lopez*,[1] has held that students may be suspended and expelled from school as long as they are afforded certain due process safeguards. At a minimum, suspensions of 10 days or less require informal notice of the charges and the opportunity for some sort of hearing. If the student denies the charges, the student must be told of the evidence and given the opportunity for rebuttal. These standards are flexible depending on the nature and severity of the infraction and the intended punishment. Stricter adherence to due process is required for more severe infractions and penalties. Suspensions of more than 10 days or expulsions would require more due process.[2] For example, a student facing expulsion should be given a quasi-judicial hearing that would include the right to be represented by counsel and the opportunity to present and cross-examine witnesses.

Students with disabilities facing disciplinary sanctions have additional rights that place extra due process requirements on school officials. Since an expulsion results in a deprivation of educational opportunity, and possibly a deprivation of the rights guaranteed by the Individuals with Disabilities Education Act (IDEA),[3] further safeguards must be employed. IDEA makes little mention of discipline; however, many of its provisions have implications for the disciplinary process.[4] The U.S. Supreme Court, in *Honig v. Doe*,[5] has suggested that IDEA was passed to prevent school districts from excluding students whose disabilities resulted in behavior problems.

## EXPULSION IS A CHANGE IN PLACEMENT

Courts have consistently held that school districts may not impose the severe disciplinary sanction of expulsion on a student with disabilities unless additional due process procedures have been provided to the student. Almost as soon as IDEA was implemented, a case in which a school district intended to expel a special education student found its way to the court system.[6] The student, who had a history of behavior problems, had been suspended for 10 days as a result of her involvement in school-wide disturbances. The superintendent recommended that she be expelled for the remainder of the school year, but her attorney initiated administrative appeals under IDEA. The attorney then argued in court that an expulsion, while administrative appeals were pending, would violate IDEA's status quo provision.[7] The district court in Connecticut agreed, holding that an expulsion was a change in placement and that a change in placement could take place only after IDEA's procedures have been followed.[8] Several other courts also have held that an expulsion, since it results in the termination of all educational services, is a change in placement.[9] Under these rulings a school district is required to treat an expulsion as it would any other change in placement.

The Ninth Circuit Court of Appeals has outlined the additional due process procedures a school district must follow when attempting to expel a student with disabilities.[10] According to the court, written notice must be given to the parents, the evaluation and placement team must be convened to determine the reason for the misconduct and consider the appropriateness of the current placement, an evaluation of the student's current educational needs must be conducted, the parents must be informed of their rights to appeal, and the student must be allowed to remain in the then current placement until all issues are resolved.

An Indiana district court stated that it was clear that Congress, in passing IDEA, intended to limit a school district's right to expel a student with disabilities.[11] That sentiment has been echoed by the U.S. Supreme Court, which stated that when Congress passed IDEA it intended to strip schools of the authority they previously had to exclude disabled students, particularly those with emotional difficulties.[12] Agreeing that an expulsion is a change in placement, the high Court held that IDEA's status quo provision prevented the exclusion of students with disabilities for disruptive behavior.

## MANIFESTATION OF THE DISABILITY DOCTRINE

The federal district court in Indiana held that a school district may not expel a special education student whose misbehavior is caused by the disability, but may expel the student if the misbehavior is not caused by the disability.[13] The court emphasized, however, that this determination must be made through IDEA's change in placement procedures. The Fifth Circuit Court of Appeals agreed with this principle, adding that the determination of whether the misconduct was a manifestation of the student's disability must be made by a specialized and knowledgeable group of persons.[14] That court also placed the burden on school officials to raise the question of whether the misconduct is a manifestation of the disability.

Establishing the nexus between a student's misbehavior and disability is not a difficult task. The Fourth Circuit Court of Appeals held that such a connection did exist even though a committee of special education professionals determined that a relationship between the student's disability and misbehavior did not exist.[15] The student was classified as learning disabled but his Individualized Education Program (IEP) indicated that he had borderline intelligence and difficulty behaving. He was expelled after he acted as a go-between in several drug transactions. When the dispute over the expulsion reached the court level, the trial court found that the student's learning disabilities caused him to have a poor self-image that caused him to seek peer approval by acting as the go-between in the drug transactions. The court also found that his learning disabilities prevented him from understanding the consequences of his actions. The appeals court affirmed, holding that the district court's finding was not clearly erroneous. The appeals court added that to allow an expulsion in such an instance would not be fair or in keeping with IDEA since the student would be expelled for behavior over which he had no control.

## PROVISION OF SERVICES DURING
## AN EXPULSION

Even if school officials are able to establish that a nexus between the student's disability and misconduct does not exist, and thus are able to expel the student, they still may be required to provide special education services during the expulsion period. The Fifth Circuit Court of Appeals held that even when the proper procedures are used under the proper circumstances and a student is expelled, a complete cessation of educational services during the expulsion period is not authorized.[16]

However, the Ninth Circuit Court of Appeals held that when a student with disabilities is properly expelled, the school district may cease providing all educational services, just as it could in any other case.[17] To do otherwise, according to the court, would amount to asserting that all acts of a child with disabilities are attributable to the disability. Although the U.S. Supreme Court heard an appeal of this case, it did not review this aspect of the circuit court's decision.

The U.S. Department of Education, however, has issued policy letters expressing the view that the IDEA requirement that a free appropriate public education be provided to all students with disabilities applied to students serving long-term suspensions or expulsions resulting from misconduct that was not a manifestation of their disabilities.[18] According to these letters, it appears that the Department of Education agrees with the Fifth Circuit's interpretation of IDEA's requirements in this regard. Although these policy letters are advisory, school officials should provide special education services to any students with disabilities who have been expelled.

## TRANSFER TO AN ALTERNATE PLACEMENT

School districts may, however, transfer a disruptive student to an alternate, even more restrictive, placement if the student's behavior interferes with the education of others or creates a dangerous situation. A comment to IDEA's least restrictive environment regulations indicates that where a student with disabilities is so disruptive in the regular classroom that the education of other students is significantly impaired, the needs of the student with disabilities cannot be met in that environment and a regular class placement may not be appropriate.[19] In spite of the recent emphasis on inclusion, most courts agree that a disruptive student's effect on the operation of a general education classroom can be considered when determining the least restrictive environment for that student.[20]

The district court in Connecticut stated that students with disabilities are not immune from discipline and are not entitled to participate in programs if their behavior disrupts the educational process for others.[21] The court indicated that school authorities may change the placement of a disruptive student to a more restrictive one by following procedures consistent with IDEA. The Fourth Circuit Court of Appeals also stated that when the student's disruptive behavior is caused by the disability, consideration should be made for a change in educational placement.[22] One court, stressing that nothing in IDEA deprives school officials of their ever-present right to maintain order and discipline, has even suggested that the change in placement could occur involuntarily.[23]

The U.S. Supreme Court, stating that school officials are not left powerless to deal with dangerous students, has suggested that school officials may seek to reach an agreement for an alternate placement with the parents of a student who poses a safety risk to others.[24] If the parents adamantly refuse to consent to the change in placement, school officials may seek the aid of the courts. The Court has ruled that in this situation school officials may not be required to exhaust their administrative remedies prior to bringing court action. In appropriate cases the courts could issue a temporary order preventing a dangerous student from attending school. The courts also could order a temporary alternate placement, such as homebound instruction. However, the burden clearly is on school authorities to show that the student is dangerous and that no other alternative except exclusion is feasible.

## EXCLUSION PENDING PLACEMENT REVIEW PROCEEDINGS

As indicated in the preceding section, the U.S. Supreme Court has ruled that courts may enjoin dangerous students from attending school if the school district and parents cannot agree on an alternate placement. If the school district and parents cannot reach an agreement, the administrative appeals process would be set in motion. The Supreme Court's ruling gives the courts the authority to issue a temporary order regarding the student's educational situation until those proceedings are final. Although the school district would not be required to exhaust administrative remedies prior to seeking such a temporary order, the permanent placement dispute still would be subject to the administrative process.

In a case that was decided three years before the *Honig* decision, a district court in Mississippi upheld a school district's refusal to allow a student who had engaged in disruptive sexual conduct to return to school.[25] The student initially had been suspended, but during his suspension he was placed by the youth court in a state hospital. Upon his release he attempted to return to school, but school officials proposed a placement in a private facility. The student rejected all offered options and initiated due process appeals. He claimed that during the pendency of those proceedings he was entitled to return to his former public school placement. The school district, citing a possible danger to other students due to his psychosexual disorder, refused to readmit him. The district court held that the school district's actions were reasonable and did not violate IDEA. The appeals court affirmed.

A district court in Texas issued an order enjoining a student it found to be dangerous from attending general education classes after the student's parents rejected a proposal that the student attend a behavior management class.[26] School officials testified that the student had committed numerous behavioral infractions, including assaults on students and teachers, destruction of school property, self-injurious acts, use of profanity, and threats to kill himself and others. The court ruled that pending completion of administrative hearings, the student could either attend the recommended behavior management class or receive homebound instruction.

## SUSPENSIONS

Although the courts have put restrictions on a school district's authority to expel a student with disabilities, they have consistently held that less harsh forms of discipline, such as suspensions, may be imposed without any additional due process safeguards. The district court in Connecticut, while holding that an expulsion was a change in placement, stated that school authorities could temporarily suspend students with disabilities who were disruptive.[27] In several of the other expulsion decisions, the courts have indicated that short suspensions are not subject to IDEA's change in placement requirements.[28]

In a case in which a brief suspension was imposed on a student for verbally abusing a teacher, a district court in Illinois specifically held that a suspension was not a change in placement.[29] Characterizing a suspension as a sanction designed to teach the student, the court found that the loss of classwork during the suspension period did not outweigh the educational value of the suspension.

The U.S. Supreme Court ruled that school districts may suspend a student with disabilities for up to 10 days if the student poses an immediate threat to the safety of others.[30] The Court suggested that the suspension could provide a cooling-down period during which school authorities and the parents could work out an agreement for an alternate, more appropriate, placement. The suspension period provides school administrators with the authority to immediately remove a dangerous student to protect the safety of others.[31] Unfortunately, the Court did not specify whether the 10-day limit on suspensions was cumulative within one year or consecutive. This question, however, is generally addressed through state policies.[32] In the absence of specific state law policies or guidelines, school administrators would be prudent to view the 10-day limit as cumulative. This view would be consistent with a long line of case law that treats serial suspensions as expulsions.

Courts have consistently held that an expulsion by any other name is still an expulsion. Suspensions are defined as short-term exclusions from school and expulsions as long-term exclusions. Tradition holds that anything over 10 days procedurally is the equivalent of an expulsion. The U.S. Supreme Court, in the *Goss* decision discussed at the beginning of this chapter, indicated that greater due process would be required for suspensions of more than 10 days.

The district court in Indiana stated that the prohibition against expulsions included informal expulsions, such as indefinite suspensions.[33] By the same token the Supreme Court of Nebraska held that sending a student home and telling his parents that he could not return constituted an expulsion.[34] An Ohio district court held that a suspension of several months, even when home tutoring was provided during the suspension period, was a change in placement.[35] The court indicated that suspensions of one or two weeks would have been acceptable.

These court decisions do not require school authorities to provide any due process safeguards over and above those outlined in the *Goss* v. *Lopez* decision. Thus, when it comes to a suspension, a student with disabilities may be treated in the same manner as any other student.

## OTHER DISCIPLINARY SANCTIONS

It is not uncommon for school officials to place a continually disruptive student on a reduced day schedule under the theory that the student's misbehavior is due to an inability to tolerate a full day of instruction. The Ninth Circuit Court of Appeals held that a reduction in the schedule of a special education student for disciplinary purposes was a change in placement subject to IDEA's procedures.[36] The student had been placed on a half-day schedule following several incidents of misconduct. Although his guardians agreed to the reduction in schedule, it was accomplished without providing the full due process safeguards required by IDEA for a change in placement.

A district court in Indiana, a state that authorizes corporal punishment, held that paddling a student with disabilities, taping his mouth, and providing him with an isolated seating arrangement did not violate his rights.[37] Finding that these punishments were not excessive and were within school officials' common law privileges, the court stated that school officials were entitled to substantial discretion in handling day-to-day discipline. Noting that the student in this case received the same punishment any other child would have, the judge remarked, "An elementary school cannot be subjugated by the tyrannical behavior of a nine-year-old child."[38]

Many special education teachers commonly employ a technique known as "time-out" as part of a behavior modification program. Time-out refers to the removal of a child from a setting for a specified and limited period of time. Generally, the student is placed in a secluded area of the classroom set aside for this purpose or a separate time-out room. The Tenth Circuit Court of Appeals held that such a short-term disciplinary measure as time-out or an in-school suspension does not constitute a change in placement.[39] However, the court did indicate that in-class disciplinary methods, since they were matters relating to the education of the child, were subject to IDEA's administrative appeals process if the parents objected to them. The Eighth Circuit Court of Appeals also has held that an in-school suspension, even when it limits the student's access to special education classes and resources, does not violate the student's substantive due process rights.[40] The court noted that an in-school suspension furthered the school district's legitimate interest in maintaining order and discipline.

While these paragraphs indicate that IDEA does not limit a school district's right to use normal disciplinary sanctions, short of expulsion, with a special education student, it should be noted that state policies may impose some restrictions. For example, some states may limit the number of days a student may be placed on an in-school suspension if the student is not allowed to attend special education classes during the suspension period. If the student is being deprived of special education services, the state may treat an in-house suspension in the same manner as an out-of-building suspension so that it would count toward the 10-day limitation placed on suspensions.

A state court in Pennsylvania held that an in-school suspension amounted to a de facto or constructive suspension because the student chose to go home rather than report for the in-school suspension.[41] The court reasoned that since school officials continued to assign in-school suspensions after it became abundantly clear that the student would opt to go home, they knew that an in-school suspension would result in the student's exclusion. Since the total number of days the student was excluded from school exceeded the maximum allowed by state law, the court held that school officials acted contrary to the mandates of IDEA regarding student exclusions.

## TREATMENT OF STUDENTS UNDERGOING AN EVALUATION

Students who have been identified as disabled are entitled to the additional due process protections of IDEA when harsh disciplinary sanctions may be imposed that would affect the delivery of special education services. The question has arisen as to how students who are undergoing an evaluation, but who have not yet been classified as disabled, are to be treated.

This issue arose in an early Connecticut case that was settled by a consent decree agreed to by the parties to the litigation. The consent decree stipulated that a child undergoing an evaluation would be treated in a similar manner as a child already identified as disabled.[42] However, about the same time a district court in Minnesota, noting that IDEA's procedures are designed to minimize the risk of misclassifying students, held that to treat a student suspected of being disabled as disabled would violate the law.[43] Since the student in this case had not been identified as disabled, the court ruled that school officials had no obligation to treat her as a special education student when imposing disciplinary sanctions.

However, the disciplinary process may not interfere with a student's right to be evaluated and identified. In other words, if a student undergoing an evaluation is disciplined, the evaluation may not be halted during the disciplinary period.[44] Also, as soon as school officials are aware that a student is disabled, they have an obligation to provide the student with the full protections of IDEA.[45]

The Connecticut consent decree also stipulated that students who are continually disruptive would be referred for an evaluation.[46] Since constant misbehavior may be an indication of an underlying, unidentified disability, this would appear to be a prudent practice in light of the affirmative obligations school districts have under IDEA to locate and identify all students with disabilities.[47]

## INDIVIDUALIZED DISCIPLINE PROGRAM

A school district may develop an individualized disciplinary program and incorporate it into a special education student's IEP; however, students with disabilities are not necessarily entitled to an individualized disciplinary program. The district court in Maryland held that each IEP must be individually tailored to meet the needs of the student, but subject to that requirement, the policies outlined in the student handbook could be made applicable to a student with disabilities.[48]

Although an individualized disciplinary policy may not be required, it is not a bad idea. In the case of a special education student who has a history of behavioral problems, a prudent special educator would clearly spell out in the student's IEP what was expected of the student and what sanctions would be imposed if those expectations were not met. As was seen earlier, one court has held that in-class disciplinary methods are subject to IDEA's administrative appeals process; however, if school personnel act in accordance with a valid IEP, it is unlikely that their actions will be overturned by a hearing officer or court. As with all special education instructional methods, the behavior management program spelled out in the IEP must be developed according to accepted practices in the field.

## EFFECT ON THE JUVENILE COURT

The procedures and requirements outlined in this chapter refer only to disciplinary sanctions imposed by the schools. These court rulings do not affect the ability of the courts to impose sanctions of their own in cases involving criminal complaints. This would even involve actions that may have arisen in the school setting. A family court in New York specifically rejected a parent's contention that the *Honig* decision divested it of jurisdiction in a truancy proceeding.[49] The court held that *Honig* did not divest the courts of subject matter jurisdiction.

## SUMMARY

One of the more controversial issues that has come before the courts since the implementation of IDEA concerns the imposition of disciplinary sanctions on students with disabilities. This issue is not directly addressed by the act or its implementing regulations; thus, school administrators must turn to case law for guidance. Although there is no direct reference to discipline in IDEA, many of its provisions, such as those governing a change in placement, have implications for the application of disciplinary sanctions on special education students.

This is a very delicate issue as it pits the duty of school administrators to maintain order, discipline, and a safe environment in schools against the special education students' rights to receive a free appropriate public education in the least restrictive environment. The authority of school officials to maintain discipline should not be undermined. However, a student should not be denied the rights accorded by IDEA if the student's misconduct is caused by the student's disability.

The case law, as it has emerged in the past two decades, clearly strikes an appropriate balance. School officials may impose disciplinary sanctions as long as they follow procedures that will not deprive special education students of their rights. School officials may impose normal disciplinary sanctions, including suspensions, on special education students by following general procedures and providing normal due process.

Restrictions are placed on school authorities, however, when they wish to impose more drastic sanctions such as an expulsion or attempt to change the student's placement for disciplinary reasons. Basically, in these situations the due process procedures in IDEA replace the normal due process protections.

School district personnel first must determine if the student's offensive behavior was a manifestation of the student's disability. If it was, the student may not be expelled. This determination must be made by a specialized and knowledgeable group of persons such as the district's evaluation and placement team. School districts may, however, temporarily suspend a disruptive or dangerous student and attempt to negotiate another, possibly more restrictive, placement with the student's parents. If an alternate placement can be agreed on, the student's placement can be changed.

If the school district and the parents cannot agree on an alternate placement, that disagreement, like any other IEP disagreement, is subject to IDEA's administrative appeals process. If the school district feels that the student is dangerous and does not wish to have the student attend school while awaiting a final administrative determination, the school district may seek court intervention. If the court agrees that the student's presence in school creates a dangerous situation, the court may enjoin the student from attending school and may order an alternate placement on a temporary basis. However, the school district must show, by a preponderance of the evidence, that the student is dangerous and must be excluded.

If the school district's evaluation and placement team determines that there is no causal connection between the student's disability and misconduct, the student may be expelled. However, during the expulsion period the student must be provided with educational services. This would require the school district to either provide homebound instruction or arrange for an alternate placement.

Although additional requirements are placed on school authorities when disciplining students with disabilities, they have not been left totally hamstrung. School officials may take swift action, in the form of a suspension, to deal with an immediate situation that is deemed dangerous. If a dispute develops between the parents and school district over the appropriate long-term placement, IDEA provides a mechanism to settle that dispute. In the meantime, the courts can provide an immediate short-term solution. However, the school district will bear the burden of showing that the student's exclusion is necessary.

It is far better to anticipate a problem and prevent one from escalating. If a student is known to have disabilities that may result in misbehavior, school officials should take steps to address those problems. An appropriate IEP that specifically contains goals, objectives, and methods for behavior modification should be developed. Specific recommendations for dealing with disruptive behavior should be included in that IEP. Those recommendations may be consistent with, or even identical to, the procedures outlined in the student handbook; however, as long as they meet the student's individual needs, they are acceptable.

## ENDNOTES

1. *Goss* v. *Lopez*, 419 U.S. 565, 95 S. Ct. 729, 42 L. Ed.2d 725 (1975).
2. Hudgins, H.C. and Vacca, R.S. (1991). *Law and Education: Contemporary Issues and Court Decisions*. Charlottesville, VA: The Michie Company.
3. 20 U.S.C. § 1401 et seq.
4. Sorenson, G. (1993). Update on Legal Issues in Special Education Discipline. *Education Law Reporter, 81*, 399–410.
5. *Honig* v. *Doe*, 484 U.S. 305, 108 S. Ct. 592, 98 L. Ed.2d 686, 43 Ed.Law Rep. 857 (1988).
6. *Stuart* v. *Nappi*, 443 F. Supp. 1235 (D. Conn. 1978).
7. 20 U.S.C. § 1415(e)(3). See Chapter 3 for a discussion of IDEA's status quo provision and change in placement requirements.
8. Before a special education student's placement can be changed, the school district must notify the parents of their intent to change the placement and give the parents the opportunity to object. If the parents object to the change in placement and administrative appeals are initiated, the child's placement may not be changed while those proceedings are pending unless the parents agree to the change. 20 U.S.C. §§ 1415(b)(1)(C) and 1415(e)(3).
9. *S-1* v. *Turlington*, 635 F.2d 342 (5th Cir. 1981); *Blue* v. *New Haven Board of Education*, EHLR 552:401 (D. Conn. 1981); *Kaelin* v. *Grubbs*, 682 F.2d 595, 5 Ed.Law Rep. 710 (6th Cir. 1982); *Honig* v. *Doe*, 484 U.S. 305, 108 S. Ct. 592, 98 L. Ed.2d 686, 43 Ed.Law Rep. 857 (1988).
10. *Doe* v. *Maher*, 793 F.2d 1470, 33 Ed.Law Rep. 125 (9th Cir. 1986), *aff'd on other grounds sub nom. Honig* v. *Doe*, 484 U.S. 305, 108 S. Ct. 592, 98 L. Ed.2d 686, 43 Ed.Law Rep. 857 (1988).
11. *Doe* v. *Koger*, 480 F. Supp. 225 (N.D. Ind. 1979).
12. *Honig* v. *Doe*, 484 U.S. 305, 108 S. Ct. 592, 98 L. Ed.2d 686, 43 Ed.Law Rep. 857 (1988).
13. *Doe* v. *Koger*, 480 F. Supp. 225 (N.D. Ind. 1979).
14. *S-1* v. *Turlington*, 635 F.2d 342 (5th Cir. 1981). *Also see Kaelin* v. *Grubbs*, 682 F.2d 595, 5 Ed.Law Rep. 710 (6th Cir. 1982).
15. *School Board of the County of Prince William* v. *Malone*, 762 F.2d 1210, 25 Ed.Law Rep. 141 (4th Cir. 1985).
16. *S-1* v. *Turlington*, 635 F.2d 342 (5th Cir. 1981). *Also see Board of Trustees of Pascagoula Municipal Separate School District* v. *Doe*, 508 So.2d 1081, 40 Ed.Law Rep. 1090 (Miss. 1987).

17. *Doe v. Maher,* 793 F.2d 1470, 33 Ed.Law Rep. 125 (9th Cir. 1986), *aff'd on other grounds sub nom. Honig v. Doe,* 484 U.S. 305, 108 S. Ct. 592, 98 L. Ed.2d 686, 43 Ed.Law Rep. 857 (1988).

18. *New Letter,* EHLR 213:258 (OSERS 1989); *Davis Letter,* 16 EHLR 734 (OSERS 1989); *Symkowick Letter,* 17 EHLR 469 (OSERS 1991); *Smith Letter,* 18 IDELR 685 (OSERS 1992).

19. 34 C.F.R. § 300.552 Note.

20. See Chapter 5 for additional information on the least restrictive environment provision.

21. *Stuart v. Nappi,* 443 F. Supp. 1235 (D. Conn. 1978).

22. *School Board of the County of Prince William v. Malone,* 762 F.2d 1210, 25 Ed.Law Rep. 141 (4th Cir. 1985). *Also see Southeast Warren Community School District v. Department of Public Instruction,* 285 N.W.2d 173 (Iowa 1979); *Doe v. Koger,* 480 F. Supp. 225 (N.D. Ind. 1979).

23. *Victoria L. v. District School Board of Lee County, Florida,* EHLR 552:265, *aff'd* 741 F.2d 369, 19 Ed.Law Rep. 478 (11th Cir. 1984).

24. *Honig v. Doe,* 484 U.S. 305, 108 S. Ct. 592, 98 L. Ed.2d 686, 43 Ed.Law Rep. 857 (1988).

25. *Jackson v. Franklin County School Board,* 606 F. Supp. 152, 24 Ed.Law Rep. 185 (S.D. Miss. 1985), *aff'd* 765 F.2d 535, 25 Ed.Law Rep. 1080 (5th Cir. 1985).

26. *Texas City Independent School District v. Jorstad,* 752 F. Supp. 231, 64 Ed.Law Rep. 1064 (S.D. Tex.).

27. *Stuart v. Nappi,* 443 F. Supp. 1235 (D. Conn. 1978).

28. *See, for example, Doe v. Koger,* 489 F. Supp. 225 (N.D. Ind. 1979); *Kaelin v. Grubbs,* 682 F.2d 595, 5 Ed.Law Rep. 710 (6th Cir. 1982).

29. *Board of Education of Peoria v. Illinois State Board of Education,* 531 F. Supp. 148, 2 Ed.Law Rep. 1032 (C.D. Ill. 1982).

30. *Honig v. Doe,* 484 U.S. 305, 108 S. Ct. 592, 98 L. Ed.2d 686, 43 Ed.Law Rep. 857 (1988).

31. Osborne, A. G. (1988). Dangerous Handicapped Students Cannot Be Excluded From the Public Schools. *Education Law Reporter, 46,* 1105–1113.

32. For example, Massachusetts has specific requirements school districts must follow when suspensions for a special education student will accumulate to more than 10 days in a school year. These regulations require the evaluation team to reconvene to determine if the student's misconduct is a manifestation of the disability or a result of an inappropriate placement. If the determination is positive in this regard, a new placement must be recommended. If the determination is negative the student may be suspended for more than 10 days, but services must continue during the suspension period. 603 C.M.R. 28.00 ¶ 338.0.

33. *Doe v. Koger,* 480 F. Supp. 225 (N.D. Ind. 1979). *Also see Sherry v. New York State Education Department,* 479 F. Supp. 1328 (W.D.N.Y. 1979).

34. *Adams Central School District v. Deist,* 334 N.W.2d 775, 11 Ed.Law Rep. 1020 (Neb. 1983), *modified* 338 N.W.2d 591, 13 Ed.Law Rep. 846 (Neb. 1983).

35. *Lamont X. v. Quisenberry,* 606 F. Supp. 809, 24 Ed.Law Rep. 772 (S.D. Ohio 1984).

36. *Doe* v. *Maher,* 793 F.2d 1470, 33 Ed.Law Rep. 125 (9th Cir. 1986), *aff'd on other grounds sub nom. Honig* v. *Doe,* 484 U.S. 305, 108 S. Ct. 592, 98 L. Ed.2d 686, 43 Ed.Law Rep. 857 (1988).
37. *Cole* v. *Greenfield-Central Community Schools,* 657 F. Supp. 56, 39 Ed.Law Rep. 76 (S.D. Ind. 1986).
38. *Id.,* 657 F. Supp. at 63, 39 Ed.Law Rep. at 83.
39. *Hayes* v. *Unified School District No. 377,* 877 F.2d 809, 54 Ed.Law Rep. 450 (10th Cir. 1989).
40. *Wise* v. *Pea Ridge School District,* 855 F.2d 560, 48 Ed.Law Rep. 1098 (8th Cir. 1988).
41. *Big Beaver Falls Area School District* v. *Jackson,* 624 A.2d 806, 82 Ed.Law Rep. 861 (Pa. Commw. Ct. 1993).
42. *P-1* v. *Shedd,* EHLR 551:164 (D. Conn. 1979). *Also see Hacienda La Puente Unified School District of Los Angeles* v. *Honig,* 976 F.2d 487, 77 Ed.Law Rep. 1117 (9th Cir. 1992), where the court interpreted sections of the California special education laws to invoke IDEA's procedural protections even when the student in question did not have a previously identified disability but was subsequently determined to be disabled.
43. *Mrs. A.J.* v. *Special School District No. 1,* 478 F. Supp. 418 (D. Minn. 1979).
44. Osborne, A.G. (1984). *An Examination of Handicapped Students' Rights to Education and Appropriate Placement Under Federal Law.* Doctoral Dissertation: Boston College. University Microfilms International 8415613.
45. *Doe* v. *Rockingham County School Board,* 658 F. Supp. 403, 39 Ed.Law Rep. 590 (W.D. Va. 1987).
46. *P-1* v. *Shedd,* EHLR 551:164 (D. Conn. 1979).
47. 20 U.S.C. § 1412(2)(C).
48. *Pratt* v. *Board of Education of Frederick County,* 501 F. Supp. 232 (D. Md. 1980).
49. *In re Thomas W.,* 560 N.Y.S.2d 227, 62 Ed.Law Rep. 1122 (N.Y. Fam. Ct. 1989).

# 8

# REMEDIES

When a school district fails to provide a student with disabilities with a free appropriate public education, the courts are empowered to grant appropriate relief.[1] The relief granted may involve reimbursement of tuition and other costs borne by the parents in unilaterally obtaining appropriate services for the child. In situations where the parents are not able financially to obtain private services, awards of compensatory educational services may be granted. If the parents are forced into litigation to gain an appropriate education for the student, they may be entitled to reimbursement for their legal costs as well. Generally, however, appropriate relief does not include an award of punitive damages. As will be shown in this chapter, many of these rights to reimbursement and equitable relief have been gained either as a result of court decisions or legislative action taken in response to a court decision.

## DAMAGES

The term *damages,* by its broad definition, refers to monetary relief that is awarded to compensate an aggrieved party for a loss.[2] The term *damages,* as used in this chapter, however, is defined in a narrower context. It refers to a monetary award given to a person injured by the actions of another for punitive purposes.[3] A compensatory award, such as reimbursement for tuition and other out-of-pocket expenses, is not considered to be a damages award for purposes of this section. Compensatory awards are treated separately in this chapter. In the special education context, courts in the past few years have treated punitive damages as a separate entity from compensation for lost services.[4] The author has chosen to follow that distinction in this chapter.

## Failure to Provide an Appropriate Education

As a rule, courts have held that damages are not available under the Individuals with Disabilities Education Act (IDEA)[5] unless a school district fails to comply with the act's procedural provisions in a flagrant manner. The Seventh Circuit Court of Appeals, in a case in which the parents were actually looking for tuition reimbursement, held that monetary awards were not available under IDEA unless exceptional circumstances existed.[6] One of the exceptional circumstances enumerated by the court is when the school district has acted in bad faith by failing to comply with IDEA's procedural provisions in an egregious fashion. Although this case involved an award of tuition reimbursement, other courts have either cited the Seventh Circuit's decision or used an analogous reasoning in determining that damages are not available under IDEA because that court viewed a reimbursement award as an award for damages.[7]

The Seventh Circuit's treatment of reimbursement as a damages award has specifically been struck down by the U.S. Supreme Court;[8] however, the legal reasoning that damages are available only when the school district acted in bad faith has survived. The Fifth Circuit Court of Appeals has stated that a damages award is not consistent with the goals of IDEA and that appropriate relief does not include punitive damages when the school district acted in good faith.[9] Similarly, a district court in Virginia held that damages were not available unless it could be shown that the school district acted in bad faith or committed an act of intentional discrimination.[10]

The First Circuit Court of Appeals, in reversing a district court's punitive damages award, stated that such an award would hinder, rather than help, the purposes of IDEA since the award would result in fewer available funds to spend on educating students with disabilities.[11] The district court had awarded damages because the school district's failure to provide appropriate transportation resulted in the student's exclusion from school. The district court reasoned that by not educating the student, the school district saved money and was unjustly enriched. The appeals court specifically rejected the unjust enrichment theory, finding that available funds were spent on programs that benefitted all special education students.

A New York district court held that damages are allowed for bad faith or egregious failure to comply with IDEA; however, they are not warranted when the school district makes a good faith effort to provide an appropriate placement but commits a misjudgment.[12] However, a district court in

Michigan held that when a court finds that a school district's placement is not appropriate, it is limited to fashioning an appropriate placement.[13] That court held that damages were not available even if the parents could show that school officials acted in bad faith or grossly misused their professional discretion.

## Tort Negligence

The purpose of a tort remedy is to compensate individuals for injuries that result from the unreasonable conduct of others.[14] A tort is a civil wrong committed against someone's person or property.[15] Torts may result from either intentional or unintentional acts. In order to receive a damages award, a litigant must show negligence on the part of the person allegedly committing the tort. Awards may be granted to compensate for the actual loss as well as for punitive purposes.[16]

A state court decision from Louisiana indicates that school districts will not be held liable for injuries received by students who have been mainstreamed as long as the mainstreaming was reasonable. The court held that a school district was not liable for injuries received on the playground by a student with mental retardation.[17] The student was injured by two other students who had engaged in horseplay. Her mother filed suit claiming an increased level of supervision should have been provided. The trial court had awarded damages ruling that the student should have been segregated because of her disabilities. The appeals court reversed, holding that the student was mainstreamed in accordance with state law and that the program developed for her was appropriate, thus the school district was not negligent.

A California state court held that tort damages were not available under IDEA for a claim that students had been denied a free appropriate public education.[18] The court held that the appropriate remedy for a denial of services would be an award of compensatory educational services. Similarly, a state court in Michigan held that damages for negligence were not recoverable under IDEA for a school district's failure to properly evaluate a student.[19] The court stated that there was no indication that Congress intended for the act to serve as a vehicle for a private cause of action for damages.

The Sixth Circuit Court of Appeals ruled that IDEA does not create any right to recover damages for loss of earning power attributed to the failure to provide an appropriate education.[20] The student had sued to recover lost wages allegedly resulting from an insufficient education. That same court in another case also held that a student could not receive a damages award for an emotional injury allegedly suffered by the student who was wrongfully barred from participating in sports.[21]

## Damages under Section 1983

Section 1983 of the Civil Rights Act of 1871[22] provides for punitive damages designed to punish and discourage individuals who deprive others of rights, privileges, and immunities secured by the Constitution and laws of the United States.[23] Courts have held, however, that since aggrieved persons cannot recover damages under IDEA, they may not recover damages under section 1983 for any violation of rights secured by IDEA.[24]

# TUITION REIMBURSEMENT

IDEA stipulates that while any administrative hearings or judicial action involving a placement dispute is pending, the student is to remain in his or her current educational placement unless the parents and school district or state agree otherwise.[25] Unfortunately, however, due process proceedings under IDEA may take several months or even years. Parents who feel that the child's current placement is not appropriate may not wish to have the child remain in that placement for the length of time it takes to reach a final settlement. Often parents in this situation have opted to remove the child from the current placement and enroll him or her in a private facility. When parents prevail in this situation they feel that they should be reimbursed for the tuition and other expenses associated with the private placement in addition to receiving prospective relief.

Although this issue is now well settled, in the early years of IDEA it was very controversial.[26] Due to disagreement among the appeals court circuits, the U.S. Supreme Court was called on to settle the controversy in 1985.[27] However, the litigation has not ended as new issues have emerged regarding the interpretation and application of the case law created by the Court.

## Early Decisions

In the early years of IDEA most courts followed the reasoning of a decision by the Seventh Circuit Court of Appeals that reimbursement was available only if one of two exceptional circumstances existed to warrant the unilateral action by the parents.[28] The two exceptional circumstances were if the child's health would have been endangered if alternative arrangements had not been made by the parents or if school officials acted in bad faith by failing to comply with IDEA's procedural requirements in an egregious fashion. Several appeals courts in other circuits[29] as well as numerous district courts ruled in a similar fashion.

However, a ruling by the First Circuit Court of Appeals rejected the rationale that reimbursement was available only in exceptional circumstances.[30] The First Circuit held that reimbursement was generally available to parents who unilaterally enrolled their child in a private school as long as the private school was determined to be the appropriate placement. The First Circuit reasoned that reimbursing parents for their expenses put all parties in the position they would have been in if the school district had provided the appropriate placement from the beginning. Although that ruling was not appealed, a second ruling along the same lines by that same court was appealed.[31]

## Supreme Court Decides Reimbursement Issue

In *Burlington School Committee* v. *Department of Education*[32] the U.S. Supreme Court upheld the First Circuit's decision that IDEA allowed reimbursement as long as the parents' chosen placement was determined to be the appropriate placement for the student. The high Court held that by empowering the courts to grant appropriate relief, Congress intended to include retroactive relief as an available remedy. The Court reasoned that reimbursement merely required the school district to pay the expenses it would have been paying all along if it had developed a proper Individualized Education Program (IEP) from the beginning. If reimbursement were not available, the Court stated, the student's right to a free appropriate public education, the parents' right to fully participate in developing an appropriate IEP, and IDEA's procedural safeguards would be less than complete.

The Court ruled that a parental violation of IDEA's status quo provision did not constitute a waiver of tuition reimbursement. The Court warned, however, that parents who make unilateral placements do so at their own financial risk since they would not be reimbursed if the school district proposed, and had the capacity to implement, an appropriate IEP.

## Reimbursement Ordered under *Burlington*

The *Burlington* decision did not end the legal controversy over reimbursement. In the years since the Court issued its verdict in 1985 the lower courts have been flooded with lawsuits seeking reimbursement for private school expenses. Many of these cases have been straightforward and the courts have made tuition reimbursement awards after finding that *Burlington's* conditions were met.[33]

Tuition reimbursement awards have been denied in a number of cases where the courts first determined that the school district had offered and had the capacity to implement an appropriate IEP.[34] In the majority of these cases the courts determined that the program offered by the school district met the standards for an appropriate education under the Supreme Court's *Rowley*[35] decision. Once a court has determined that the school district's proposed IEP is appropriate, it does not need to examine the appropriateness of the parents' chosen placement.

## Parents' Chosen Placement Must Be Appropriate but Need Not Be Perfect

The *Burlington* decision indicates that parents will be reimbursed for private school costs if their chosen placement is held to be appropriate and the school district's proposed placement is held to be inappropriate. However, the courts, recognizing that parents are not experts when it comes to making educational placements, do not expect the parents to make the exact required placement. As long as the parents' chosen placement is found to be more appropriate than the placement proposed by the school district, the courts will award reimbursement, even if the parents' placement is not identical to the one that is finally determined to be appropriate. However, the parents will not be reimbursed fully if the courts find that their chosen placement went well beyond what was required and was thus more costly than necessary. The amount of advice and counsel a school district provides parents seeking to make a unilateral placement may determine the extent of the reimbursement award.

A Fifth Circuit Court of Appeals decision is illustrative.[36] In this case the parents of a multidisabled child, who were seeking summer programming, unilaterally arranged for services for two consecutive summers while litigation was pending. The court awarded reimbursement for the first summer after finding that the services the mother secured were less than appropriate but were better than no services at all. However, the court found that the mother's choice for the second summer may have provided more than was necessary. The court remanded the case back to the district court to determine whether full or partial reimbursement was due. In making its determination, the lower court was instructed to consider the mother's efforts in securing a placement, the existence of more suitable programs, and the cooperation offered by the school district.

Parents making unilateral placements may not have as many options available to them as are available to the school district. Thus, the parents may not necessarily be able to make the exact appropriate placement decision. However, courts have held that reimbursement is still an available remedy. A district court in Texas ordered the school district to reimburse the mother of an autistic student for costs associated with after-school and summer services after a hearing officer determined that a residential placement was required.[37] The court held that the fact that the mother did not obtain the precise services the student required did not preclude a reimbursement award, especially since she could not afford to provide the residential placement herself. Another court held that parents could be reimbursed for unilaterally obtained services even when they were not provided by state certified personnel since the school district had failed to offer an appropriate IEP in a timely fashion.[38]

In another case in which the court determined that a residential placement was required, it was troubled by the fact that the parents had chosen one in Tokyo, Japan.[39] The court held that the parents were entitled to some reimbursement but was not convinced that a placement so far from home was necessary. The court held off making a reimbursement award so that it could hear additional evidence. Similarly, the Supreme Court of New Jersey held that parents who had chosen a residential placement when a private day school was sufficient to provide an appropriate education were not entitled to full reimbursement.[40] The court awarded reimbursement for the student's educational expenses at the school but not for room and board expenses.

Parents will not be granted a tuition reimbursement award for a unilaterally obtained placement if it is not appropriate, even when the school district also failed to offer an appropriate IEP. In a Connecticut case, the district court held that the school district's IEP was not appropriate since district personnel committed several procedural errors, but that the parents' chosen placement was not appropriate either.[41] The school the parents had chosen was not staffed by professionals who could deliver the special education services the student needed since they were not properly certified in special education. The court held that an award of tuition reimbursement was not warranted. A state court in Ohio denied a reimbursement award for the services of an aide the parents had hired privately after determining that even with the aide the student did not receive an appropriate education.[42] Under these circumstances the student may be entitled to an award of compensatory educational services, however.

## Reimbursement at Schools that Do Not Meet State Standards

The issue of whether parents can be reimbursed for a unilateral placement at a school that does not meet state educational standards has been controversial.[43] IDEA states that a free appropriate public education means special education and related services that, among other things, meet the state's educational standards.[44] IDEA also gives the states the responsibility for ensuring that the programs offered at private schools meet state standards.[45] Most states have a list of private schools and facilities that have been approved by the state educational agency for placement of special education students. In the early years of IDEA courts, based on these provisions, held that reimbursement was not available if the student was placed in an unapproved private school. However, the U.S. Supreme Court has held otherwise.

Over the years the federal district and appeals courts have heard several cases in which parents sought reimbursement for unilateral placements in private schools that were not on their state's list of approved special education facilities. In the majority of these cases the courts held that parents could not be reimbursed for such placements, even if the school district had failed to offer an appropriate placement. In these decisions the courts held that since school districts could not place students in an unapproved facility, parents could not be reimbursed if they unilaterally did so.[46] Since an unapproved facility does not meet state standards, the courts reasoned that the educational program it provided was not legally appropriate regardless of how good it might be. One court even held that parents could not be reimbursed for unilaterally placing their child in an unapproved private school when there was no approved facility available that was willing to accept the child.[47]

Although the majority of courts held that reimbursement was not available if the parents' chosen facility was not approved by the state, not all courts agreed. The Supreme Judicial Court of Massachusetts held that reimbursement was required as long as the parents' chosen facility was appropriate, even if it was not approved by the state.[48] The court stated that if the parents and school district had agreed to a nonapproved placement, nothing prevented school officials from seeking state approval for the placement.

The Fourth Circuit Court of Appeals created a conflict among the federal appeals circuits when it held that the parents of a learning disabled student were entitled to be reimbursed for tuition at an unapproved private school.[49] In a unanimous decision, the U.S. Supreme Court settled the controversy by affirming the Fourth Circuit's decision in *Florence County School District Four* v. *Carter.*[50] In this case the student's parents, dissatisfied with the school district's IEP, placed the student in an unapproved private school. Eventually, the district court held that the school district's IEP was inadequate and ordered reimbursement for the private school. The appeals court affirmed, holding that the private school, even though it was not state approved and did not fully comply with IDEA, provided an educational program that met the *Rowley*[51] standard. The appeals court held that when a school district has defaulted on its obligations under IDEA, reimbursement for a placement at a facility that has not been approved by the state is not forbidden as long as the educational program provided at the school meets the *Rowley* standard.

In affirming the decision, the Supreme Court emphasized that IDEA was intended to ensure that students with disabilities received an education that was both appropriate and free. The Court stated that to bar reimbursement under the circumstances of this case would defeat those statutory purposes. The Court noted that public school officials who wished to avoid reimbursing parents of students with disabilities for private school costs could either give the student an appropriate education in a public school setting or place the student in an appropriate private school. The high Court found that IDEA gave courts broad discretion in fashioning equitable relief for students and parents when a school district defaulted on its obligation to provide an appropriate education.

The Ninth Circuit Court of Appeals, citing the Supreme Court's *Carter* decision, awarded reimbursement to the parents of an autistic student who had been enrolled unilaterally by his parents in a private clinic that was not certified to provide special education services.[52] The court found that the school district had failed to offer an appropriate placement and that the student had received educational benefit from his placement at the private clinic. A district court in Maryland, also citing *Carter,* has held that parents were entitled to be reimbursed for tuition expenses at a private school that was not approved to provide special education services since evidence indicated that the student received an appropriate education at the school.[53] In that case the parents enrolled the student in the private school when the school district failed to offer an appropriate IEP six months after their request for an evaluation.

## School District Must Be Given the Opportunity to Act

In *Burlington* the Supreme Court held that parents who have violated the status quo provision did not waive their right to reimbursement in doing so. However, several post-*Burlington* cases indicate that they will waive their right to reimbursement if they make a unilateral move before giving the school district the opportunity to change the IEP the parents claim is inappropriate. The parents must notify the school district that they are dissatisfied with the IEP and allow school officials to take appropriate action. Failure to do this may result in a reduced reimbursement award or a total denial of reimbursement.

School districts must be given the opportunity to propose an educational placement before the parents take unilateral action. If the parents do not give the school district this opportunity, they will not be reimbursed. A state court in Washington held that reimbursement is allowed only after the school district has proposed an inappropriate placement.[54] In this case the parents had enrolled the student in a private school and requested tuition assistance. The school district informed the parents that it would first have to evaluate the child and determine his eligibility for special education. The student's mother refused to allow the evaluation. The state court held that since the school district had not even been given the opportunity to evaluate the student, reimbursement was not available.

In the Washington case the student had never received special education services. In another case, where the student had received services for several years, the Eighth Circuit Court of Appeals held that reimbursement was not available because the school district had not been given the opportunity to make changes to the student's educational program.[55] The student had regressed and the school district wanted to meet to discuss the situation; however, the parents made a unilateral placement change before the meeting could be held. The court found that there was no indication that the school district would have refused to make a change in the student's program and that they were entitled to have the opportunity to make changes. The court emphatically stated that school officials must be put on notice that the parents disagree with the student's educational program and must be given the opportunity to voluntarily make a change in placement before parents are justified in taking unilateral action.

Similarly, the Ninth Circuit Court of Appeals affirmed a district court's finding that parents were not entitled to be reimbursed for expenses they incurred in providing services for their son for the time period before they requested preparation of an IEP.[56] The district court had held that the school district's IEP was not appropriate but that reimbursement was available only for the time period after the parents and school district disagreed over the placement. A Texas district court also awarded reimbursement to a parent who had unilaterally obtained additional services for her child, but not for the time period prior to her challenging the school district's IEP.[57]

## Reimbursement Granted when School District Commits Procedural Errors

The fact that a school district has an appropriate educational program for the student is not sufficient to preclude a reimbursement award. The appropriate placement must be called for in a properly executed IEP. Procedural errors have been held to be sufficient grounds for awarding reimbursement for unilateral placements. Under *Rowley* an educational placement is not appropriate if it is not called for in a properly executed IEP.

The Third Circuit Court of Appeals held that reimbursement was warranted when the school district proposed an appropriate program but the IEP was determined to be defective on procedural grounds.[58] The school district had made a proposal for a placement that was deemed appropriate but failed to write an IEP for that proposal. Similarly, the Fourth Circuit Court of Appeals affirmed a reimbursement award after holding that a school district failed to provide an appropriate education.[59] The district court had held that the school district's program was not appropriate because of procedural defects; specifically, it failed to conduct annual reviews and involve the parents in the IEP process.

School districts must be given the opportunity to evaluate a student and propose an appropriate placement. However, they may be liable for tuition reimbursement if they do not properly evaluate the student. The Fourth Circuit Court of Appeals has held that parents are justified in making a unilateral placement when the school district fails to propose an appropriate placement because it improperly evaluated the student.[60] The court held that the parents did not waive their right to reimbursement when they removed the child from the public schools before school personnel conducted further assessments and proposed a final IEP.

## Parental Delays Do Not Preclude Reimbursement

Parents are not precluded from being reimbursed if they cause delays in the hearing process according to a ruling by a district court in New York.[61] In this case the parents' choice of a private school was eventually held to be the appropriate placement. In the action seeking reimbursement the school district argued that the parents had caused several delays in the proceedings and should not be reimbursed for the period of any delay. The court, however, simply stated that this argument had no merit. The school district would have been responsible for the private school tuition for the entire time period whether there were delays in the proceedings or not.

The federal district court in New Jersey has held that parents do not waive their right to reimbursement by failing to initiate review proceedings seeking reimbursement for a period of time after making their unilateral placement.[62] In this case the parents had waited two years before filing their claim. The court could find no basis in either case law or state regulations to deny the award and held that doing so would not be in accord with IDEA. State statutes of limitations could, however, impose a limit on the time frame in which a parent may file a reimbursement claim.[63]

## Reimbursement for Related Services

Courts consistently have awarded reimbursement for the costs of related services as well as for tuition. Related services are supportive services that may be required to help a student with disabilities benefit from special education.[64] In most of these cases the related services were provided at a private school in conjunction with special education services. However, in some instances courts have awarded reimbursement for the costs of privately obtained related services when the school district failed to provide them in conjunction with a public special education placement. The criteria for reimbursement of related services is similar to the criteria for reimbursement of tuition expenses: The parents must show that the related services were required for the student to receive an appropriate education.

Several courts have awarded reimbursement for the costs of psychotherapy or counseling services.[65] In several of these cases the therapeutic services were provided to students who had been placed in private schools or psychiatric facilities because of emotional difficulties. In others, however, the counseling services were obtained privately by the parents to supplement the services the student received in a public school setting. Regardless of the setting where the student received the special education services, parents receiving a reimbursement award have shown that the student would not have benefitted from those services without psychotherapy or counseling.

A federal district court in New York awarded reimbursement for the nonmedical costs associated with a psychiatric hospitalization.[66] The state had agreed to pay the tuition costs of the educational component of the placement, and the student's health insurance picked up the medical expenses. However, certain therapeutic and maintenance costs associated with the placement were left unfunded. The court held that when a student's medical, social, or emotional problems create or are intertwined with the educational problem, the state is liable for the costs of the required residential placement.

Students cannot benefit from special education services if they cannot get to them. Thus, transportation is a related service that must be provided by the school district. Students attending private schools at public expense must be provided with appropriate transportation. Many of the tuition reimbursement awards cited in previous sections included reimbursement for other necessary costs such as tuition.[67] However, reimbursement also has been awarded to parents of students attending public schools when the school district failed to provide appropriate transportation. The First Circuit Court of Appeals reimbursed the father of a student with physical disabilities for transporting the student himself after the school district failed to make appropriate arrangements.[68] In another case a district court in New York reimbursed a care provider for costs associated with transporting a student to an educational facility for students with physical disabilities.[69] That award included reimbursement for hiring a babysitter to watch other children while she transported the student to the center.

Courts also have awarded reimbursement for various other related services such as occupational therapy,[70] speech therapy,[71] and private tutoring.[72] In the latter case the student attended a parochial school and the public school district failed to offer an appropriate IEP for special education services. The student's parents hired a private tutor to provide the student with special education while due process appeals were pending. However, reimbursement will not be awarded for related services associated with a private school program if the school district had offered an appropriate education and the parents chose to enroll the student at the private school at their own expense.[73] One court has awarded reimbursement for the costs of lodging for the student and his mother that were necessary because the facility the student attended was not within daily commuting distance of the family's residence.[74]

## Hearing Officer May Grant Reimbursement Awards

Although all of the reimbursement awards cited here were granted by the courts, parents do not necessarily have to go to court to obtain reimbursement. Hearing officers have the authority to grant reimbursement awards along with other forms of appropriate equitable relief. A district court in North Carolina held that reimbursement was included within IDEA's provision that a hearing may be held on any matter relating to a free appropriate public education.[75] The court also indicated that Congress did not intend to give courts any greater powers of equity than those given to a hearing officer.

## COMPENSATORY EDUCATIONAL SERVICES

Awards of compensatory educational services have been granted by the courts during the past few years in situations where the school district did not provide an appropriate education, but the student's parents did not have the financial means to obtain alternate services. Thus, the parents were forced to allow the student to remain in the inappropriate program while administrative hearings were pending. In many cases the child lost several years of an appropriate education during the appeals process and the parents sought compensation. Generally, compensatory services are provided during a time period when the student would not be otherwise eligible for services. In most of the compensatory services cases, the courts have applied the *Burlington* rationale when determining whether compensatory services were warranted.

## Compensatory Services Granted

Several courts have held that courts were given the authority to award compensatory services when they were empowered by Congress to fashion an appropriate remedy to cure a deprivation of rights secured by IDEA. These courts have ruled that compensatory services, like reimbursement, merely compensate the student for the inappropriate education received while placement issues were in dispute or the school district failed to act properly. The theory behind compensatory educational services awards is that an appropriate remedy is not limited to those parents who can afford to provide their children with an alternate educational placement while litigation is pending.[76] Generally, compensatory services must be provided for a time period equal to the time the student was denied services.[77] Compensatory awards may be granted even after the student has passed the ceiling age for eligibility under IDEA.[78]

An Eleventh Circuit Court of Appeals decision is illustrative. That court held that an award of compensatory educational services was similar to an award of tuition reimbursement in that it was necessary to preserve the student's right to a free appropriate public education.[79] The court stated that without compensatory services awards a student's rights under IDEA would depend on the parents' ability to privately obtain services during due process hearings. Similarly, the Eighth Circuit Court of Appeals held that compensatory educational services were available to the parent of a student with disabilities who could not afford to provide appropriate educational services himself during the lengthy court battle.[80] In granting the compensatory education award, the court stated that Congress did not intend for a child's entitlement to a free appropriate public education to rest upon the parents' ability to pay for the costs of the placement up front. Another court stated that if compensatory services were not available, the parents would be given a Pyrrhic victory because the student's right to a free appropriate public education would be illusory.[81]

The Second Circuit Court of Appeals awarded compensatory services to a student who had multiple disabilities after the school he had been attending closed and it took the hearing officer over one year to rule on another placement option.[82] During the interim period the student did not receive any educational services. The court held that the student should not be deprived of a free appropriate public education because his parents could not afford a private placement while awaiting the final outcome of the placement litigation. Students who may be denied services during disciplinary exclusions that are later held to be inappropriate also are entitled to compensatory services.[83]

In one of the first cases granting compensatory services the Supreme Judicial Court of Massachusetts found that a student's special education services had been terminated prematurely by the inappropriate conferring of a high school diploma.[84] The court determined that the student had not met the requirements for the diploma and was graduated solely so that special education services could be discontinued. While the dispute was pending the student reached the ceiling age for eligibility under state law. The court held that he was entitled to receive compensatory services to make up for the education he lost after the diploma was improperly conferred.

Students may receive compensatory services even after they earn a valid high school diploma. The district court in Massachusetts awarded compensatory educational services to a student who had earned a high school diploma after determining that the school district had failed to follow proper procedures.[85] The court stated that the fact that the student had earned a diploma was not an indication that she had not required special education services, but rather, it was an indication that she succeeded despite the school district's shortcomings. The school district was ordered to provide services equal in scope to what it should have provided prior to the student's graduation. A New York district court also held that a student who had graduated was entitled to compensatory educational services while attending college but not in the form of college tuition.[86] Similarly, a New Hampshire district court ordered a school district to provide compensatory services to a student after he graduated from high school or reached the ceiling age of eligibility to compensate him for a period of time when he was denied educational services.[87]

Hearing officers have the power to grant awards of compensatory educational services. As with the power to grant tuition reimbursement, courts have held that hearing officers may fashion appropriate relief, and that sometimes requires an award of compensatory services.[88]

## Compensatory Services Denied

As with tuition reimbursement, compensatory services are available only when it can be shown that the student was not provided with a free appropriate public education as mandated by IDEA.[89] However, a district court in Tennessee denied an award of compensatory education even after determining that a homebound program the student had been receiving was not appropriate.[90] The court felt that compensatory education was not warranted because the school district and the parents had not been aware of the existence of an appropriate program. Thus, since the school district had not taken any action that resulted in the denial of a free appropriate public education, the court held that it was not required to provide compensatory services.

## ATTORNEY FEES

IDEA contains one of the most comprehensive mechanisms for dispute resolution ever created by Congress. However, litigation is costly. Many parents, after succeeding in their litigation against the school district, have felt that they also should be reimbursed for their costs in bringing the legal action. Many felt that they achieved a hollow victory if they succeeded in showing that the school district had failed to provide the free appropriate public education their children were entitled to receive under IDEA but were left with large legal bills. Initially, most courts viewed an award of attorney fees as an award for damages.[91]

In 1984 the U.S. Supreme Court held that recovery of legal expenses was not available under IDEA.[92] Congress responded by amending IDEA in 1986 with the Handicapped Children's Protection Act (HCPA).[93] HCPA allows courts to provide an award of reasonable attorney fees to parents who have prevailed against the school district in any action or proceeding brought pursuant to IDEA. The award is to be based on the prevailing rates in the community in which the case arose. The courts have the authority to determine what is a reasonable amount of time to have spent preparing and arguing the case in terms of the issues litigated. The award may be limited if the school district made a settlement offer more than 10 days before the proceedings began that was equal to or more favorable than the final relief obtained. The fee award also may be reduced if the court finds that the parents unreasonably protracted the dispute, the attorney's hourly rate was excessive, or the time spent and legal services furnished were excessive in light of the issues litigated. The HCPA was made retroactive to July 4, 1984, the day before the Supreme Court declared that attorney fees were not available under IDEA.[94]

Hearing officers do not have the authority to grant an attorney fees award.[95] HCPA reserves that authority for the courts. However, parents do not always have to go to court to recover their legal expenses. An agreement may be worked out with the school district for payment of the parents' legal expenses. If parents are required to file court action to recover attorney fees, and they are successful in that action, they may recover their costs in filing the fee petition as well.[96] Since hearing officers cannot award attorney fees, parents do not need to exhaust administrative remedies prior to filing a fee petition.[97]

## Prevailing Parents

One of the most frequently litigated issues under the HCPA concerns the issue of whether the parents had actually prevailed in the litigation. On its face the issue seems simple enough: if the parents won, they prevailed. However, with law nothing is simple. Most special education disputes involve multiple issues, and the parents may have prevailed on only some of them. Courts have generally defined a prevailing parent as one who succeeded on most of the issues litigated. However, in some situations where the parents have not prevailed on all issues, the courts have granted partial awards.

### Full Awards

Courts generally will grant a full award when the parents have prevailed on the major issue in the litigation even if they did not prevail on some minor issues. In most of these situations the work performed litigating the minor issues was inseparable from the major issue, was insignificant compared to the major issue, or was performed in conjunction with the work completed for the major issue.[98]

A district court in Texas awarded attorney fees after determining that the parents were the prevailing party because they had acquired the primary relief they sought.[99] Similarly, the district court in Connecticut granted a full fees award when the parents prevailed on the principal issue in their suit.[100]

The district court in Oregon awarded full fees to a parent who was unsuccessful in obtaining a restraining order but still achieved the primary goal of the litigation: access to an administrative hearing.[101] Similarly, the Eleventh Circuit Court of Appeals awarded attorney fees to a parent who had obtained the most significant relief sought, a free appropriate public education.[102]

Parents may still be given full reimbursement of their legal expenses even if they do not prevail on all issues. Generally, full awards will be granted if the time spent litigating the various issues cannot be easily apportioned on an issue-by-issue basis. The Sixth Circuit Court of Appeals awarded attorney fees to parents who did not receive the residential placement they had requested but succeeded in obtaining additional services because the legal relationship between the school district and parents had changed as a result of the litigation.[103] In another case a district court in Ohio held that parents were entitled to a full fee award because the matters before the administrative hearing were intertwined and could not be viewed as a series of separate claims and the parents got most of what they asked for.[104]

In a very interesting case a district court in Georgia awarded attorney fees to parents who obtained relief not from the courts but from the state legislature.[105] The parents had filed a lawsuit but the state legislature enacted a law that resolved the dispute while the litigation was pending. The district court determined that the parents' lawsuit prompted the action by the state legislature and awarded attorney fees. Similarly, a district court in New York partially reimbursed the father of a student with disabilities after determining that his lawsuit contributed to enactment of new legislation.[106]

### Partial Awards

Partial awards are granted when the parents do not prevail on the most significant issue litigated but do prevail on some of the issues presented. Parents also may be given only a partial attorney fees award when they prevail on some of their claims, and the various claims litigated are distinct enough so that the work done on each claim can be distinguished from the work done on all others. The requested fee award also may be reduced for various other reasons. For example, if the court feels the hourly rate requested or number of hours billed was excessive or finds fault with the time sheets submitted by the attorney, an adjustment may be made in the requested fee award.

A district court in New York stated that fees cannot be recovered for unsuccessful claims that are distinct in all respects from successful claims.[107] Partial fees were granted since the parents had prevailed on a placement issue. Similarly, a district court in Illinois reduced a fee award after determining that the parents had succeeded on a major claim but had failed on several other issues.[108]

Courts have reduced requested fee awards for a variety of reasons. The district court in Rhode Island found that the time spent litigating a fees petition was excessive and reduced the requested amount accordingly.[109] The court also held that the parents were entitled to receive fee reimbursement for work completed only up until the time they achieved their objective. A district court in Indiana reduced a requested fee amount after ruling that the parents' counsel had unnecessarily protracted the proceedings.[110] The Fourth Circuit Court of Appeals reduced a requested award in part because of insufficient record keeping.[111]

Courts do not always reduce awards by determining the exact cost of litigating each issue and reducing the award by the amount of fees charged for litigating the issues in which the parents did not prevail. Sometimes awards are adjusted in proportion to the overall success and failure of the litigation. For example, the district court in New Jersey found it difficult to apportion legal costs issue-by-issue so it simply reduced the requested fee award by 50 percent since the parents had not achieved their primary objective but were successful on several other significant issues.[112] Similarly, the Fourth Circuit Court of Appeals affirmed a district court's reduced fees award because the parents had achieved limited success.[113]

## Parents Have Not Prevailed

Parents cannot recover their legal expenses if the school district is the prevailing party. Naturally, parents who do not succeed on any of their claims do not achieve prevailing party status.[114] As was discussed in the previous section, parents may receive limited reimbursement if they prevail on at least some of their claims. Parents will not be awarded attorney fees, however, if their legal relationship with the school district is not altered as a result of the litigation. Parents also are not the prevailing party if the changes that occur are not a direct result of the litigation but are caused by other factors.

The Second Circuit Court of Appeals held that parents who succeeded in obtaining a temporary restraining order preventing the state from discharging a student from a state-operated facility did not achieve prevailing party status because the merits of the case were never addressed.[115] After receiving the restraining order the student's mother removed the student from the state-operated facility and enrolled him in a private school. Similarly, a district court in Illinois ruled that parents who withdrew their request for a hearing were not entitled to attorney fees even though the school district changed its placement recommendation.[116] The court found that the school district modified its recommendation because of changes in the student's academic performance, not because of the impending due process hearing. In another case a Mississippi district court denied a requested fees award even though the parents had prevailed on some issues because they never allowed the hearing officer's decision to be implemented.[117] The court held that since the IEP ordered by the hearing officer was not implemented, the legal relationship between the parties never changed.

As was shown earlier in this section, parents are sometimes given partial reimbursement of their legal expenses if they obtain some, but not all, of the relief sought. However, if the relief obtained is insignificant, courts may not grant even a partial award. The Seventh Circuit Court of Appeals denied an award of attorney fees even though the parents had obtained some relief that conferred a benefit on the student.[118] The court determined that the value of those benefits was wiped out by the ultimate outcome of the lawsuit.

A district court in Michigan denied an award of attorney fees after finding that the plan ultimately agreed on, although it was accepted by the parents, was far less than the school district originally offered.[119] The court stated that the attorney had not improved the parents' position but, rather, had unnecessarily aggrandized and protracted the misunderstanding between the parties. Similarly, the Fourth Circuit Court of Appeals denied an award of attorney fees in part because it determined that the problem complained of by the parents could have been resolved without resort to the administrative or judicial forums.[120] The Second Circuit Court of Appeals held that the guardian of a student with disabilities was not entitled to an attorney fees award after the lawsuit was dismissed by the district court due to her failure to exhaust administrative remedies, even though she eventually reached a settlement agreement with the school district.[121]

A three judge panel of the Fourth Circuit Court of Appeals awarded attorney fees after determining that a lawsuit was at least partially responsible for a Department of Education letter ruling that modified the state's procedures. However, that decision was later overturned following a rehearing by the entire court. In the latter decision the court held that the fact that a lawsuit may act as a catalyst for post-litigation changes in a defendant's conduct cannot suffice to establish the plaintiff as the prevailing party.[122]

## Fees Are Available for Administrative Proceedings

The HCPA provides for the recovery of attorney fees to parents who prevail in "any action or proceeding" brought under IDEA's dispute resolution provision.[123] The meaning of the term *any action or proceeding* has been in dispute. Many school districts have claimed that it refers only to court action and that attorney fees are not recoverable for work performed at the administrative hearing level. After some controversy, it is now well settled that attorney fees are available for representation at administrative hearings even if the dispute is settled without court action. It also is well settled that a lawsuit can be filed solely for the purpose of recovering legal expenses.

The leading and most controversial case on the topic was decided by the federal appeals court for the District of Columbia in 1990.[124] Initially, a divided three-judge panel held that the language Congress used in the HCPA provided for an award of attorney fees only in cases where the losing party in an administrative action appealed to the courts and prevailed in the judicial action.[125] According to that decision fees could not be awarded to a parent who prevailed at the administrative level and brought judicial action only to obtain attorney fees. Since this decision was contrary to the majority of decisions that had been handed down by other appeals court circuits[126] and district courts,[127] the court granted a rehearing *en banc.*

Following the rehearing the appeals court vacated its previous decision and held that attorney fees were available for administrative proceedings. This time the court found that Congress, using the term *any action or proceeding,* meant to authorize fees for parents who prevailed in a civil action or an administrative proceeding. The court further found that the legislative history of HCPA supported that interpretation. Since that decision, courts have been unanimous in holding that parents who prevail at the administrative level many recover their legal expenses.[128] The district court for the District of Columbia also awarded fees to parents who obtained a court order to enforce the decision of a hearing officer.[129]

## Settlement Offers

School districts can lessen their liability by attempting to reach a settlement with the parents before the administrative hearings begin. One section of HCPA states that fees are not available for any legal representation that occurs after the school district makes a written settlement offer if the final relief obtained by the parent is not more favorable to the parents than the offer of settlement. The settlement offer must be made at least 10 days before the scheduled start of the due process hearing.[130]

The settlement offer does not need to be identical to the final administrative decision to stop the attorney's time clock from ticking. A Tennessee district court held that parents were not entitled to an award of attorney fees when the final relief they obtained was substantially similar to the last offer the school district made before the hearing.[131] Similarly, the district court in Rhode Island denied a fees award after determining that the school district's final settlement offer, although different from the final relief obtained, was not more favorable.[132] In its opinion the court chastised the parents for failing to make a good faith attempt at settlement and for being utterly inflexible regarding settlement.

Several courts have held that parents are entitled to collect attorney fees for legal work completed up to the time of the settlement offer, even when the hearing is canceled because the settlement offer was accepted.[133] The Eighth Circuit Court of Appeals refused to award fees to a parent who had filed for an administrative hearing before giving the school district the opportunity to alter the student's educational placement.[134]

## Attendance at Meetings Prior to a Hearing

It is well settled that the phrase *any action or proceeding* includes administrative hearings and courts have awarded fees for work completed preparing for a hearing even when the hearing was canceled because a settle-ment was reached. It is also fair to assume that Congress did not intend for school districts to be paying for attorneys to accompany dissatisfied parents to all meetings where the student's placement or program is discussed. Congress envisioned that parents and school district personnel would work together. Disagreements may arise, but most can be worked out without the involvement of the legal profession. In other situations, however, the presence of an attorney at a meeting prior to a hearing may help bring about a quick settlement. Courts have been asked to demarcate the point at which an attorney's involvement was warranted. The deter-mining factor may be how school officials initially responded to the parents' dissatisfaction.

A district court in California held that fees are properly awarded for services performed prior to an administrative hearing such as for a settlement process or mediation conferences.[135] The district court for the District of Columbia decreed that nothing in HCPA precluded an award of attorney fees for work done in preparation for filing a complaint or for an attorney's presence at IEP meetings if such attendance was necessary to gain an appropriate placement.[136] However, the district court in Maine ruled that the plain language of IDEA and its legislative history indicated that recovery of attorney fees arising from representation at IEP team meetings was not authorized.[137] The court stated that allowing recovery of legal fees for these meetings would only encourage adversarial conduct, a result that is not in keeping with the purpose of IDEA.

## Fees to Public Agency Attorneys

Many parents use the services of an attorney from a public advocacy agency. These agencies generally provide low-cost or free legal services to parents on a sliding scale fee arrangement. The courts have held that when parents who are represented by public agency attorneys prevail in a special education action, the attorney is entitled to be reimbursed at the prevailing rate in the community even if that rate is higher than the rate the parent would have been charged.

The Sixth Circuit Court of Appeals, in examining the legislative history of HCPA, found that Congress intended for publicly funded attor-neys to be compensated at prevailing rates.[138] The court held that an award of attorney fees was available to prevailing parents regardless of whether their attorney was associated with a private organization or public agency. Similarly, the Eleventh Circuit Court of Appeals held that the fact that prevailing parents had not paid their attorney was irrelevant to a fees award.[139] The court held that the right to an attorney fees award did not depend on the parents' financial status or the availability of free legal assistance.

## Fees to Lay Advocates and Pro Se Attorneys

Many parents, particularly in the early stages of a dispute, rely on the services of a lay advocate to advise them and represent them in meetings with the school district. Although the services of a lay advocate may be beneficial to resolving the dispute, since they are not attorneys, they may not be reimbursed for legal representation under HCPA. Also, it has been held that parents who represent themselves may not be compensated under HCPA, even if they are members of the bar.

The Third Circuit Court of Appeals held that IDEA, as amended by HCPA, did not contain any provisions granting fees for representation by lay advocates.[140] In this particular case the lay advocate acted as the parents' representative in administrative hearings. State law prohibited nonlawyers from receiving a fee for representing parties in administrative hearings so the district court denied a requested fee award. In affirming, the appeals court held that Congress did not intend to limit a state's control over the practice of law when it passed HCPA. Many legal advocates work under the direction of attorneys. In this capacity it is likely that reimbursement for their services would be allowed as part of the attorney's costs.[141] In fact, in the Third Circuit case, the appeals court stated that the advocate could charge a fee as an educational consultant.

The district court in Maryland held that HCPA should be interpreted consistently with Title VII of the Civil Rights Act of 1964,[142] and that under Title VII a litigant's *pro se* status constituted a special circumstance that justified a denial of a fee award.[143] The court further found that Congress's purpose in passing IDEA would not be advanced and fairness would not be served by awarding fees to the father of a student with disabilities just because he was an attorney. Similarly, a district court in New York held that payment could not be awarded to a plaintiff who worked as a paralegal in his own lawsuit.[144] However, the federal appeals court for the District of Columbia held that a school district waived its argument against the availability of fee awards to pro se litigants by failing to raise it in its original opposition of a fee award.[145]

## Expert Witnesses

HCPA allows parents to recover other costs of bringing a special education legal action along with being reimbursed for attorney fees. In particular, parents may receive remuneration for the costs of hiring expert witnesses.

Several district courts have held that parents may include the costs of expert witnesses in their request for an attorney fees award.[146] A district court in Georgia even held that parents were entitled to be reimbursed for the services of an expert who did not testify but who did contribute to the development of the case.[147] However, the district court in New Jersey would not reimburse parents for the full costs of an expert witness because it felt that although the expert witness was helpful, the use of an expert was not necessary.[148] The Third Circuit Court of Appeals held that even though a lay advocate could not be reimbursed for legal representation, she could charge a fee for services as an expert witness or an educational consultant.[149]

## Retroactive Provision

When HCPA was passed many school districts were surprised by the retroactive clause of the statute. Although the act was passed in 1986 Congress decreed that it applied to any actions or proceedings that were still pending on July 4, 1984. School districts found themselves liable for legal expenses in cases the administrators felt were well behind them. Some school districts unsuccessfully challenged the constitutionality of the retroactive provision, and others questioned whether certain cases actually were pending on July 4, 1984.

Courts have been unanimous in holding that there is no constitutional bar to the retroactive provision of HCPA. A decision by the Second Circuit Court of Appeals is illustrative.[150] That court affirmed the lower court's holding that the retroactive provision was not unconstitutional because it was rationally related to a legitimate legislative purpose: to enable parents to utilize the attorney of their choice. The appeals court added that Congress was acting pursuant to its fourteenth amendment enforcement powers and that the retroactive provision had the rational purpose of furthering IDEA's goals by encouraging parents and attorneys to vindicate the rights of students with disabilities. Other courts have held that the retroactive provision is not unconstitutional and is consistent with Congress's spending power.[151]

After Congress passed HCPA numerous settled court cases were resurrected solely for the purpose of recovering attorney fees. The courts were asked to determine if some of them were pending on the effective date of the legislation. Among the first such cases the district court for the District of Columbia and the Seventh Circuit Court of Appeals held that the term *pending* included pending fee applications.[152] However, the Eleventh Circuit Court of Appeals refused to reopen a case in which a final unappealed judgment denying attorney fees had been rendered before the date the statute was enacted.[153]

## Special Circumstances

In several situations school districts have asked courts to deny an attorney fees award claiming that special circumstances existed to make such an award unjust. The Ninth Circuit Court of Appeals stated that the retroactive provision of HCPA does not create a special circumstance.[154] The court stated that a necessary evil of making awards retroactively is that settled expectations may be upset. The court held that when considering whether special circumstances exist that would justify a denial of attorney fees, courts must examine whether awarding fees would further Congressional intent and consider the balance of equities.[155]

## Awards to School Districts

HCPA allows for recovery of legal expenses by prevailing parents. It does not give school districts the right to seek reimbursement for their legal expenses if they prevail in the litigation. However, courts may award fees to school districts, using their general powers of equity, if it is determined that the parents' lawsuit was frivolous or the parents' actions unnecessarily prolonged the litigation.

The First Circuit Court of Appeals held that a school district was entitled to reimbursement of legal expenses under Appellate Rule 38[156] after concluding that the parents' lawsuit was "completely devoid of merit and plagued by unnecessary delay."[157] The court found that the parents had engaged in tactics throughout the proceedings that led to undue delays and failed to cooperate in negotiations to settle the dispute.

A district court in New York denied a prevailing school district's request for attorney fees based on the claim that the parents brought the action in bad faith.[158] The court found that both parties proceeded in good faith and should bear their own costs.

## ELEVENTH AMENDMENT IMMUNITY

The U.S. Constitution's Eleventh Amendment provides the states with immunity from lawsuits in the federal courts. Congress may abrogate the states' immunity with respect to a particular law if it expresses its intent to do so in clear and unmistakable language within the statute.[159] In 1989, after some controversy in the lower courts,[160] the U.S. Supreme Court held that states were immune from liability in cases arising under IDEA.[161] The Court, in *Dellmuth* v. *Muth,* declared that when Congress passed IDEA, it did not abrogate the states' sovereign immunity since it had not stated its intent to do so in clear and unmistakable language within the act itself.[162]

The Court, declaring that Congress's intent to abrogate must be both unequivocal and textual, held that since IDEA did not mention either the Eleventh Amendment or sovereign immunity, this standard had not been met.

Congress acted quickly to amend the law in 1990 to specifically abrogate the states' Eleventh Amendment immunity. This time Congress employed clear and unmistakable language to declare that the states "shall not be immune under the eleventh amendment to the Constitution of the United States from suit in Federal court for a violation of this Act."[163] The amendment applied to any violations that occurred in whole or in part after October 30, 1990.

A district court in Illinois held that the 1990 amendment explicitly abrogated the states' Eleventh Amendment immunity and was controlling over the Supreme Court's *Muth* decision for any violations that occurred after the effective date of October 30, 1990.[164] Since certain alleged violations in the case before it were ongoing, the court held that they defeated a sovereign immunity defense. Similarly, a district court in New York held that the state was immune from lawsuits for any violations of IDEA that occurred before October 30, 1990, but could be held liable for harm that continued past that date.[165] However, the Second Circuit Court of Appeals held that violations cannot be considered to be ongoing just because a student failed to secure the relief he sought in administrative hearings that were concluded well before the effective date of the abrogation amendment.[166]

## SUMMARY

The courts are empowered to grant appropriate relief when a school district fails to provide an appropriate education as called for in IDEA. In most situations the appropriate relief is to order the school district to provide a free appropriate public education in the future. However, numerous lawsuits have been filed seeking compensation for the district's past failure to provide the services the student was entitled to receive under IDEA. The courts have used their powers of equity to provide the parents of students with disabilities with various forms of compensation for lost services and out-of-pocket expenses. On two occasions, U.S. Supreme Court decisions have caused Congress to amend IDEA.

It is well settled that punitive damages are not available in special education litigation unless it can be shown that the school district violated the student's rights in an egregious fashion. School districts will not be held responsible for monetary awards of a punitive nature if their actions were made in good faith but did not live up to the mandates of

IDEA. Most courts have adopted the position that any funds used to pay a damages award will reduce the funds available to provide educational programs. Consistent with the holdings that punitive damages will not be levied against a school district, absent blatant intentional disregard for a student's rights, lawsuits alleging educational malpractice have not been successful.

Following a great deal of legal controversy, the U.S. Supreme Court declared that parents are entitled to be reimbursed for tuition and other costs of providing their children with an appropriate education when the school district failed to do so. However, to be reimbursed, the parents must show that the school district failed to offer an appropriate program and the services the parents obtained privately were appropriate. Parents, in appropriate circumstances, may be reimbursed even if the private school they chose was not state-approved. In addition to tuition for private school placements, parents also may be reimbursed for the costs of related services.

In some situations in which it was eventually determined that the school district failed to provide a free appropriate public education, the parents were unable to procure the needed services privately while the dispute was pending. In these situations the student may have lost several months or years of appropriate educational services. The courts have held that an appropriate remedy under these circumstances is an award of compensatory educational services. Compensatory services generally are provided during a time period when the student otherwise would not be eligible for services. For example, a court may extend a student's eligibility for services beyond the date when services would normally be terminated.

After the U.S. Supreme Court ruled that parents who successfully brought a lawsuit against a school district could not be reimbursed for their legal expenses, Congress amended IDEA to provide for recovery of attorney fees by prevailing parents in a special education dispute. If the parents ultimately are declared to be the prevailing party in the litigation, they may sue for reimbursement of all legal expenses incurred as a result of the school district's failure to provide an appropriate education. Courts have even awarded attorney fees when the lawsuit prompted new legislation or changes in state policy. Reduced fee awards will be granted in situations where the parents may not have prevailed on all of the issues litigated, but did prevail on some significant issues. Fee awards also may be reduced if the school district made a settlement offer that was rejected by the parents but was equal to or more favorable than the final relief the parents obtained. Courts will reduce the requested fee award if it is excessive in view of the issues litigated.

The Eleventh Amendment of the U.S. Constitution provides states with immunity to lawsuits in the federal courts unless that immunity is specifically abrogated by Congress when it passes a specific piece of legislation. Congress acted to amend IDEA once again after the U.S. Supreme Court declared that states were immune from IDEA lawsuits in the federal courts. Congress added language to IDEA that specifically abrogated the states' sovereign immunity in litigation under IDEA.

The remedies the courts have fashioned over the years have had the effect of ensuring that students with disabilities will not be deprived of the free appropriate public education they are guaranteed under IDEA and that their parents will not have to bear any personal expenses in securing those rights. School districts can be held financially liable for their failures to provide students with disabilities with the educational services to which they are entitled. Since it is less costly to provide the needed services from the outset than it is to reimburse parents for obtaining those services privately along with their legal expenses, the incentive exists for school districts to implement the law as Congress intended.

## ENDNOTES

1. 20 U.S.C. § 1415(e)(2).
2. Zirkel, P. A. and Osborne, A. G. (1987). Are Damages Available in Special Education Suits? *Education Law Reporter, 42,* 497–508.
3. *See* Black, H.C. (1979). *Black's Law Dictionary, Fifth Edition.* St. Paul, MN: West Publishing Co.
4. *See, for example, Burlington School Committee* v. *Department of Education of the Commonwealth of Massachusetts,* 471 U.S. 359, 105 S. Ct. 1996, 85 L. Ed.2d 385, 23 Ed.Law Rep. 1189 (1985).
5. 20 U.S.C. § 1401 et seq.
6. *Anderson* v. *Thompson,* 658 F.2d 1205 (7th Cir. 1981).
7. *Powell* v. *DeFore,* 699 F.2d 1078, 9 Ed.Law Rep. 492 (11th Cir. 1983); *Marvin H.* v. *Austin Independent School District,* 714 F.2d 1348, 13 Ed.Law Rep. 210 (5th Cir. 1983); *Gary A.* v. *New Trier High School District No. 203,* 796 F.2d 940, 33 Ed.Law Rep. 1052 (7th Cir. 1986); *Barnett* v. *Fairfax County School Board,* 721 F. Supp. 755, 56 Ed.Law Rep. 802 (E.D. Va. 1989), *aff'd* 927 F.2d 146, 66 Ed.Law Rep. 64 (4th Cir. 1991); *Valerie J.* v. *Derry Cooperative School District,* 771 F. Supp. 492, 69 Ed.Law Rep. 1076 (D.N.H. 1991).
8. *Burlington School Committee* v. *Department of Education of the Commonwealth of Massachusetts,* 471 U.S. 359, 105 S. Ct. 1996, 85 L. Ed.2d 385, 23 Ed.Law Rep. 1189 (1985).
9. *Marvin H.* v. *Austin Independent School District,* 714 F.2d 1348, 13 Ed.Law Rep. 210 (5th Cir. 1983).
10. *Barnett* v. *Fairfax County School Board,* 721 F. Supp. 755, 56 Ed.Law Rep. 802 (E.D. Va. 1989), *aff'd* 927 F.2d 146, 66 Ed.Law Rep. 64 (4th Cir. 1991). *Also see Kelly K.* v. *Town of Framingham,* 36 Mass. App. Ct. 483, 633 N.E.2d 414, 91 Ed.Law Rep. 274 (Mass. App. Ct. 1994).

11. *Hurry v. Jones,* 734 F.2d 879, 17 Ed.Law Rep. 774 (1st Cir. 1984).
12. *Gerasimou v. Ambach,* 636 F. Supp. 1504, 33 Ed.Law Rep. 665 (E.D.N.Y. 1986).
13. *Sanders v. Marquette Public Schools,* 561 F. Supp. 1361, 11 Ed.Law Rep. 171 (W.D. Mich. 1983).
14. Evans, W.J. (1992). Torts. In Thomas, S.B. (ed.) *The Yearbook of Education Law 1992.* Topeka, KS: The National Organization of Legal Problems of Education.
15. Gatti, R.D. and Gatti D.J. (1975). *Encyclopedic Dictionary of School Law.* West Nyack, NY: Parker Publishing Co.
16. Nolte, M. C. (1980). *Nolte's School Law Desk Book.* West Nyack, NY: Parker Publishing Co.
17. *Brooks v. St. Tammany Parish School Board,* 510 So.2d 51, 40 Ed.Law Rep. 1323 (La. App. Ct. 1987).
18. *White v. State of California,* 240 Cal. Rptr. 732, 42 Ed.Law Rep. 262 (Ca. Ct. App. 1987).
19. *Johnson v. Clark,* 418 N.W.2d 466, 44 Ed.Law Rep. 689 (Mich. Ct. App. 1987).
20. *Hall v. Knott County Board of Education,* 941 F.2d 402, 69 Ed.Law Rep. 242 (6th Cir. 1991).
21. *Crocker v. Tennessee Secondary School Athletic Association,* 980 F.2d 382, 79 Ed.Law Rep. 389 (6th Cir. 1992).
22. 42 U.S.C. § 1983.
23. Hudgins, H. C. and Vacca, R. S. (1991). *Law and Education: Contemporary Issues and Court Decisions.* Charlottesville, VA: The Michie Co. For a discussion of the relationship between section 1983 and IDEA, see Chapter 4 of this text.
24. *Barnett v. Fairfax County School Board,* 721 F. Supp. 755, 56 Ed.Law Rep. 802 (E.D. Va. 1989), *aff'd* 927 F.2d 146, 66 Ed.Law Rep. 64 (4th Cir. 1991); *Crocker v. Tennessee Secondary School Athletic Association,* 980 F.2d 382, 79 Ed.Law Rep. 389 (6th Cir. 1992).
25. 20 U.S.C. § 1415(e)(3).
26. Osborne, A.G. (1989). Reimbursement of Private School Tuition to Parents Since *Burlington. Remedial and Special Education, 10(5),* 58–62.
27. *Burlington School Committee v. Department of Education of the Commonwealth of Massachusetts,* 471 U.S. 359, 105 S. Ct. 1996, 85 L. Ed.2d 385, 23 Ed.Law Rep. 1189 (1985).
28. *Anderson v. Thompson,* 658 F.2d 1205 (7th Cir. 1981).
29. *Stemple v. Board of Education of Prince George's County,* 623 F.2d 893 (4th Cir. 1980); *Mountain View-Los Altos Union High School v. Sharron B.H.,* 709 F.2d 28, 11 Ed.Law Rep. 845 (9th Cir. 1983); *Marvin H. v. Austin Independent School District,* 714 F.2d 1348, 13 Ed.Law Rep. 210 (5th Cir. 1983); *Rowe v. Henry County School Board,* 718 F.2d 115, 13 Ed.Law Rep. 945 (4th Cir. 1983); *Department of Education, State of Hawaii v. Katherine D.,* 727 F.2d 809, 16 Ed.Law Rep. 378 (9th Cir. 1983); *Tatro v. State of Texas,* 703 F.2d 823, 10 Ed.Law Rep. 73 (5th Cir. 1983), *aff'd sub nom. Irving Independent School District v. Tatro,* 468 U.S. 883, 104 S. Ct. 3371, 82 L. Ed.2d 664, 18 Ed.Law Rep. 138 (1984); *Scokin v. Texas,* 723 F.2d 432, 15 Ed.Law Rep. 122 (5th Cir. 1984).
30. *Doe v. Brookline School Committee,* 722 F.2d 910, 15 Ed.Law Rep. 72 (1st Cir. 1983).

31. *Town of Burlington* v. *Department of Education, Commonwealth of Massachusetts,* 736 F.2d 773, 18 Ed.Law Rep. 278 (1st Cir. 1984).
32. *Burlington School Committee* v. *Department of Education of the Commonwealth of Massachusetts,* 471 U.S. 359, 105 S. Ct. 1996, 85 L. Ed.2d 385, 23 Ed.Law Rep. 1189 (1985).
33. *See, for example, McKenzie* v. *Smith,* 771 F.2d 1527, 27 Ed.Law Rep. 465 (D.C. Cir. 1985); *Hall* v. *Vance County Board of Education,* 774 F.2d 629, 27 Ed.Law Rep. 1107 (4th Cir. 1985); *Board of Education of East Windsor Regional School District* v. *Diamond,* 808 F.2d 987, 36 Ed.Law Rep. 1136 (3d Cir. 1986); *Jenkins* v. *State of Florida,* 815 F.2d 629, 38 Ed.Law Rep. 909 (11th Cir. 1987), 931 F.2d 1469, 67 Ed.Law Rep. 493 (11th Cir. 1991); *Jefferson County Board of Education* v. *Breen,* 853 F.2d 853, 48 Ed.Law Rep. 382 (11th Cir. 1988); *Babb* v. *Knox County School System,* 965 F.2d 104, 75 Ed.Law Rep. 767 (6th Cir. 1992); *Slack* v. *State of Delaware Department of Public Instruction,* 826 F. Supp. 115, 84 Ed.Law Rep. 944 (D. Del. 1993).
34. *See, for example, Wexler* v. *Westfield Board of Education,* 784 F.2d 176 (3d Cir. 1986); *Gregory K.* v. *Longview School District,* 811 F.2d 1307, 37 Ed.Law Rep. 1104 (9th Cir. 1987); *Hudson* v. *Wilson,* 828 F.2d 1059, 41 Ed.Law Rep. 830 (4th Cir. 1987); *Knight* v. *District of Columbia,* 877 F.2d 1025, 54 Ed.Law Rep. 791 (D.C. Cir. 1989); *Doe* v. *Defendant I,* 898 F.2d 1186, 59 Ed.Law Rep. 619 (6th Cir. 1990); *David H.* v. *Palmyra Area School District,* 769 F. Supp. 159, 69 Ed.Law Rep. 428 (M.D. Pa. 1990) *aff'd without published opinion* 932 F.2d 959 (3d Cir. 1991); *Doe* v. *Board of Education of Tullahoma City Schools,* 9 F.3d 455, 87 Ed.Law Rep. 354 (6th Cir. 1993); *Bonnie Ann F.* v. *Calallen Independent School District,* 835 F. Supp. 340, 87 Ed.Law Rep. 95 (S.D. Tex. 1993).
35. *Board of Education of the Hendrick Hudson Central School District* v. *Rowley,* 458 U.S. 176, 102 S. Ct. 3034, 73 L. Ed.2d 690, 5 Ed.Law Rep. 34 (1982). See Chapter 5 for a discussion of this case and the Court's definition of an appropriate education.
36. *Alamo Heights Independent School District* v. *State Board of Education,* 790 F.2d 1153, 32 Ed.Law Rep. 445 (5th Cir. 1986).
37. *Garland Independent School District* v. *Wilks,* 657 F. Supp. 1163, 39 Ed.Law Rep. 92 (N.D. Tex. 1987).
38. *Delaware County Intermediate Unit #25* v. *Martin K.,* 831 F. Supp. 1206, 86 Ed.Law Rep. 147 (E.D. Pa. 1993).
39. *Drew P.* v. *Clarke County School District,* 676 F. Supp. 1559, 44 Ed.Law Rep. 250 (M.D. Ga. 1987), *aff'd* 877 F.2d 927, 54 Ed.Law Rep. 456 (11th Cir. 1989).
40. *Lascari* v. *Board of Education of the Ramapo Indian Hills Regional High School District,* 560 A.2d 1180, 54 Ed.Law Rep. 1244 (N.J. 1989).
41. *P.J.* v. *State of Connecticut State Board of Education,* 788 F. Supp. 673, 74 Ed.Law Rep. 1117 (D. Conn. 1992).
42. *Cremeans* v. *Fairland Local School District Board of Education,* 633 N.E.2d 570, 91 Ed.Law Rep. 280 (Ohio App. Ct. 1993).
43. Parkinson, J. R. (1992). Parents' Unilateral Placement of a Disabled Child in an Unapproved Private School: A "Free Appropriate Public Education?" *Education Law Reporter, 76,* 893–912.

44. 20 U.S.C. § 1401(a)(18)(B). *Also see Board of Education of the Hendrick Hudson Central School District* v. *Rowley,* 458 U.S. 176, 102 S. Ct. 3034, 73 L. Ed.2d 690, 5 Ed.Law Rep. 34 (1982).

45. 20 U.S.C. § 1413(a)(4)(B)(ii).

46. *Schimmel* v. *Spillane,* 630 F. Supp. 159, 31 Ed.Law Rep. 468 (E.D. Va. 1986), *aff'd* 819 F.2d 477, 39 Ed.Law Rep. 999 (4th Cir. 1987); *Taglianetti* v. *Cronin,* 97 Ill. Dec. 547, 493 N.E.2d 29, 32 Ed.Law Rep. 711 (Ill. Ct. App. 1986); *Doe* v. *Anrig,* 651 F. Supp. 424, 37 Ed.Law Rep. 511 (D. Mass. 1987); *Hiller* v. *Board of Education of the Brunswick Central School District,* 687 F. Supp. 735, 47 Ed.Law Rep. 951 (N.D.N.Y. 1988); *B.G.* v. *Cranford Board of Education,* 702 F. Supp. 1140, 51 Ed.Law Rep. 470 (D.N.J. 1988), *amended* 702 F. Supp. 1158, 51 Ed.Law Rep. 488 (D.N.J. 1988); *Tucker* v. *Bay Shore Union Free School District,* 873 F.2d 563, 53 Ed.Law Rep. 434 (2d Cir. 1989); *Straube* v. *Florida Union Free School District,* 801 F. Supp. 1164, 78 Ed.Law Rep. 390 (S.D.N.Y. 1992); *Fagan* v. *District of Columbia,* 817 F. Supp. 161, 82 Ed.Law Rep. 403 (D.D.C. 1993).

47. *Antkowiak* v. *Ambach,* 838 F.2d 635, 44 Ed.Law Rep. 129 (2d Cir. 1988).

48. *Carrington* v. *Commissioner of Education,* 535 N.E.2d 212, 52 Ed.Law Rep. 209 (Mass. 1989). This ruling may be contrasted with an earlier one by the federal district court in the same state that ruled that a school district was not responsible for room and board expenses at a facility that was not state-approved for special education because under state law placements could only be made in approved facilities. *Doe* v. *Anrig,* 651 F. Supp. 424, 37 Ed.Law Rep. 511 (D. Mass. 1987).

49. *Carter* v. *Florence County School District Four,* 950 F.2d 156, 71 Ed.Law Rep. 633 (4th Cir. 1991). This decision may be contrasted with an earlier Fourth Circuit decision in *Schimmel* v. *Spillane,* 819 F.2d 477, 39 Ed.Law Rep. 999 (4th Cir. 1987) cited above. In *Schimmel* the court affirmed a district court's denial of reimbursement to parents who had placed a student in an unapproved private school.

50. *Florence County School District Four* v. *Carter,* ___ U.S. ___, 114 S. Ct. 361, 126 L. Ed.2d 284, 86 Ed.Law Rep. 41 (1993).

51. *Board of Education of the Hendrick Hudson Central School District* v. *Rowley,* 458 U.S. 176, 102 S. Ct. 3034, 73 L. Ed.2d 690, 5 Ed.Law Rep. 34 (1982).

52. *Union School District* v. *Smith,* 15 F.3d 1519, 89 Ed.Law Rep. 449 (9th Cir. 1994).

53. *Gerstmyer* v. *Howard County Public Schools,* 850 F. Supp. 361, 91 Ed.Law Rep. 569 (D. Md. 1994).

54. *Hunter* v. *Seattle School District No. 1,* 731 P.2d 19, 37 Ed.Law Rep. 362 (Wash. Ct. App. 1987).

55. *Evans* v. *District No. 17 of Douglas County,* 841 F.2d 824, 45 Ed.Law Rep. 543 (8th Cir. 1988).

56. *Ash* v. *Lake Oswego School District,* 766 F. Supp. 852, 68 Ed.Law Rep. 683 (D. Or. 1991), *aff'd* 980 F.2d 585, 79 Ed.Law Rep. 408 (9th Cir. 1992).

57. *Garland Independent School District* v. *Wilks,* 657 F. Supp. 1163, 39 Ed.Law Rep. 92 (D. Tex. 1987).

58. *Muth* v. *Central Bucks School District,* 839 F.2d 113, 44 Ed.Law Rep. 1037 (3d Cir. 1988), *rev'd and rem'd on other grounds sub nom. Dellmuth* v. *Muth,* 491 U.S. 223, 109 S. Ct. 2397, 105 L. Ed.2d 181, 53 Ed.Law Rep. 792 (1989).
59. *Board of Education of the County of Cabell* v. *Dienelt,* 843 F.2d 813, 46 Ed.Law Rep. 64 (4th Cir. 1988).
60. *Hudson* v. *Wilson,* 828 F.2d 1059, 41 Ed.Law Rep. 830 (4th Cir. 1987).
61. *Eugene B.* v. *Great Neck Union Free School District,* 635 F. Supp. 753, 33 Ed.Law Rep. 187 (E.D.N.Y. 1986).
62. *Bernardsville Board of Education* v. *J.H.,* 817 F. Supp. 14, 82 Ed.Law Rep. 392 (D.N.J. 1993).
63. See Chapter 4 for a discussion of state statutes of limitations.
64. See Chapter 6 for a discussion of related services.
65. *Max M.* v. *Thompson,* 566 F. Supp. 1330, 12 Ed.Law Rep. 761 (N.D. Ill. 1983), 592 F. Supp. 1437, 20 Ed.Law Rep. 489 (N.D. Ill. 1984), *sub nom. Max M.* v. *Illinois State Board of Education,* 629 F. Supp. 1504, 31 Ed.Law Rep. 437 (N.D. Ill. 1986); *Gary A.* v. *New Trier High School District No. 203,* 796 F.2d 940, 33 Ed.Law Rep. 1052 (7th Cir. 1986); *Doe* v. *Anrig,* 651 F. Supp. 424, 37 Ed.Law Rep. 511 (D. Mass. 1987); *Tice* v. *Botetourt County School Board,* 908 F.2d 1200, 61 Ed.Law Rep. 1207 (4th Cir. 1990); *Babb* v. *Knox County School System,* 965 F.2d 104, 75 Ed.Law Rep. 767 (6th Cir. 1992); *Straube* v. *Florida Union Free School District,* 801 F. Supp. 1164, 78 Ed.Law Rep. 390 (S.D.N.Y. 1992).
66. *Vander Malle* v. *Ambach,* 667 F. Supp. 1015, 41 Ed.Law Rep. 913 (S.D.N.Y. 1987).
67. *See, for example, Northeast Central School District* v. *Sobol,* 584 N.Y.S.2d 525, 75 Ed.Law Rep. 890 (N.Y. 1992); *Union School District* v. *Smith,* 15 F.3d 1519, 89 Ed.Law Rep. 449 (9th Cir. 1994).
68. *Hurry* v. *Jones,* 734 F.2d 879, 17 Ed.Law Rep. 774 (1st Cir. 1984).
69. *Taylor* v. *Board of Education of Copake-Taconic,* 649 F. Supp. 1253, 36 Ed.Law Rep. 1206 (N.D.N.Y. 1986).
70. *Rapid City School District* v. *Vahle,* 922 F.2d 476, 65 Ed.Law Rep. 65 (8th Cir. 1990).
71. *Johnson* v. *Lancaster-Lebanon Intermediate Unit 13, Lancaster City School District,* 757 F. Supp. 606, 66 Ed.Law Rep. 227 (E.D. Pa. 1991).
72. *W.G. and B.G.* v. *Board of Trustees of Target Range School District No. 23, Missoula, Montana,* 789 F. Supp. 1070, 75 Ed.Law Rep. 254 (D. Mont. 1991), *aff'd* 960 F.2d 1479 (9th Cir. 1992).
73. *Dreher* v. *Amphitheater Unified School District,* 797 F. Supp. 753, 77 Ed.Law Rep. 211 (D. Ariz. 1992), *aff'd* 22 F.3d 228, 91 Ed.Law Rep. 32 (9th Cir. 1994).
74. *Union School District* v. *Smith,* 15 F.3d 1519, 89 Ed.Law Rep. 449 (9th Cir. 1994).
75. *S-1* v. *Spangler,* 650 F. Supp. 1427, 37 Ed.Law Rep. 208 (M.D.N.C. 1986), *vac'd and rem'd due to mootness* 832 F.2d 294, 42 Ed.Law Rep. 717 (4th Cir. 1987), *on remand* (unpublished opinion); *aff'd sub nom. S-1* v. *State Board of Education,* 6 F.3d 160, 86 Ed.Law Rep. 56 (4th Cir. 1993), *rehearing en banc, rev'd* 21 F.3d 49, 90 Ed.Law Rep. 1006 (4th Cir. 1994). Courts also have held that hearing officers may grant awards of compensatory educational services. *See Cocores* v. *Portsmouth, NH School District,* 779 F. Supp. 203 (D.N.H. 1991); *Big Beaver*

*Falls Area School District* v. *Jackson,* 615 A.2d 910, 78 Ed.Law Rep. 888 (Pa. Commw. Ct. 1992).

76. *White* v. *State of California,* 240 Cal. Rptr. 732, 42 Ed.Law Rep. 262 (Cal. Ct. App. 1987); *Lester H.* v. *Gilhool,* 916 F.2d 865, 63 Ed.Law Rep. 458 (3d Cir. 1990); *Todd D.* v. *Andrews,* 933 F.2d 1576, 67 Ed.Law Rep. 1065 (11th Cir. 1991); *Manchester School District* v. *Christopher B.,* 807 F. Supp. 860, 79 Ed.Law Rep. 865 (D.N.H. 1992); *Murphy* v. *Timberlane Regional School District,* 973 F.2d 13, 77 Ed.Law Rep. 28 (1st Cir. 1992), *on rem'd* 819 F. Supp. 1127, 82 Ed.Law Rep. 798 (D.N.H. 1993), *aff'd* 22 F.3d 1186, 91 Ed.Law Rep. 62 (1st Cir. 1994).

77. *See, for example, Valerie J.* v. *Derry Cooperative School District,* 771 F. Supp. 483, 69 Ed.Law Rep. 1067 (D.N.H. 1991); *Manchester School District* v. *Christopher B.,* 807 F. Supp. 860, 79 Ed.Law Rep. 865 (D.N.H. 1992); *Big Beaver Falls Area School District* v. *Jackson,* 624 A.2d 806, 82 Ed.Law Rep. 861 (Pa. Commw. Ct. 1993).

78. *See, for example, Pihl* v. *Massachusetts Department of Education,* 9 F.3d 184, 87 Ed.Law Rep. 341 (1st Cir. 1993).

79. *Jefferson County Board of Education* v. *Breen,* 853 F.2d 853, 48 Ed.Law Rep. 382 (11th Cir. 1988).

80. *Miener* v. *Missouri,* 800 F.2d 749, 34 Ed.Law Rep. 1014 (8th Cir. 1986).

81. *Cremeans* v. *Fairland Local School District Board of Education,* 633 N.E.2d 570, 91 Ed.Law Rep. 280 (Ohio App. Ct. 1993).

82. *Burr* v. *Ambach,* 863 F.2d 1071, 50 Ed.Law Rep. 964 (2d Cir. 1988), *vac'd and rem'd* 109 S.Ct. 3209, 54 Ed.Law Rep. 410 (1989), *on rem'd sub nom. Burr* v. *Sobol,* 888 F.2d 258, 56 Ed.Law Rep. 1126 (2d Cir. 1989).

83. *Big Beaver Falls Area School District* v. *Jackson,* 624 A.2d 806, 82 Ed.Law Rep. 861 (Pa. Commw. Ct. 1993). See Chapter 7 for additional information concerning disciplinary exclusions.

84. *Stock* v. *Massachusetts Hospital School,* 467 N.E.2d 448, 19 Ed.Law Rep. 637 (Mass. 1984). *Also see Mrs. C.* v. *Wheaton,* 916 F.2d 69, 63 Ed.Law Rep. 93 (2d Cir. 1990). Compensatory services were awarded after special education services were prematurely terminated.

85. *Puffer* v. *Raynolds,* 761 F. Supp. 838, 67 Ed.Law Rep. 536 (D. Mass. 1988).

86. *Straube* v. *Florida Union Free School District,* 801 F. Supp. 1164, 78 Ed.Law Rep. 390 (S.D.N.Y. 1992).

87. *Valerie J.* v. *Derry Cooperative School District,* 771 F. Supp. 483, 69 Ed.Law Rep. 1067 (D.N.H. 1991).

88. *Cocores* v. *Portsmouth, NH School District,* 779 F. Supp. 203 (D.N.H. 1991); *Big Beaver Falls Area School District* v. *Jackson,* 615 A.2d 910, 78 Ed.Law Rep. 888 (Pa. Commw. Ct. 1992).

89. *Timms* v. *Metropolitan School District,* EHLR 554:361 (S.D. Ind. 1982), *aff'd* 718 F.2d 212, 13 Ed.Law Rep. 951 (7th Cir. 1983); *amended* 722 F.2d 1310, 15 Ed.Law Rep. 951 (7th Cir. 1983); *Martin* v. *School Board of Prince George County,* 348 S.E.2d 857, 35 Ed.Law Rep. 302 (Va. Ct. App. 1986); *Garro* v. *State of Connecticut,* 23 F.3d 734, 91 Ed.Law Rep. 478 (2d Cir. 1994).

90. *Brown* v. *Wilson County School Board,* 747 F. Supp. 436, 63 Ed.Law Rep. 525 (M.D. Tenn. 1990).

91. *See, for example, Diamond v. McKenzie*, 602 F. Supp. 632, 23 Ed.Law Rep. 100 (D.D.C. 1985).
92. *Smith v. Robinson*, 468 U.S. 992, 104 S. Ct. 3457, 82 L. Ed.2d 746, 18 Ed.Law Rep. 148 (1984).
93. Codified at 20 U.S.C. § 1415(e)(4)(B).
94. Osborne, A. G. and DiMattia, P. (1991). Attorney Fees Are Available for Administrative Proceedings Under the EHA. *Education Law Reporter, 66,* 909–920.
95. *Mathern v. Campbell County Children's Center*, 674 F. Supp. 816, 43 Ed.Law Rep. 699 (D. Wyo. 1987).
96. *See, for example, Angela L. v. Pasadena Independent School District*, 918 F.2d 1188, 64 Ed.Law Rep. 350 (5th Cir. 1990).
97. *J.G. v. Board of Education of the Rochester City School District*, 648 F. Supp. 1452, 36 Ed.Law Rep. 696 (W.D.N.Y. 1986), *aff'd* 830 F.2d 444, 42 Ed.Law Rep. 52 (2d Cir. 1987); *Esther C. v. Ambach*, 535 N.Y.S.2d 462 (N.Y. App. Div. 1988); *Sidney K. v. Ambach*, 535 N.Y.S.2d 468, 50 Ed.Law Rep. 1120 (N.Y. App. Div. 1988).
98. *Taylor v. Board of Education of Copake-Taconic*, 649 F. Supp. 1253, 36 Ed.Law Rep. 1206 (N.D.N.Y. 1986); *Fontenot v. Louisiana Board of Elementary and Secondary Education*, 805 F.2d 1222, 36 Ed.Law Rep. 61 (5th Cir. 1986), 835 F.2d 117, 43 Ed.Law Rep. 45 (5th Cir. 1988); *Yaris v. Special School District of St. Louis County*, 661 F. Supp. 996, 40 Ed.Law Rep. 315 (E.D. Mo. 1987); *Holmes v. District of Columbia*, 680 F. Supp. 40, 45 Ed.Law Rep. 688 (D.D.C. 1988); *Turton v. Crisp County School District*, 688 F. Supp. 1535, 48 Ed.Law Rep. 210 (M.D. Ga. 1988); *Drew P. v. Clarke County School District*, 877 F.2d 927, 54 Ed.Law Rep. 456 (11th Cir. 1989); *Rapid City School District v. Vahle*, 733 F. Supp. 1364, 59 Ed.Law Rep. 1083 (D.S.D. 1990), *aff'd* 922 F.2d 476, 65 Ed.Law Rep. 65 (8th Cir. 1990); *Angela L. v. Pasadena Independent School District*, 918 F.2d 1188, 64 Ed.Law Rep. 350 (5th Cir. 1990); *Grace B. v. Lexington School Committee*, 762 F. Supp. 416, 67 Ed.Law Rep. 660 (D. Mass. 1991); *Edwards-White v. District of Columbia*, 785 F. Supp. 1022, 73 Ed.Law Rep. 943 (D.D.C. 1992); *Hacienda La Puente Unified School District of Los Angeles v. Honig*, 976 F.2d 487, 77 Ed.Law Rep. 1117 (9th Cir. 1992); *Remis v. New Jersey Department of Human Services*, 815 F. Supp. 141, 81 Ed.Law Rep. 762 (D.N.J. 1993); *Phelan v. Bell*, 8 F.3d 369, 87 Ed.Law Rep. 46 (6th Cir. 1993).
99. *Kristi W. v. Graham Independent School District*, 663 F. Supp. 86, 40 Ed.Law Rep. 792 (N.D. Tex. 1987). *Also see Borengasser v. Arkansas State Board of Education*, 996 F.2d 196, 84 Ed.Law Rep. 35 (8th Cir. 1993).
100. *Barbara R. v. Tirozzi*, 665 F. Supp. 141 (D. Conn. 1987).
101. *Neisz v. Portland Public School District*, 684 F. Supp. 1530, 47 Ed.Law Rep. 167 (D. Or. 1988).
102. *Mitten v. Muscogee County School District*, 877 F.2d 932, 54 Ed.Law Rep. 461 (11th Cir. 1989).
103. *Krichinsky v. Knox County Schools*, 963 F.2d 847, 75 Ed.Law Rep. 158 (6th Cir. 1992). *Also see Angela L. v. Pasadena Independent School District*, 918 F.2d 1188, 64 Ed.Law Rep. 350 (5th Cir. 1990); *Hall v. Detroit Public Schools*, 823 F. Supp.

1377, 84 Ed.Law Rep. 205 (E.D. Mich. 1993) [however, the court did reduce the amount of the award in this case because it felt that the attorney's bill was excessive given the nature of the lawsuit].

104. *Moore* v. *Crestwood Local School District,* 804 F. Supp. 960, 78 Ed.Law Rep. 796 (N.D. Ohio 1992). *Also see Massachusetts Department of Public Health* v. *School Committee of Tewksbury,* 841 F. Supp. 449, 88 Ed.Law Rep. 1060 (D. Mass. 1994).

105. *Grinsted* v. *Houston County School District,* 826 F. Supp. 482, 84 Ed.Law Rep. 953 (M.D. Ga. 1993).

106. *Heldman* v. *Sobol,* 846 F.3d 285, 90 Ed.Law Rep. 106 (S.D.N.Y. 1994).

107. *Burr* v. *Sobol,* 748 F. Supp. 97, 63 Ed.Law Rep. 830 (S.D.N.Y. 1990). *For previous action in the same case, see Burr* v. *Ambach,* 683 F. Supp. 46, 46 Ed.Law Rep. 585 (S.D.N.Y. 1988).

108. *Max M.* v. *Illinois State Board of Education,* 684 F. Supp. 514, 46 Ed.Law Rep. 942 (N.D. Ill.), *aff'd* 859 F.2d 1297, 49 Ed.Law Rep. 1125 (7th Cir. 1988). *Also see Muth* v. *Central Bucks School District,* 839 F.2d 113, 44 Ed.Law Rep. 1037 (3d Cir. 1988), *rev'd on other grounds sub nom. Dellmuth* v. *Muth,* 491 U.S. 223, 109 S. Ct. 2397, 105 L. Ed.2d 181, 53 Ed.Law Rep. 792 (1989); *Puffer* v. *Raynolds,* 761 F. Supp. 838, 67 Ed.Law Rep. 536 (D. Mass. 1988).

109. *Mr. D.* v. *Glocester School Committee,* 711 F. Supp. 66, 53 Ed.Law Rep. 864 (D.R.I. 1989). *Also see Hall* v. *Detroit Public Schools,* 823 F. Supp. 1377, 84 Ed.Law Rep. 205 (E.D. Mich. 1993).

110. *Howey* v. *Tippecanoe School Corporation,* 734 F. Supp. 1485, 60 Ed.Law Rep. 457 (N.D. Ind. 1990).

111. *In re Conklin,* 946 F.2d 306, 70 Ed.Law Rep. 351 (4th Cir. 1991).

112. *Field* v. *Haddonfield Board of Education,* 769 F. Supp. 1313, 69 Ed.Law Rep. 724 (D.N.J. 1991). *Also see E.M.* v. *Millville Board of Education,* 849 F. Supp. 312, 91 Ed.Law Rep. 96 (D.N.J. 1994) where the court reduced the requested fees by 25% to account for the partial defeat of the parent's claims.

113. *In re Conklin,* 946 F.2d 306, 70 Ed.Law Rep. 351 (4th Cir. 1991).

114. *Wheeler* v. *Towanda Area School District,* 950 F.2d 128, 71 Ed.Law Rep. 621 (3d Cir. 1991). In this case all of the parents' claims were rejected by the hearing officer but they requested attorney fees anyway.

115. *Christopher P.* v. *Marcus,* 915 F.2d 794, 63 Ed.Law Rep. 64 (2d Cir. 1990).

116. *Brown* v. *Griggsville Community Unit School District No. 4,* 817 F. Supp. 734, 82 Ed.Law Rep. 417 (C.D. Ill. 1993), *aff'd* 12 F.3d 681, 88 Ed.Law Rep. 63 (7th Cir. 1993). *Also see Combs* v. *School Board of Rockingham County,* 15 F.3d 357, 89 Ed.Law Rep. 366 (4th Cir. 1994) [court held that changes to the student's IEP made by the school district did not result from an administrative hearing].

117. *Livingston* v. *DeSoto County School District,* 782 F. Supp. 1173, 72 Ed.Law Rep. 790 (N.D. Miss. 1992).

118. *Hunger* v. *Leininger,* 15 F.3d 664, 89 Ed.Law Rep. 421 (7th Cir. 1994).

119. *Fischer* v. *Rochester Community Schools,* 780 F. Supp. 1142, 72 Ed.Law Rep. 180 (E.D. Mich. 1991).

120. *Combs* v. *School Board of Rockingham County,* 15 F.3d 357, 89 Ed.Law Rep. 366 (4th Cir. 1994).

121. *W.G.* v. *Senatore,* 18 F.3d 60, 89 Ed.Law Rep. 1080 (2d Cir. 1994).

122. *S-1* v. *State Board of Education of North Carolina,* 6 F.3d 160, 86 Ed.Law Rep. 56 (4th Cir. 1993), *rev'd* 21 F.3d 49, 90 Ed.Law Rep. 1006 (4th Cir. 1994).
123. 20 U.S.C. § 1415(e)(4)(B).
124. *Moore* v. *District of Columbia,* 907 F.2d 165, 61 Ed.Law Rep. 477 (D.C. Cir. 1990).
125. *Moore* v. *District of Columbia,* 886 F.2d 335, 56 Ed.Law Rep. 435 (D.C. Cir. 1989).
126. *Eggers* v. *Bullitt County School District,* 854 F.2d 892, 48 Ed.Law Rep. 796 (6th Cir. 1988); *Duane M.* v. *Orleans Parish School Board,* 861 F.2d 115, 51 Ed.Law Rep. 365 (5th Cir. 1988); *Mitten* v. *Muscogee County School District,* 877 F.2d 932, 54 Ed.Law Rep. 461 (11th Cir. 1989); *McSombodies (No. 1)* v. *Burlingame Elementary School District,* 886 F.2d 1558, 56 Ed.Law Rep. 477 (9th Cir. 1989); *McSombodies (No. 2)* v. *San Mateo City School District,* 886 F.2d 1559, 56 Ed.Law Rep. 478 (9th Cir. 1989), *supplemented* 897 F.2d 975, 59 Ed.Law Rep. 327 (9th Cir. 1990).
127. *Burpee* v. *Manchester School District,* 661 F. Supp. 731, 40 Ed.Law Rep. 305 (D.N.H. 1987); *Michael F.* v. *Cambridge School Department,* EHLR 558:269 (D. Mass. 1987); *School Board of the County of Prince William* v. *Malone,* 662 F. Supp. 999, 40 Ed.Law Rep. 761 (E.D. Va. 1987); *Prescott* v. *Palos Verdes Peninsula Unified School District,* 659 F. Supp. 921 (C.D. Cal. 1987); *Kristi W.* v. *Graham Independent School District,* 663 F. Supp. 86, 40 Ed.Law Rep. 792 (N.D. Tex. 1987); *Unified School District No. 259* v. *Newton,* 673 F. Supp. 418, 43 Ed.Law Rep. 56 (D. Kan. 1987); *Robert D.* v. *Sobol,* 688 F. Supp. 861, 48 Ed.Law Rep. 197 (S.D.N.Y. 1988); *Chang* v. *Board of Education of Glen Ridge Township,* 685 F. Supp. 96, 47 Ed.Law Rep. 182 (D.N.J. 1988); *Turton* v. *Crisp County School District,* 688 F. Supp. 1535, 48 Ed.Law Rep. 210 (M.D. Ga. 1988); *Williams* v. *Boston School Committee,* 709 F. Supp. 27, 52 Ed.Law Rep. 1035 (D. Mass. 1989).
128. *Grace B.* v. *Lexington School Committee,* 762 F. Supp. 416, 67 Ed.Law Rep. 660 (D. Mass. 1991); *Reid* v. *Board of Education, Lincolnshire-Prairie View School District,* 765 F. Supp. 965, 68 Ed.Law Rep. 400 (N.D. Ill. 1991); *Barlow-Gresham Union High School District No. 2* v. *Mitchell,* 940 F.2d 1280, 69 Ed.Law Rep. 203 (9th Cir. 1991); *Moore* v. *Crestwood Local School District,* 804 F. Supp. 960, 78 Ed.Law Rep. 796 (N.D. Ohio 1992).
129. *Capiello* v. *District of Columbia,* 779 F. Supp. 1, 71 Ed.Law Rep. 802 (D.D.C. 1991).
130. 20 U.S.C. § 1415(e)(4)(D).
131. *Hyden* v. *Board of Education of Wilson County,* 714 F. Supp. 290, 54 Ed.Law Rep. 532 (M.D. Tenn. 1989).
132. *Mr. L. and Mrs. L.* v. *Woonsocket Education Department,* 793 F. Supp. 41, 76 Ed.Law Rep. 398 (D.R.I. 1992).
133. *Shelly C.* v. *Venus Independent School District,* 878 F.2d 862 (5th Cir. 1989); *E.P.* v. *Union County Regional High School District No. 1,* 741 F. Supp. 1144, 62 Ed.Law Rep. 198 (D.N.J. 1989); *Barlow-Gresham Union High School District No. 2* v. *Mitchell,* 940 F.2d 1280, 69 Ed.Law Rep. 203 (9th Cir. 1991).
134. *Johnson* v. *Bismarck Public School District,* 949 F.2d 1000, 71 Ed.Law Rep. 403 (8th Cir. 1991).

135. *Masotti v. Tustin Unified School District,* 806 F. Supp. 221, 79 Ed.Law Rep. 459 (C.D. Cal. 1992). *Also see E.M. v. Millville Board of Education,* 849 F. Supp. 312, 91 Ed.Law Rep. 96 (D.N.J. 1994).
136. *Medford v. District of Columbia,* 691 F. Supp. 1473, 48 Ed.Law Rep. 1206 (D.D.C. 1988).
137. *Fenneman v. Gorham,* 802 F. Supp. 543, 78 Ed.Law Rep. 698 (D. Me. 1992).
138. *Eggers v. Bullitt County School District,* 854 F.2d 892, 48 Ed.Law Rep. 796 (6th Cir. 1988).
139. *Mitten v. Muscogee County School District,* 877 F.2d 932, 54 Ed.Law Rep. 461 (11th Cir. 1989).
140. *Arons v. New Jersey State Board of Education,* 842 F.2d 58, 45 Ed.Law Rep. 1008 (3d Cir. 1988).
141. One court has indicated that paralegal expenses qualify as part of an award for legal fees; *Heldman v. Sobol,* 846 F. Supp. 285, 90 Ed.Law Rep. 106 (S.D.N.Y. 1994).
142. 42 U.S.C. § 2000e et seq.
143. *Rappaport v. Vance,* 812 F. Supp. 609, 81 Ed.Law Rep. 64 (D. Md. 1993).
144. *Heldman v. Sobol,* 846 F. Supp. 285, 90 Ed.Law Rep. 106 (S.D.N.Y. 1994).
145. *Kattan v. District of Columbia,* 995 F.2d 274, 83 Ed.Law Rep. 982 (D.C. Cir. 1993).
146. *Chang v. Board of Education of Glen Ridge Township,* 685 F. Supp. 96, 47 Ed.Law Rep. 182 (D.N.J. 1988); *Turton v. Crisp County School District,* 688 F. Supp. 1535, 48 Ed.Law Rep. 210 (M.D. Ga. 1988); *Aronow v. District of Columbia,* 780 F. Supp. 46, 72 Ed.Law Rep. 100 (D.D.C. 1992), *amended* 791 F. Supp. 318, 75 Ed.Law Rep. 1049 (D.D.C. 1992).
147. *Id. Turton v. Crisp County School District,* 688 F. Supp. 1535, 48 Ed.Law Rep. 210 (M.D. Ga. 1988).
148. *E.M. v. Millville Board of Education,* 849 F. Supp. 312, 91 Ed.Law Rep. 96 (D.N.J. 1994).
149. *Arons v. New Jersey State Board of Education,* 842 F.2d 58, 45 Ed.Law Rep. 1008 (3d Cir. 1988).
150. *Counsel v. Dow,* 666 F. Supp. 366, 41 Ed.Law Rep. 593 (D. Conn. 1987), *aff'd* 849 F.2d 731, 47 Ed.Law Rep. 414 (2d Cir. 1988).
151. *Rollison v. Biggs,* 656 F. Supp. 1204, 38 Ed.Law Rep. 1028 (D. Del. 1987), *rehearing* 660 F. Supp. 875, 40 Ed.Law Rep. 208 (D. Del. 1987); *Doe v. Watertown School Committee,* 701 F. Supp. 264, 51 Ed.Law Rep. 124 (D. Mass. 1988); *Abu-Sahyun v. Palo Alto Unified School District,* 843 F. Supp. 1250, 46 Ed.Law Rep. 72 (9th Cir. 1988); *James v. Nashua School District,* 720 F. Supp. 1053, 56 Ed.Law Rep. 481 (D.N.H. 1989).
152. *Capello v. District of Columbia Board of Education,* 669 F. Supp. 14, 42 Ed.Law Rep. 103 (D.D.C. 1987); *Tonya K. v. Board of Education of the City of Chicago,* 847 F.2d 1243, 47 Ed.Law Rep. 45 (7th Cir. 1988).
153. *Georgia Association of Retarded Citizens v. McDaniel,* 855 F.2d 805, 48 Ed.Law Rep. 1134 (11th Cir. 1988).
154. *Abu-Sahyun v. Palo Alto Unified School District,* 843 F.2d 1250, 46 Ed.Law Rep. 72 (9th Cir. 1988).

155. *Also see Independent School District No. 623, Roseville, MN v. Digre,* 893 F.2d 987, 58 Ed.Law Rep. 92 (8th Cir. 1990); *Northeast Central School District v. Sobol,* 584 N.Y.S.2d 525, 75 Ed.Law Rep. 890 (N.Y. 1992).
156. Fed.R.App.P. 38.
157. *Caroline T. v. Hudson School District,* 915 F.2d 752 at 757, 63 Ed.Law Rep. 56 at 61 (1st Cir. 1990).
158. *Hiller v. Board of Education of the Brunswick Central School District,* 743 F. Supp. 958, 62 Ed.Law Rep. 974 (N.D.N.Y. 1990).
159. *Atascadero State Hospital v. Scanlon,* 473 U.S. 234, 105 S. Ct. 3142, 87 L. Ed.2d 171 (1985).
160. *See, for example, David D. v. Dartmouth School Committee,* 775 F.2d 411, 28 Ed.Law Rep. 70 (1st Cir. 1985) where the court held that Congress abrogated the states' eleventh amendment immunity when it passed IDEA *and Gary A. v. New Trier High School District No. 203,* 796 F.2d 940, 33 Ed.Law Rep. 1052 (7th Cir. 1986) where the court held that Congress did not abrogate the states' sovereign immunity.
161. *Dellmuth v. Muth,* 491 U.S. 223, 109 S. Ct. 2397, 105 L. Ed.2d 181, 53 Ed.Law Rep. 792 (1989).
162. Osborne, A. G. (1990). States' Eleventh Amendment Immunity Is Not Abrogated by the EHA. *Education Law Reporter, 56,* 1099–1105.
163. P.L. 101-476, *codified at* 20 U.S.C. § 1403.
164. *Joshua B. v. New Trier Township High School District 203,* 770 F. Supp. 431, 69 Ed.Law Rep. 797 (N.D. Ill. 1991).
165. *Straube v. Florida Union Free School District,* 778 F. Supp. 774, 71 Ed.Law Rep. 725 (S.D.N.Y. 1991), 801 F. Supp. 1164, 78 Ed.Law Rep. 390 (S.D.N.Y. 1992).
166. *Garro v. State of Connecticut,* 23 F.3d 734, 91 Ed.Law Rep. 478 (2d Cir. 1994).

# 9

# ADDITIONAL ISSUES

There are a number of issues under the Individuals with Disabilities Education Act (IDEA)[1] that have not been litigated frequently. Nevertheless, these issues are important. Due to the lack of litigation on these issues, currently there is not sufficient information to warrant writing separate chapters on each. Thus, several miscellaneous topics have been grouped together for treatment in this chapter. The fact that there has not been much litigation on these issues in the past does not mean that there will be little litigation in the future.

## MINIMUM COMPETENCY TESTS

During the past several years many educational reform movements have called for greater accountability in the nation's classrooms. Minimum competency tests, or basic skills tests, have been developed and are being administered in many states to address the need for greater accountability. These tests may be used either as a graduation requirement to assure that students receiving a diploma have a specified knowledge base or to identify students who have not achieved competency in basic skills and thus may require remedial instruction.

States have the authority to develop and administer minimum competency tests. States also have the authority to establish graduation requirements. It is now well settled that states may require students to pass a minimum competency test to receive a standard high school diploma. However, when these tests are used as a graduation requirement, they must be a valid measure of what has been taught and students must be given sufficient notice that they must pass a minimum competency test to receive a standard diploma. Naturally, minimum competency tests may not be racially, linguistically, or ethnically discriminatory.[2]

Courts that have ruled on the issue have held that students with disabilities may be required to pass a minimum competency test to receive a standard high school diploma.[3] However, to be a valid diploma requirement, students expected to take the test must be given sufficient notice and their Individualized Education Programs (IEPs) should include instruction in the areas to be tested.

Students with disabilities taking minimum competency tests may require some modifications. School districts may be required to modify how a test is administered but would not be required to modify the actual content of the test. For example, a blind student should be given a braille version of the test or a student with physical disabilities may need assistance writing or filling in the circles on a machine scored answer sheet. However, school districts would not be required to develop and administer a test with fewer items or easier items for a student with intellectual impairments.[4] Basically, school officials are required to provide modifications that will allow the student to take the test but do not need to modify the item content.

## STUDENTS WITH AIDS

It is well settled that students with AIDS or other infectious diseases may not be excluded from school unless there is an unusually high risk of transmission of the disease. The fact that a student has AIDS does not, by itself, qualify the student for special education services.[5] However, as the student's illness progresses, the student may qualify as other health impaired under IDEA. A student with AIDS would be entitled to special education services if, due to illness, the student's academic performance is adversely affected.[6]

Students who have AIDS who qualify for special education services because they have one of the disabilities listed in IDEA[7] may not be denied those services because they also are afflicted with AIDS.[8] These students also may not be segregated from other students unless the risk of transmission of the disease is greater than normal and cannot be reduced by following normal prophylactic procedures.[9] Our current state of medical knowledge indicates that exclusion of a student with AIDS from the public schools under these stipulations would be an extremely rare occurrence.

# RESPONSIBILITY OF INSURANCE CARRIERS

IDEA's regulations clearly indicate that insurance companies are not relieved of any obligations they may have to provide services to a child with a disability simply because those services also may be available to the child under IDEA.[10] Courts consistently have ruled that insurance companies or other third party payers may not use IDEA to absolve their responsibilities to an insured party or client.

On two separate occasions a district court in Pennsylvania has dismissed lawsuits by insurance companies seeking to have school districts assume the responsibility for providing special education and related services to students who had disabilities resulting from injuries sustained in automobile accidents.[11] In each case the court held that the insurance company did not have standing to sue because only students and their parents may invoke the provisions of IDEA. However, in dicta, the judge hearing these cases stated that IDEA does not alter or disturb the relationship between parents and their insurer or shift obligations from an insurance company to a school district.

The Second Circuit Court of Appeals held that a student who required the services of a nurse 24 hours a day was entitled to have the nursing services provided in school by Medicaid.[12] In a previous action the court had held that the school district was not responsible for providing a full-time nurse under IDEA's related services provision.[13] In the present case the court ruled that providing private duty nursing services in the school setting was basically equivalent to providing those same services in the student's home and was the responsibility of Medicaid.

Insurance companies are not required to provide or pay for any services that are educational in nature and clearly are not covered by the insurance policy. A New York state court held that a school for children with dyslexia was an academic institution and not a hospital as defined by the parents' insurance policy.[14] The court found that the school and the services it provided were not medically approved or recognized as a method for remediating dyslexia. Thus, the court held that the insurance company was not responsible for the student's tuition at the private school.

# RELATIONSHIP OF IDEA TO THE VACCINE ACT

The National Childhood Vaccine Injury Act of 1986[15] provides compensation to children who suffer permanent damage after receiving a vaccine. Several courts have held that students are entitled to receive compensation for services that may be required beyond those provided under IDEA. These courts have reasoned that students are entitled under the Vaccine Act to a higher level of services than those required by IDEA.

The U.S. Claims Court held that a student who suffered neurological damage related to the administration of a diphtheria, pertussis, and tetanus (DPT) vaccination was entitled to an award of damages for special education and related services, even though the student would receive services under IDEA, because the service provided by the school district could be inadequate to meet the student's tremendous needs.[16] In a similar case involving a student who suffered vaccine-related learning disabilities, the U.S. Court of Federal Claims held that the Vaccine Act endeavors to restore the injured party to his or her former status.[17] According to the court's ruling, what may be an acceptable plan under IDEA may not be adequate under the Vaccine Act and the student may require compensation for services that are not addressed in the IEP. In a separate case that same court held that services that are normally provided under federal and state special education laws were not sufficient to meet the unique needs of a student who had multiple disabilities resulting from the DPT vaccine.[18]

These decisions indicate that children who suffer serious injuries as a result of receiving a DPT vaccination are entitled to a level of compensation that will provide services above and beyond those provided under IDEA. This stems from the fact that IDEA was intended to provide only a basic floor of opportunity to students with disabilities[19] while the Vaccine Act's intent was to make the injured party whole again. However, the intent of the Vaccine Act is not to provide duplicate coverage. Compensation would not be allowed for services that are already available under IDEA or state special education laws. Although no cases were found originating in a state whose laws provide a greater level of services than IDEA, it is reasonable to assume that students in these states would not fare as well under the Vaccine Act. For example, in states whose special education laws mandate a level of services designed to maximize a student's potential,[20] the student's IEP may provide a sufficient level of special education and related services to adequately address the student's disabilities. Students in those states may not be entitled to more under the Vaccine Act.

However, the Vaccine Act does not relieve school districts of any obligations under IDEA to students whose disabilities result from the DPT vaccine. Regardless of the source of the student's disabilities, school districts are obligated to provide at least the minimum level of services mandated by IDEA. The fact that the student may be entitled to additional compensation from the Vaccine Act does not alter the school district's basic responsibility to provide the student with a free appropriate public education.

## DISBURSEMENT OF FEDERAL FUNDS

Federal special education funds are disbursed by the U.S. Department of Education to local school districts through the state educational agency. The state educational agency may delegate responsibility for disbursement to its chief state school officer. In a Louisiana case the state Board of Elementary and Secondary Education disagreed with the Superintendent of Education's disbursement of funds received by the state under IDEA and notified the U.S. Department of Education of its concerns.[21] After an audit the federal government agreed that funds had been misapplied and ordered the state to refund $700,000. The state objected since it had not disbursed the funds. However, the Fifth Circuit Court of Appeals held that the state agency was the actual recipient of the funds and was responsible for overseeing the expenditure of the funds.

IDEA provides that federal funds are to be used to defray the excess costs of educating students with disabilities.[22] Under this provision federal funds may not be used to supplant state funds for special education. The Ninth Circuit Court of Appeals held that this provision requires maintenance of fiscal effort, even if this requires a reallocation of funds.[23] If costs decline, the court held, funds must be used to provide new programs that the school district previously could not afford. The only exceptions to the maintenance of expenditures requirement exist when there is a decrease in enrollment or if there had been unusual expenditures in the previous year.

The Fourth Circuit Court of Appeals held that IDEA requires a hearing whenever the federal Department of Education attempts to discontinue funding to a state based on a perceived violation of the Act's provisions.[24] The federal education department had withheld $50 million in Virginia's IDEA funds because the state plan indicated that students with disabilities could be disciplined in the same manner as other students if their misbehavior was unrelated to their disability. The education department informed the state that it could not discontinue services to expelled special education students even if the discipline resulted from behavior that stemmed from the disability. After the state failed to change the regulation in question the department notified it that funds would be withheld. The funds were withheld pending a hearing on the matter. In ruling that notice and a hearing were required before the funds were actually withheld, the court commented, "It seems only proper that a department which so

emphasizes procedural fairness on the part of states would exercise that same fairness in its dealings with them."[25]

## EFFECT ON THE JUVENILE COURTS

The procedures and requirements of IDEA apply to actions by the school districts but do not interfere with the jurisdiction of the courts in juvenile matters. Courts have held that IDEA does not restrict or limit the authority of juvenile courts. A state court in Louisiana held that IDEA applied only to a school system's authority to place students but did not limit the authority of the juvenile court to order homebound instruction after determining that a student was a child in need of supervision.[26] Similarly, a family court in New York held that IDEA did not divest it of jurisdiction in a truancy proceeding.[27]

## RATE SETTING AT PRIVATE SCHOOLS

Private schools and facilities that provide special education and related services are licensed and regulated by the state. Tuition and other charges at these facilities may be established by the state educational agency if public funds are used to pay these costs. The Supreme Judicial Court of Massachusetts held that an individual special education student attending a private facility is not entitled under IDEA to have tuition set at a particular figure.[28] The court ruled that if the facility could not provide the educational program called for in the student's IEP, the student could challenge his placement at that facility through IDEA's due process mechanism. However, the court found that state and federal laws did not entitle the student to payment of a particular rate to a particular provider.

Once it has been determined that a private school is the appropriate placement for a student, the school district must pay the tuition rate established for that school. The federal district court for the District of Columbia ruled that a school district cannot refuse to pay the tuition rate established by private schools.[29] The students in this case had been placed in the private schools pursuant to decisions of independent hearing officers. The school district refused to pay the tuition set by the private schools and, instead, paid a rate it established arbitrarily. The court held that the school district's actions were without justification after finding that the tuition established by the private schools was reasonable.

# POLICY LETTERS

As has been shown in this book, special education is governed by statutes, regulations, and court decisions. However, from time to time the U.S. Department of Education issues policy letters that are intended to either clarify administrative regulations or provide an interpretation of what is required by the federal law. These policy letters may be issued in response to a question raised by a state or local school district official. Generally, they are published in the *Federal Register* and frequently are reproduced by several looseleaf law reporting services. The Seventh Circuit Court of Appeals held that a policy letter issued by the Department of Education regarding its interpretation of requirements for providing services to students with disabilities who have been expelled was an interpretive rule not subject to the Administrative Procedures Act's (APA)[30] notice and comment requirements.[31] The APA outlines public notice procedures that must be followed if a federal agency promulgates a legislative rule. The court found that the letter was not a legislative rule but, rather, simply stated what the Department thought IDEA required.

# STUDENT RECORDS

Under the Family Educational Rights and Privacy Act of 1974 (FERPA)[32] school districts are required to provide eligible students with certain rights regarding the confidentiality of their educational records. Although these rights are available to all students, they are reiterated in IDEA's regulations.[33] FERPA provides parents and students over the age of 18 with the right to inspect their educational records and request that they be amended if there is a disagreement over their contents. FERPA further restricts access to a student's school records by a third party.

Parents have the right to inspect and review any educational records relating to their child that are maintained by the school district. The right to inspect the records also includes the right to have the records interpreted and explained. Parents are entitled to receive copies of the records; however, school districts may charge a fee for the copies.

If a student or parent feels that any records are incorrect or misleading they may request that the records be amended. If the school district refuses to amend the records the parents may contest that denial through a due process hearing. If the final outcome of the hearing is that the records do not need to be amended, the parents have the right to attach a statement commenting on the information in the records. The parents' comment

must be maintained with the records and included whenever the records are disseminated.

Parental permission must be obtained before any records are disseminated to a third party, and a log must be kept of any such third party dissemination of records. A school district must take steps to ensure that personally identifiable information is not disclosed and that the confidentiality of records is maintained. In one case a district court in Connecticut held that a school district violated the parents' privacy rights when it released the names of the student and parents to a local newspaper after a due process hearing.[34]

Since most students are minors their privacy rights must be protected. For that reason the names of many students are withheld from published court opinions. The Eighth Circuit Court of Appeals, noting that strong public policy favors protection of the privacy of minors where sensitive matters are concerned, held that court proceedings under IDEA can be closed to the public.[35] The court further noted that IDEA restricts the release of information concerning students with disabilities without parental permission. To safeguard that information and prevent stigmatization of the student, the court ruled that access to the courtroom could be restricted and the files could be sealed.

## PROGRAMS FOR INFANTS AND TODDLERS

In 1986 Congress amended the federal special education law to insert a discretionary grant program for states that wanted to provide special education services to children with disabilities from birth through the age of 2.[36] The purpose of these grants is to provide financial assistance to states to develop and implement "a statewide, comprehensive, coordinated, multidisciplinary, interagency program of early intervention services for infants and toddlers with disabilities and their families."[37]

The grants are to be used to provide direct services and support services to eligible children and their families. Eligible infants and toddlers are those who are experiencing developmental delays in one or more of the following areas: cognitive development, physical development, language and speech development, psychosocial development, or self-help skills.[38] In addition, children who have a physical or mental condition that has a high probability of resulting in a developmental delay are eligible.[39]

The preschool amendment specifies that a written Individualized Family Service Plan (IFSP) is to be developed for each eligible child.[40] An IFSP is similar to an IEP except that it also addresses the needs of the child's family. The IFSP is to be based on a multidisciplinary assessment of the unique strengths and needs of the infant or toddler and an identification of services appropriate to meet those needs. In addition, the agency must conduct an assessment of the resources, priorities, and concerns of the family with an intent to identify the supports and services that would be needed to enhance the family's ability to meet the developmental needs of the infant or toddler.

Since the preschool amendment calls for interagency cooperation in the delivery of services to infants and toddlers and their families, the regulations implementing the amendment specify that each family must be provided with an individual who is responsible for coordinating all services across agency lines.[41] The purpose of the coordinator is to provide a single point of contact to help parents obtain the services and assistance they need and to provide an ongoing process to assist the families in gaining access to early intervention services. The amendments also contain procedural safeguards similar to those found in IDEA for school-aged students with disabilities and their parents.[42] While the preschool amendments call for interagency cooperation, the state education agency is ultimately accountable for the provision of services.[43]

## SUMMARY

IDEA and its regulations contain a myriad of provisions. The major provisions of the law have been discussed in previous chapters of this book. This chapter included information on several minor but important provisions of the law. These provisions are unique in that they have generated little controversy or litigation since IDEA became effective in 1977. School officials need to be aware of these provisions as well as those that have been more controversial.

The call for greater accountability in the schools will increase the pressure on school districts to ascertain that those students receiving a standard high school diploma have achieved a certain level of competence. It is likely that states increasingly will mandate that students must pass minimum competency tests as a graduation requirement. This in turn has serious implications for special education students, many of whom may not have the skills to pass these tests. Pressure may be put on school districts to develop alternate paths to high school graduation for special education students.

It is well settled that students with AIDS or other infectious diseases cannot be excluded from the public schools or denied services because of their illnesses. As the AIDS epidemic continues to spread among the adolescent population, school districts may be required to provide more services to students who qualify as other health impaired under IDEA.

As the costs of providing special education services continue to escalate, school districts must tap into any available resources. A frequently overlooked source of funding lies with insurance policies. Students who have disabilities as a result of injuries sustained in accidents may be entitled to remedial services under the terms of an insurance policy. Similarly, health insurance policies and Medicaid may provide coverage for some therapeutic, health-related, and diagnostic services. The Vaccine Act also provides compensation to students who are disabled as a result of an adverse reaction to a vaccination. Frequently, students may be entitled to a higher level of services under the Vaccine Act than under IDEA.

Federal funds for special education are funneled to school districts through the state educational agency. Each state has adopted its own mechanism for channeling those funds to local school districts. Regardless of the methods used to appropriate federal funds, the state educational agency remains the recipient of those funds and is legally responsible for their disbursement. Federal funds are to be used to supplement, not supplant, the programs offered by the state or local school districts. This requires that the amount of money appropriated by the state and local school districts remains constant unless there is a decline in enrollment or unusual expenditures in a previous year.

IDEA was passed to provide students with disabilities with access to a free appropriate public education in the least restrictive environment. Nothing in its provisions may be used to limit the power of juvenile courts to adjudicate matters involving students with disabilities, however.

Some students with disabilities may be placed by the school district in a private educational facility. These facilities must be approved by the state educational agency that also has the authority to establish appropriate tuition charges for students educated at these facilities at public expense. However, this does not give any student the right to have his or her tuition established at a particular rate. If a particular facility cannot provide the necessary services at the established rate, the student may use IDEA's due process mechanism to challenge the placement, but cannot insist on payment of a higher rate of tuition.

From time to time the federal Department of Education issues policy letters explaining its position on matters concerning the implementation of IDEA. As long as these letters are interpretive and do not establish legislative rules, they are not subject to the public notice and comment requirements of the Administrative Procedures Act.

Students with disabilities are entitled to a degree of privacy and confidentiality. To ensure that confidentiality the Department of Education has included the requirements of the Family Educational Rights and Privacy Act into IDEA's regulations. This act provides parents with access to student records and the right to request that any information contained in the record be amended. This does not mean that school officials must amend the records just because a request to do so has been received. However, if the school district decides not to amend the records, it must provide the parents with a hearing on the matter. If the outcome of the hearing is that the records need not be amended, the parents have the right to attach information of their own to the records. This information must be maintained and disseminated with the student's records. A third party may not have access to a student's records without parental permission. When records are disseminated to a third party, the school district must log the dissemination. The confidentiality requirements of IDEA extend to all aspects of a student's special education program, including any litigation that occurs.

As a result of several amendments to IDEA a discretionary grant program currently exists to assist states in providing early intervention services to infants and toddlers with disabilities and their families. The goal of these amendments was to create interagency cooperation in the delivery of services to eligible preschoolers and their families. Many of the services are geared toward assisting the families with meeting the needs of children who have developmental delays.

It is impossible to present information on all issues that could conceivably result in litigation under IDEA. This chapter included information on less litigated provisions of IDEA that could have an important impact on a school district's delivery of special education services. At some time in the future any of these issues could generate more litigation. Each issue represents an area of special education law that could be problematic for a school district. Issues that today are infrequently litigated could become the hot topics of tomorrow. Prudent school administrators must be aware of all issues, regardless of how controversial they have been in the past.

## ENDNOTES

1. 20 U.S.C. § 1400 et seq.
2. *Debra P. v. Turlington*, 730 F.2d 1405, 16 Ed.Law Rep. 1120 (11th Cir. 1984).
3. *Board of Education of Northport-East Northport Union Free School District v. Ambach*, 469 N.Y.S.2d 699, 15 Ed.Law Rep. 342 (N.Y. 1983); *Anderson v. Banks*, 520 F. Supp. 472 (S.D. Ga. 1981), *modified* 540 F. Supp. 761, 4 Ed.Law Rep. 1127 (S.D. Ga. 1982); *Brookhart v. Illinois State Board of Education*, 697 F.2d 179, 8 Ed.Law Rep. 608 (7th Cir. 1983).
4. *Brookhart v. Illinois State Board of Education*, 697 F.2d 179, 8 Ed.Law Rep. 608 (7th Cir. 1983).

5. *Robertson* v. *Granite City Community Unit School District No. 9,* 684 F. Supp. 1002, 46 Ed.Law Rep. 1147 (S.D. Ill. 1988).
6. 34 C.F.R. § 300.7(b)(8).
7. 20 U.S.C. § 1401(a)(1)(A).
8. *Parents of Child, Code No. 870901W* v. *Coker,* 676 F. Supp. 1072, 44 Ed.Law Rep. 231 (E.D. Ok. 1987).
9. *Robertson* v. *Granite City Community Unit School District No. 9,* 684 F. Supp. 1002, 46 Ed.Law Rep. 1147 (S.D. Ill. 1988); *Martinez* v. *School Board of Hillsborough County, Florida,* 861 F.2d 1502, 50 Ed.Law Rep. 359 (11th Cir. 1988), *on remand* 711 F. Supp. 1066, 53 Ed.Law Rep. 1176 (M.D. Fla. 1989).
10. 34 C.F.R. § 300.301(b).
11. *Allstate Insurance Company* v. *Bethlehem Area School District,* 678 F. Supp. 1132, 45 Ed.Law Rep. 122 (E.D. Pa. 1987); *Gehman* v. *Prudential Property and Casualty Insurance Company,* 702 F. Supp. 1192, 51 Ed.Law Rep. 497 (E.D. Pa. 1989).
12. *Detsel* v. *Sullivan,* 895 F.2d 58, 58 Ed.Law Rep. 897 (2d Cir. 1990).
13. *Detsel* v. *Board of Education of Auburn Enlarged City School District,* 820 F.2d 587, 40 Ed.Law Rep. 79 (2d Cir. 1987). See Chapter 6 for a discussion of this and related cases.
14. *Schonfeld* v. *Aetna Life Insurance and Annuity Company,* 593 N.Y.S.2d 250, 80 Ed.Law Rep. 943 (N.Y. App. Div. 1993).
15. 42 U.S.C. § 300aa-1 et seq.
16. *Stotts* v. *Secretary of the Department of Health and Human Services,* 21 Cl. Ct. 352 (Cl. Ct. 1991).
17. *Thomas* v. *Secretary of the Department of Health and Human Services,* 27 Fed. Cl. 384, 79 Ed.Law Rep. 897 (Fed. Cl. 1992).
18. *McClendon* v. *Secretary of the Department of Health and Human Services,* 28 Fed. Cl. 1, 81 Ed.Law Rep. 813 (Fed. Cl. 1993).
19. *See Board of Education of the Hendrick Hudson Central School District* v. *Rowley,* 458 U.S. 176, 102 S. Ct. 3034, 73 L. Ed.2d 690, 5 Ed.Law Rep. 34 (1982).
20. *See, for example, David D.* v. *Dartmouth School Committee,* 775 F.2d 411, 28 Ed.Law Rep. 70 (1st Cir. 1986).
21. *Louisiana State Board of Elementary and Secondary Education* v. *United States Department of Education,* 881 F.2d 204, 55 Ed.Law Rep. 369 (5th Cir. 1989).
22. 20 U.S.C. § 1414(a)(2)(B).
23. *State of Washington* v. *U.S. Department of Education,* 905 F.2d 274, 60 Ed.Law Rep. 1118 (9th Cir. 1990).
24. *Virginia Department of Education* v. *Riley,* 23 F.3d 80, 91 Ed.Law Rep. 82 (4th Cir. 1994); *citing* 20 U.S.C. § 1416.
25. *Id.* 23 F.3d at 86, 91 Ed.Law Rep. at 88.
26. *State of Louisiana in the Interest of B.C., Jr.,* 610 So.2d 204, 80 Ed.Law Rep. 445 (3d Cir. 1992).
27. *In re Thomas W.,* 560 N.Y.S.2d 227, 62 Ed.Law Rep. 1122 (N.Y. Fam. Ct. 1989).
28. *Behavior Research Institute* v. *Secretary of Administration,* 577 N.E.2d 297, 69 Ed.Law Rep. 514 (Mass. 1991).
29. *Fisher* v. *District of Columbia,* 828 F. Supp. 87, 85 Ed.Law Rep. 53 (D.D.C. 1993).
30. 5 U.S.C. § 553.

31. *Metropolitan School District of Wayne Township, Marion County, Indiana* v. *Davila,* 969 F.2d 485, 76 Ed.Law Rep. 386 (7th Cir. 1992).
32. 20 U.S.C. § 1232g.
33. 34 C.F.R. §§ 300.560–300.576.
34. *Sean R.* v. *Board of Education of the Town of Woodbridge,* 794 F. Supp. 467, 76 Ed.Law Rep. 785 (D. Conn. 1992).
35. *Webster Groves School District* v. *Pulitzer Publishing Co.,* 898 F.2d 1371, 59 Ed.Law Rep. 630 (8th Cir. 1990).
36. Education of the Handicapped Amendments, P.L. 99-457 (1986). Additional provisions were added by P.L. 100-630 (1988), P.L. 101-476 (1990), and P.L. 102-119 (1991).
37. 34 C.F.R. § 303.1(a).
38. 20 U.S.C. § 1472(1)(A).
39. 20 U.S.C. § 1472(1)(B).
40. 20 U.S.C. § 1477.
41. 34 C.F.R. § 303.22.
42. 20 U.S.C. § 1480.
43. Ballard, J., Ramirez, B. & Zantal-Wiener, K. (1987). *Public Law 94-142, Section 504, and Public Law 99-457: Understanding what they are and are not.* Reston, VA: Council for Exceptional Children.

# 10

# ANTI-DISCRIMINATION LAWS

In addition to the Individuals with Disabilities Education Act (IDEA),[1] students with disabilities have rights under and are protected by two other significant pieces of legislation. The first, section 504 of the Rehabilitation Act of 1973, provides that "[n]o otherwise qualified individual with a disability . . . shall, solely by reason of her or his disability, be excluded from participation in, be denied the benefits of, or be subjected to discrimination under any program or activity receiving Federal financial assistance."[2] Section 504 effectively prohibits any recipient of federal funds from discriminating against individuals with disabilities in the provision of services or employment. Section 504 applies to any agency that receives federal funds, not just the schools. The second law, the Americans with Disabilities Act (ADA),[3] was passed in 1990 to provide "a comprehensive national mandate for the elimination of discrimination against individuals with disabilities."[4] ADA was an effort by Congress to expand the scope of section 504's coverage to provide protection to individuals with disabilities throughout society.[5] It effectively extends the protections of section 504 to the private sector.

A person is considered to have a disability under section 504 if he or she has a physical or mental impairment that substantially limits one or more of his or her major life activities, has a record of such an impairment, or is regarded as having such an impairment.[6] Major life activities are defined as "functions such as caring for oneself, performing manual tasks, walking, seeing, hearing, speaking, breathing, learning, and working."[7] The Supreme Court has held that a person is otherwise qualified for purposes of section 504 if the person is capable of meeting all of a program's requirements in spite of the disability.[8] If a person is otherwise qualified, a recipient of federal funds is expected to make reasonable accommodations to allow the person to participate in the program or activity, unless doing so would create an undue hardship on the program sponsor.[9] Similar standards exist under ADA.

Whereas IDEA applies only to students up to the age of 21, section 504 and ADA apply to individuals with disabilities of all ages. Therefore, these statutes also apply to students with disabilities attending colleges or individuals with disabilities in the workplace. However, this chapter is concerned only with the effects of section 504 and ADA on elementary and secondary school students.[10] Some cases are presented that did not arise in this context but that have implications for the provision of services to elementary and secondary students.

## DISCRIMINATION PROHIBITED UNDER SECTION 504

Since school districts receive federal funds, they may not discriminate against students with disabilities. Under the mandates of section 504, students with disabilities may not be excluded from participation in any school program or activity they are otherwise qualified to participate in. However, if a student does not meet the minimum qualifications for participation, and is thus denied access to the program or activity, a discrimination claim will not be upheld. In general, section 504 requires school districts to provide students with disabilities with access to any programs or activities they would have access to if they were not disabled. This requires the removal of attitudinal as well as architectural barriers.

### Section 504 and IDEA

Section 504 offers a degree of protection against discrimination to students who have disabilities but are not eligible to receive services under IDEA. Under IDEA a student must fall into one of the categories of disabilities outlined within the statute, and must require special education services as a result of that disability, to receive services.[11] The protections of section 504 reach a much wider population, however.

One of the best examples of the broader reach of section 504 involves students who have an infectious disease. Under IDEA these students would be entitled to special education services only if their academic performance was adversely affected by the illness.[12] However, under section 504 students with an infectious disease cannot be discriminated against or excluded from the schools unless there is a high risk of transmission of the disease.[13] A case decided by a district court in Illinois is illustrative.[14] A student had been excluded from attending regular classes and all extracurricular activities after he was diagnosed as having AIDS. The court held that he was disabled under section 504 because he was regarded as having a physical impairment that substantially interfered with his life activities. The court found that since there was no significant risk of the transmission of AIDS in the classroom setting, his exclusion constituted a violation of section 504.

The majority of students with disabilities are covered by both IDEA and section 504. For this reason, lawsuits frequently are filed alleging violations of both statutes. Generally, the courts have held that compliance with IDEA regarding the provision of a free appropriate public education establishes compliance with section 504.[15] IDEA's requirements for a free appropriate public education are more stringent than those under section 504.[16] In fact, the U.S. Supreme Court has held that, when available, IDEA is the exclusive avenue by which a student with disabilities may assert a claim to a free appropriate public education.[17]

One court even has held that a school district did not violate section 504 when it offered special education services to a student with learning disabilities in a manner that was not procedurally correct.[18] The court reasoned that since the services were offered, the student was not denied those services and thus was not discriminated against. According to the court's ruling, procedural errors had to be addressed via IDEA's due process mechanism.[19] Similarly, the Fourth Circuit Court of Appeals held that a school district did not violate section 504 by refusing to provide special education services in a student's neighborhood school when the needed services were available in a centralized location.[20] Again, the student was not discriminated against since the student was not denied services.

The services provided must be appropriate, however. A district court in Michigan held that allegations of a school district's failure to provide an appropriate amount of occupational and physical therapy or to provide the therapy in the proper manner stated an actionable claim under section 504. Similarly, a district court in New Hampshire held that a student's contention that he had not been provided with educational services that adequately addressed his learning disability stated a claim under section 504.[21]

Some students who do not qualify for special education services under IDEA may be eligible for services under section 504. However, each statute has a distinct purpose, and thus, the services a student is entitled to receive may be different for each statute. A District of Columbia case illustrates this point.[22] The district court upheld the school district's determination that a student with attention deficit hyperactivity disorder

(ADHD) was not eligible for services under IDEA because his educational performance was not adversely affected by his ADHD. However, the court held that a hearing officer could order a school district to provide special education services to a student designated as otherwise qualified under section 504 in appropriate circumstances. The court emphasized, however, that section 504 does not require affirmative efforts to overcome the student's disability, but simply is designed to prevent discrimination on the basis of the disability. Thus, in some situations a school district may need to provide special education services to a disabled student to eliminate discrimination.

Many incarcerated youth may have disabilities and are entitled to receive special education services in spite of their incarcerated status.[23] A ruling by an Illinois district court indicates that section 504 is applicable to correctional facilities.[24] Since correctional facilities receive federal funds to provide educational services to inmates the court held that they fall within the scope of section 504.

## Facilities Must Be Comparable to Those for the Nondisabled

Students with disabilities may require special education classes or other services that are not always offered in the general education environment. Whenever students must be removed from the mainstream to receive services, those services must be provided in facilities that are comparable to the facilities provided for the education of nondisabled students. A district court in Pennsylvania held that the state's Secretary of Education violated section 504 by failing to ensure that the educational facilities for students with disabilities were comparable to those of nondisabled students.[25] The court emphasized that the facilities did not have to be precisely equivalent, but found that in the instant case the facilities provided were substantially unequal. The court specifically indicated that relocating special education classes to lesser facilities to accommodate classes for the nondisabled violated section 504.

## Discriminatory Impact

A district court in Arizona has held that a student does not need to prove that an act of discrimination was intentional to state a claim under section 504.[26] According to the court's ruling, failure to act to correct a situation that results in a denial of access suggests a disparate impact sufficient to state a section 504 violation. In this case the school district failed to correct architectural barriers in the student's high school that forced her to attend a high school several miles away. To get to that school the student had to commute over poor roads, aggravating her condition. Eventually, she was forced to withdraw from school.

The Second Circuit Court of Appeals has held that section 504 does not require that all students with disabilities be provided with identical benefits.[27] Noting that courts must allow for professional judgment, the court stated that a student would have to show that more suitable arrangements were available but were not offered in order to substantiate a discrimination claim under section 504.

School districts also may not discriminate against a student with disabilities on the basis of the means by which the student addresses the disability. A district court in California held that as long as the means by which a student addressed her circumstances were reasonable, school officials could not discriminate against the student on the basis of those means.[28]

## Otherwise Qualified Students with Disabilities

According to a ruling of the U.S. Supreme Court, to be considered otherwise qualified, a student with disabilities must be able to participate in the program or activity in spite of the disability with reasonable accommodations.[29] In other words, the student must meet all of the usual qualifications for participation. Although this case arose in the context of a post-secondary institution, it has implications for elementary and secondary schools. The student filing the lawsuit had been denied admission to a nursing program because she was hearing impaired. She relied on lipreading to understand speech. The college based its decision to deny her admission to the nursing program on safety considerations. The Supreme Court upheld that decision, holding that section 504 did not require educational institutions to disregard the disabilities of applicants or to make substantial modifications in their programs to allow participation. The Court emphasized that legitimate physical qualifications could be essential to participation in particular programs.[30]

A district court in Kentucky illustrated this principle when it held that a blind, multidisabled student who had been denied admission to the state's school for the blind was not otherwise qualified. The court found that the student did not meet the admission criteria that applicants must demonstrate the ability for academic and vocational learning, self-care, and independent functioning.[31] Although the court held that the state did not have to admit the student to its school for the blind, it ruled that the state was still obligated under IDEA to provide the student with a free appropriate public education. In contrast, a district court in Tennessee

held that a student who suffered from an autoimmune disease was otherwise qualified to attend a private school because she had the academic qualifications to attend the school.[32]

Parents who have disabilities also may exert rights under section 504 to allow them to participate better in their children's educational program. The Second Circuit Court of Appeals ordered a school district to provide hearing-impaired parents with the services of a sign-language interpreter so that they could participate in school-related functions.[33] The court found that as parents of students attending the school they were otherwise qualified to participate in parent-oriented activities but could not do so solely because of their disabilities.

## Reasonable Accommodations

Although section 504 does not require school districts to totally disregard the disabilities of those who wish to participate in its programs and activities, it must allow participation if doing so would only require it to make a reasonable accommodation to the individual. Substantial modifications or fundamental alterations of programs and activities are not required.[34] The requirement to provide reasonable accommodations to allow an individual with disabilities to participate does not carry with it the requirement that standards need to be lowered. Reasonable accommodations would require adaptations to allow access, but would not require the elimination of essential prerequisites to participation.

The Fifth Circuit Court of Appeals held that providing basic school health services to a student with physical disabilities that would allow the student to be present in the classroom was a reasonable accommodation.[35] In this case the student needed to be catheterized approximately every four hours. Since this procedure could be provided by a school nurse, health aide, or other trained layperson, the court held that to deny this service, and thus deny access to the educational program, violated section 504.

A district court in California ordered a school district to allow a student with disabilities to bring her service dog to school.[36] The court held that as long as the means by which the student addressed her circumstances were reasonable, section 504 protected them from scrutiny. The court further indicated that to deny the student the means to address her disability at school in the same manner as she did elsewhere amounted to unreasonable and discriminatory conduct.

In the past few years several lawsuits have been filed under IDEA seeking programs within the mainstream for students with severe disabilities.[37] In ordering inclusive placements for these students, courts also are turning to section 504 for guidance. In one case, the district court in New

Jersey held that excluding a student from the regular education classroom without first investigating and providing reasonable accommodations violated section 504.[38] The court held that a segregated special education placement may be the program of choice only when it is necessary for the child to receive educational benefit.

School districts also may be required to waive some requirements for participation in extracurricular activities as long as those requirements are not essential. For example, one court held that an athletic association was required to waive age limitation requirements to allow students who had repeated grades because of their learning disabilities to participate in sports.[39] The court found that since the association allowed waivers of other rules, a waiver of the rule prohibiting students over the age of 19 from participating was a reasonable accommodation. Similarly, preventing a transfer student from participating when the student transferred in order to receive special education services would violate section 504.[40]

In the past few years many states have instituted a requirement that students must pass a minimum competency test in order to graduate with a standard high school diploma. Under section 504 school districts would be required to modify the test-taking situation to allow students with disabilities to take these tests. However, school districts are not required to alter the content of the tests themselves.[41] Altering the content of the test to accommodate an individual's inability to learn amounts to a substantial modification. However, modifying the manner in which the test is administered to accommodate a student's disability would be reasonable.

Accommodations that are unduly costly, create an excessive monitoring burden, or expose other individuals to excessive risk are not required. For example, the Eighth Circuit Court of Appeals held that inoculating staff members against the hepatitis B virus so that a carrier of that disease could attend a learning center program went beyond the requirements of section 504.[42] Similarly, a district court in Kentucky held that a school for the blind could not be required to hire additional staff or modify the mission of the institution to accept a student who did not meet the minimum qualifications for admission to the school.[43]

## AMERICANS WITH DISABILITIES ACT

The major thrust of ADA has been to extend the protections of section 504 to the private sector; however, it also has closed loopholes that existed with section 504 by codifying judicial interpretations of that legislation.[44] Compliance with section 504 generally would translate to compliance with ADA.[45] However, in situations where ADA has adopted stricter standards, school districts are required to meet the requirements of ADA.

A school district that has made diligent good faith efforts to comply with section 504 should not run into difficulty with ADA.[46]

It is unlikely that ADA will have much of an effect on the provision of a free appropriate public education under IDEA. ADA's greatest impact will be on the employment of individuals with disabilities. Although ADA prohibits discrimination against individuals on the basis of their disabilities, it does not require the provision of a free appropriate public education.[47] IDEA still remains the major vehicle to a student's right to receive a free appropriate public education.

## Provisions of ADA

ADA's definition of a disability is almost identical to section 504's definition. As with section 504, under ADA a person is disabled if that person has an impairment that substantially limits one or more major life activities. An individual who has a record of such an impairment, or is regarded as having such an impairment, would be considered disabled under ADA as well.[48]

As with section 504, otherwise qualified individuals with disabilities must be provided with reasonable accommodations so that they may participate in programs provided by a public entity.[49] A public entity includes state or local governments, agencies, or other instrumentalities of a government.[50] Thus, schools would be public entities under ADA. Public entities are prohibited from discriminating against individuals with disabilities under ADA in much the same way that recipients of federal funds are prohibited from discriminating against individuals with disabilities under section 504.[51] ADA includes extensive requirements to provide access to public transportation for the disabled; however, public school transportation is specifically exempted from these provisions.[52]

## Court Cases

At this writing relatively few cases have been decided under the ADA and, as expected, most have been in the context of an employment situation. However, there are some cases that involve students or have relevance for students. Several recent lawsuits have been filed on the basis of both section 504 and the ADA, but generally students have received no greater relief under the ADA than they would have under section 504 alone.[53]

In several cases discussed in previous chapters courts declined to intervene in situations where a parent disagreed with the methodology used in a particular placement as long as the school district could show that the selected methodology was appropriate.[54] According to a decision from the federal district court in Nebraska, the ADA does not provide parents with any additional clout regarding the choice of methodology.[55] The court found that the method used to instruct hearing impaired students was no less effective than the method preferred by their parents and thus met the requirements of ADA.

A case decided by a district court in New York involving a law school graduate has implications for school districts when administering examinations to students with disabilities.[56] A visually impaired student had requested certain accommodations when she was scheduled to sit for the bar examination. Most of her requested accommodations were granted, but some were not. Her physician testified that the additional accommodations were necessary due to her disability. The court ordered the requested accommodations stating that the purpose of ADA was to guarantee that those with disabilities are not disadvantaged but are put on an equal footing with others. The court emphasized, however, that individuals with disabilities are not to be given an unfair advantage. The court gave great weight to the physician's testimony since there was no medical evidence to the contrary. However, another New York case involving a law school graduate indicates that applicants for an exam are not entitled to modifications just because they may have failed the exam in the past without modifications.[57] The court held that modifications to the testing situation were not required for a student who claimed to be learning disabled because expert testimony indicated that he was not disabled. The court found the testimony of an acknowledged expert on dyslexia to be credible and persuasive.

In another lawsuit that has implications for the school situation, a district court in Pennsylvania held that although a public entity was not prohibited from providing benefits, services, or advantages to individuals with disabilities or to a particular class of individuals with disabilities beyond those required by the ADA, it could not discriminate in the provision of affirmative services.[58] The court ruled that providing services to individuals with physical disabilities while not providing those same services to individuals who had physical and mental disabilities constituted discrimination since there was no rational reason for excluding those physically disabled individuals who also had mental disabilities from the benefits of the program.

In yet another case that has implications for the provision of services to public school students, a district court in Florida held that the elimination of all recreation programs for individuals with disabilities violated ADA where recreation programs were still being offered to nondisabled individuals.[59] The city had eliminated the programs due to fiscal constraints, but the court held that any benefits provided nondisabled persons must be equally made available to persons with disabilities. Therefore, since the city chose to provide recreation services to nondisabled persons, the court held that the ADA required it to provide equal opportunities for persons with disabilities to receive comparable benefits. The court further held that different or separate benefits could be provided to individuals with disabilities, if necessary, to provide them with aids, benefits, or services that are as effective as those provided to others.

## Implications of ADA for School Personnel

As was stated earlier, ADA is unlikely to have much of an impact on the delivery of special education services in elementary and secondary schools since its provisions in that regard are not substantially more extensive than those of IDEA or section 504. However, educators need to be aware of ADA's major provisions for instructional purposes. Students with disabilities who will be seeking employment and independent living will need to be aware of their rights and protections under ADA in order to engage in self-advocacy. Information about ADA should be included in the instructional programs of all secondary special education students.

## SUMMARY

IDEA remains the primary vehicle students with disabilities have to assert their rights to appropriate educational programs. However, section 504 and ADA provide all individuals with disabilities with protection against discrimination in all facets of their lives.

Under these two civil rights laws, recipients of federal funds and other public entities may not exclude individuals with disabilities from participation in their programs and activities. Reasonable accommodations may need to be provided to grant effective access to programs and activities. Reasonable accommodations could include any adjustments that do not result in a major modification of the program.

## ENDNOTES

1. 20 U.S.C. § 1400 et seq.
2. 29 U.S.C. § 794.
3. 42 U.S.C. § 12101 et seq.
4. 42 U.S.C. § 12101(b)(2).
5. *Vande Zande* v. *State of Wisconsin Department of Administration,* 851 F. Supp. 353 (W.D. Wis. 1994).
6. 29 U.S.C. § 706(7)(B).
7. 34 C.F.R. § 104.3(j)(2)(ii).

8. *School Board of Nassau County* v. *Arline*, 480 U.S. 273, 107 S. Ct. 1123, 94 L. Ed.2d 307, 37 Ed.Law Rep. 448 (1987); *Southeastern Community College* v. *Davis*, 442 U.S. 397, 99 S. Ct. 2361, 60 L. Ed.2d 980 (1979).

9. 34 C.F.R. § 104.12(a).

10. For a discussion of section 504's applicability to employment situations *see*: Beezer, B. (1991). Employment Discrimination Against Handicapped School Employees: Section 504. *Education Law Reporter, 65,* 693–712.

11. 20 U.S.C. § 1401(a)(1)(A).

12. 34 C.F.R. § 300.7(b)(8).

13. *New York State Association for Retarded Children* v. *Carey*, 612 F.2d 644 (2d Cir. 1979); *Community High School* v. *Denz*, 463 N.E.2d 998, 17 Ed.Law Rep. 885 (Ill. App. Ct. 1984); *District 27* v. *Board of Education of New York*, 502 N.Y.S.2d 325, 32 Ed.Law Rep. 740 (N.Y. Sup. Ct. 1986); *Thomas* v. *Atascadero Unified School District*, 662 F. Supp. 376, 40 Ed.Law Rep. 732 (C.D. Cal. 1987); *Ray* v. *School District of DeSoto County*, 666 F. Supp. 1524, 41 Ed.Law Rep. 632 (M.D. Fla. 1987); *Doe* v. *Belleville*, 672 F. Supp. 342, 42 Ed.Law Rep. 1125 (S.D. Ill. 1987); *Doe* v. *Dolton Elementary School District*, 694 F. Supp. 440, 49 Ed.Law Rep. 580 (N.D. Ill. 1988); *Martinez* v. *School Board of Hillsborough County*, 861 F.2d 1502, 50 Ed.Law Rep. 359 (11th Cir. 1988), *on remand* 711 F. Supp. 1066, 53 Ed.Law Rep. 1176 (M.D. Fla. 1989).

14. *Doe* v. *Dolton Elementary School District*, 694 F. Supp. 440, 49 Ed.Law Rep. 580 (N.D. Ill. 1988).

15. *See, for example, Barnett* v. *Fairfax County School Board*, 721 F. Supp. 757, 56 Ed.Law Rep. 804 (E.D. Va. 1989), *aff'd* 927 F.2d 146, 66 Ed.Law Rep. 64 (4th Cir. 1991); *Doe* v. *Alabama State Department of Education*, 915 F.2d 651, 63 Ed.Law Rep. 40 (11th Cir. 1990); *Cordrey* v. *Euckert*, 917 F.2d 1460, 63 Ed.Law Rep. 798 (6th Cir. 1990).

16. *See, for example, Colin K.* v. *Schmidt*, 715 F.2d 1, 13 Ed.Law Rep. 221 (1st Cir. 1983); *Darlene L.* v. *Illinois Board of Education*, 568 F. Supp. 1340, 13 Ed.Law Rep. 282 (N.D. Ill. 1983).

17. *Smith* v. *Robinson*, 468 U.S. 992, 104 S. Ct. 3457, 82 L. Ed.2d 746, 18 Ed.Law Rep. 148 (1984).

18. *Puffer* v. *Raynolds*, 761 F. Supp. 838, 67 Ed.Law Rep. 536 (D. Mass. 1988).

19. See Chapter 4 for a discussion of IDEA's complaint resolution procedures.

20. *Barnett* v. *Fairfax County School Board*, 927 F.2d 146, 66 Ed.Law Rep. 64 (4th Cir. 1991).

21. *I.D.* v. *Westmoreland School District*, 788 F. Supp. 634, 74 Ed.Law Rep. 1109 (D.N.H. 1992).

22. *Lyons* v. *Smith*, 829 F. Supp. 414, 85 Ed.Law Rep. 803 (D.D.C. 1993).

23. *See Green* v. *Johnson*, 513 F. Supp. 965 (D. Mass. 1982).

24. *Donnell C.* v. *Illinois State Board of Education*, 829 F. Supp. 1016 (N.D. Ill. 1993).

25. *Hendricks* v. *Gilhool*, 709 F. Supp. 1362, 53 Ed.Law Rep. 81 (E.D. Pa. 1989).

26. *Begay* v. *Hodel*, 730 F. Supp. 1001, 58 Ed.Law Rep. 1128 (D. Ariz. 1990).

27. *P.C.* v. *McLaughlin*, 913 F.2d 1033, 62 Ed.Law Rep. 881 (2d Cir. 1990).

28. *Sullivan* v. *Vallejo City Unified School District*, 731 F. Supp. 947, 59 Ed.Law Rep. 73 (E.D. Cal. 1990).

29. *Southeastern Community College* v. *Davis,* 442 U.S. 397, 60 L. Ed.2d 980 (1979).
30. *See* Wenkart, R. D. (1991). Providing a Free Appropriate Public Education Under Section 504. *Education Law Reporter, 65,* 1021–1029.
31. *Eva N.* v. *Brock,* 741 F. Supp. 626, 62 Ed.Law Rep. 112 (E.D. Ky. 1990).
32. *Thomas* v. *Davidson Academy,* 846 F. Supp. 611, 90 Ed.Law Rep. 132 (M.D. Tenn. 1994).
33. *Rothschild* v. *Grottenthaler,* 907 F.2d 286, 57 Ed.Law Rep. 832 (2d Cir. 1990).
34. *Southeastern Community College* v. *Davis,* 442 U.S. 397, 99 S. Ct. 2361, 60 L. Ed.2d 980 (1979).
35. *Tatro* v. *State of Texas,* 625 F.2d 557 (5th Cir. 1980), on remand 516 F. Supp. 968 (N.D. Tex. 1981), *aff'd* 703 F.2d 823, 10 Ed.Law Rep. 73 (5th Cir. 1983), *aff'd sub nom. Irving Independent School District* v. *Tatro,* 468 U.S. 883, 104 S. Ct. 3371, 82 L. Ed.2d 664, 18 Ed.Law Rep. 138 (1984).
36. *Sullivan* v. *Vallejo City Unified School District,* 731 F. Supp. 947, 59 Ed.Law Rep. 73 (E.D. Cal. 1990).
37. Osborne, A.G. & DiMattia, P. (1992). Mainstreaming students with severe disabilities: Implications for public policy. *ERIC Document Reproduction Service,* 354652. Osborne, A. G. & DiMattia, P. (1994). The IDEA's least restrictive environment mandate: Legal implications. *Exceptional Children, 61,* 6–14.
38. *Oberti* v. *Board of Education of the Borough of Clementon School District,* 801 F. Supp. 1393 (D.N.J. 1992), *aff'd* 995 F.2d 1204, 83 Ed.Law Rep. 1009 (3d Cir. 1993).
39. *University Interscholastic League* v. *Buchanan,* 848 S.W.2d 298, 81 Ed.Law Rep. 1145 (Tex. App. Ct. 1993). *Also see Hoot* v. *Milan Area Schools,* 853 F. Supp. 243, 92 Ed.Law Rep. 841 (E.D. Mich. 1994).
40. *Crocker* v. *Tennessee Secondary School Athletic Association,* 735 F. Supp. 753, 60 Ed.Law Rep. 502 (M.D. Tenn. 1990), *aff'd without published opinion sub nom. Metropolitan Government of Nashville and Davidson County* v. *Crocker,* 908 F.2d 973, 61 Ed.Law Rep. 1187 (6th Cir. 1990).
41. *Brookhart* v. *Illinois State Board of Education,* 697 F.2d 179, 8 Ed.Law Rep. 608 (7th Cir. 1983).
42. *Kohl* v. *Woodhaven Learning Center,* 865 F.2d 930, 51 Ed.Law Rep. 383 (8th Cir. 1989).
43. *Eva N.* v. *Brock,* 741 F. Supp. 626, 62 Ed.Law Rep. 112 (E.D. Ky. 1990).
44. Marczely, B. (1993). The Americans with Disabilities Act: Confronting the Shortcomings of Section 504 in Public Education. *Education Law Reporter, 78,* 199–207.
45. *Vande Zande* v. *State of Wisconsin Department of Administration,* 851 F. Supp. 353 (W.D. Wis. 1994).
46. Miles, A. S., Russo, C. J. and Gordon, W. M. (1991). The Reasonable Accommodations Provisions of the Americans with Disabilities Act. *Education Law Reporter, 69,* 1–8.
47. Wenkart, R. D. (1993). The Americans with Disabilities Act and Its Impact on Public Education. *Education Law Reporter, 82,* 291–302.

48. 42 U.S.C. § 12102(2). For an excellent overview of ADA's provisions *see:* Kaesberg, M.A. and Murray, K.T. (1994). Americans with Disabilities Act. *Education Law Reporter, 90,* 11-20.

49. 42 U.S.C. § 12111(9).

50. 42 U.S.C. § 12131(1).

51. 42 U.S.C. § 12132.

52. 42 U.S.C. § 12141.

53. *See, for example, Thomas* v. *Davidson Academy,* 846 F. Supp. 611, 90 Ed.Law Rep. 132 (M.D. Tenn. 1994).

54. See Chapter 5, in particular, for additional information.

55. *Petersen* v. *Hastings Public Schools,* 831 F. Supp. 742, 86 Ed.Law Rep. 122 (D. Neb. 1993).

56. *D'Amico* v. *New York State Board of Law Examiners,* 813 F. Supp. 217 (W.D.N.Y. 1993).

57. *Pazer* v. *New York State Board of Law Examiners,* 849 F. Supp. 284 (S.D.N.Y. 1994).

58. *Easley* v. *Snider,* 841 F. Supp. 668 (E.D. Pa. 1993).

59. *Concerned Parents to Save Dreher Park Center* v. *City of West Palm Beach,* 846 F. Supp. 986 (S.D. Fla. 1994).

# Epilogue:
# MANAGING THE LEGAL
# SYSTEM—PREVENTIVE LAW

As this book has shown, the Individuals with Disabilities Education Act (IDEA) provides students with disabilities and their parents with considerable substantive and procedural rights. A significant portion of the federal law was designed by Congress to protect students by ensuring compliance with the law. The due process section of IDEA[1] created a vehicle for the resolution of any dispute regarding the provision of a free appropriate public education as guaranteed by IDEA. That due process mechanism is the most elaborate system ever established by Congress for the resolution of disputes between parents and school authorities. Although Congress intended for parents and school officials to work together in developing an individualized education program (IEP) for a student with disabilities, there are some situations where the parties simply cannot agree. Thus there was a need for a dispute resolution process.

This book has provided information about hundreds of lawsuits that have been filed since the passage of IDEA. These lawsuits have involved numerous aspects of the federal special education legislation. The deluge of lawsuits is not likely to stop in the near future. Some school law commentators have stated that during the decade after implementation of IDEA, there had been a continuing increase in special education litigation.[2] Studies have shown that in the past few years the level of litigation in special education has remained constant.[3]

Special education administrators have been heard to lament that one has to be half lawyer to successfully hold that position. While having a law degree is not a prerequisite for the position, the fact remains that the special education process is very much a legal process. Successful special education practitioners have knowledge of the law and understand how the legal system operates. Those who are most successful are those who manage the legal system rather than allow the legal system to manage them. The purpose of this chapter is to provide information on how and when to access the legal system.

## PREVENTIVE LAW

The best way to deal with a legal problem is to prevent it from occurring. In the past few years school districts have been forced to budget an increased amount of money for legal fees. No one will argue that this money would be better spent on educational programs. This is most true in special education where litigation has increased faster than in any other area of school law.[4] In addition to their own legal fees, school districts may be required to reimburse parents for their legal expenses if the parents win the lawsuit.[5]

In the past few years many educators have taken an interest in an emerging area known as preventive law. The purpose of preventive law is either to preclude a legal dispute entirely or to put the school district in a favorable position if a dispute should occur.[6] Preventive law, to be most effective, must be a continuing practice within the school district. One objective of preventive law is to find permanent solutions to the situations that give rise to conflicts in the schools. Generally, it is less expensive to find those permanent solutions than to mount a defense in a protracted lawsuit.

The first step in any program of preventive law is for school administrators and special education practitioners to be knowledgeable of the legal issues in special education. Reading this book and others like it will provide school officials with a basic knowledge of the issues and the results of previous litigation. However, the law is constantly evolving. New cases are decided daily that can alter the status of the law. Several examples of this have been cited in previous chapters. School authorities must take affirmative action to stay abreast of new developments in the law.

Today there are numerous sources of information about issues and developments in education law. The National Organization on Legal Problems of Education (NOLPE) in Topeka, Kansas, publishes a *Yearbook of Education Law* that includes a chapter on special education law entitled *Individuals with Disabilities*. In addition, NOLPE publishes a monthly newsletter, *NOLPE Notes,* and reporter, *School Law Reporter,* that provide up-to-date information. Many special education journals frequently contain articles on legal issues. Professional organizations such as the Council for

Exceptional Children and NOLPE generally have several sessions at their annual conventions that address legal issues. Almost all colleges and universities with education departments offer a course on special education law. Workshops on special education law should be part of every school system's staff development program.

Much litigation arises out of misunderstandings or small differences of opinion between the parties. Much costly and embarrassing litigation could be avoided through communication and compromise. Communication between administrators, teachers, and parents is an important key to successfully avoiding litigation. When proposed special education placements are rejected by the parents, school officials should make every attempt possible to determine the reasons for the rejected individualized education program (IEP). The rejection may be due to a misunderstanding over what the proposal entails or a disagreement with only a minor aspect of the program. If the school district does not communicate, or is not willing to compromise, litigation is sure to follow.

Active listening is an important component of the communication process. When parents present a counterproposal or make additional demands, school officials must listen and give serious thought to their ideas. In the spirit of compromise, the school district should be prepared to make some concessions. If the parents' demands cannot be met, great care should be taken to explain to them why their proposal cannot be implemented.

Much litigation also arises due to the failure of school district representatives to consistently implement the district's policies. Oftentimes the district has appropriate and legally correct policies and procedures in place, but its employees fail to follow them in all situations. Training new employees and conducting ongoing staff development activities to ensure that employees are aware of all policies and procedures are critical.

Finally, one of the most important steps a school district can take in the realm of preventive law is to periodically conduct a legal audit. The audit should focus on the district's policies, procedures, and practices to ensure that they are legally correct. Since the status of the law is constantly evolving, it is important that a legal audit be repeated every couple of years. The attorney the school district uses for its special education litigation is the ideal person to conduct such an audit.

## DISPUTE RESOLUTION

Unfortunately, despite the best efforts of school authorities to prevent it, litigation will always be a fact of life in today's school systems. Honest disagreements over what constitutes an appropriate placement will occur between parents and special educators. Sometimes parents will make demands or have expectations that the school district cannot meet, and compromise will not be possible. And sometimes school district personnel will make errors.

The Individuals with Disabilities Education Act (IDEA) contains a meticulous system of dispute resolution. That mechanism was described in Chapter 4. This section outlines steps school authorities should take when parents initiate legal action.

## Mediation

Sometimes communication between school officials and parents will break down, and the parties may find it difficult to sit and work out an agreement. A mediation process can be very helpful in this situation and is explicitly encouraged by IDEA.[7] Mediation is a viable alternative for the resolution of disputed IEPs, but it cannot be used to deny or delay the parents' right to a formal due process hearing.

The parties involved in a special education dispute can engage the services of an impartial mediator who will attempt to bring them together through negotiation. Several states have provisions in their own special education laws for a formal mediation process prior to litigation.[8] However, even if the state does not explicitly provide for mediation, it is unlikely that it would be forbidden. Successful mediation depends on the willingness of school authorities to compromise. School officials must evaluate any reasonable proposals that are presented either by the parents or mediator and be prepared to offer specific counterproposals.

There are many advantages to trying mediation before proceeding to a due process hearing. First, the costs involved and the time spent on a due process hearing certainly justify the effort to mediate and hopefully avoid the hearing stage. Most important, however, is the fact that mediation can salvage a working relationship between the parties. Unfortunately, a due process hearing is an adversarial process that does little to foster a positive working relationship between parents and school officials.

## Preparing for a Hearing

Despite the best efforts of school officials, sometimes a due process hearing is inevitable. If all placement decisions have been made according to the procedures set forth in IDEA, school officials need not fear a due process hearing. However, there still is no substitute for proper preparation prior to the hearing.

Preparation for a hearing needs to begin long before it is even apparent that a hearing will take place. The key to success in an administrative hearing is to have all proper documentation to show that the school district has complied with applicable laws and procedures. It is impossible to create the proper documentation after the fact if the documentation does not exist. Thus, it is advisable to treat all special education situations as if they may someday culminate in a hearing. In other words documentation must begin the day the special education process begins and must become part of the routine.

Generally, the person responsible for presenting the school district's case will be the special education administrator. Since the special education administrator usually would become involved in the case only after problems have developed, he or she would be unfamiliar with the child's prior history. The first task for the administrator would be to gather all pertinent information for study. The administrator must become familiar with all aspects and details of the case. The decisions that will need to be made throughout the hearing process will require intricate knowledge of the student.

The requirements and qualifications for an independent hearing officer vary from state to state. In some states hearing officers are attorneys who have some knowledge of special education practices. In other states the hearing officer may be a special education professor from a local college who is well versed in special education procedures. It would be a mistake to assume that the hearing officer has detailed knowledge of the school district's programs or other available options. The task for school officials is to educate the hearing officer about the positive aspects of the school district's proposal and the weaknesses of the parents' position.

One of the most important pieces of evidence the school district must supply is the documentation that all due process procedures have been complied with. However, if this is not the case and all procedural requirements have not been met, school officials must acknowledge the error. Not all procedural errors are fatal; however, evasiveness or intentional covering up of procedural errors can be very damaging to the school district's case.

During the hearing, it is very important to make a complete presentation of the facts. It may be helpful to use visual aids such as charts, diagrams, or other graphic presentations to clarify points made during the oral argument or cross examination of expert witnesses. Careful advance preparation of these materials is necessary.

Those who will testify or present evidence on behalf of the school district must be well prepared. Rehearsals should be held. Although it is impossible to determine in advance exactly what line of questioning will be used by the opposition during cross-examination, the school district's attorney should be able to prepare all witnesses adequately for what is to come.

The school district's task in a hearing is to show that its proposed program is appropriate. According to IDEA, once it has been shown that a school district has offered an appropriate program, there is no need to examine any alternative proposals.[9] However, prudent school officials should be prepared to show why they do not feel the program favored by the parents is necessary. Many school districts have been successful in due process hearings by showing that the program favored by the parents was inadequate.

The importance of working with the school district's attorney cannot be overemphasized. Communication between school officials and their attorney is an important ingredient to success. In the next section factors to consider when choosing an attorney will be discussed.

## Selecting an Attorney

It has been observed that the party who is in the right in special education litigation is not always the victor.[10] As in any legal contest, the party that can present the best case most often wins. This being the situation, having a qualified attorney may make all the difference. The necessity of having a skilled attorney in a special education lawsuit cannot be overemphasized.

As an area of law, special education has become a specialized topic due to the tremendous amount of litigation that has occurred since IDEA was passed in 1975. School officials cannot rely on the school board attorney to defend the school district in a special education lawsuit. Although the school board attorney may be well qualified to handle most of the school district's legal affairs, he or she may not have the specialized knowledge required to adequately litigate a special education case.

School districts should retain a separate attorney to handle all their special education litigation. Many school districts use the services of a large law firm that specializes in education law. A large law firm may have one or two attorneys who further specialize in special education law. If this is the case, school officials need look no further for special education counsel.

However, if the school district is not represented by a large firm with a special education division, a separate attorney for special education litigation must be located and retained. The attorney chosen should be well versed in education law in general as well as special education law and must have experience in administrative hearing procedures since most of the litigation will be at that level. Furthermore, the attorney should be familiar with educational issues and practices such as evaluation methods, teaching techniques, and various placement options.

Naturally, an experienced and talented attorney will cost more; however, there simply is no substitute for experience.

To find a qualified attorney to handle a special education lawsuit a school district should solicit referrals from other knowledgeable parties. Since the person representing the school district in a special education lawsuit may need to confer with the school board attorney, that person would be a logical starting point. The school board attorney may have a ready list of qualified special education attorneys. Special education administrators from other districts would be another source of referrals. Finally, the county or state bar associations should be able to provide a list of attorneys specializing in special education litigation.

An attorney should be located and retained long before one is needed. The point at which a school district is under the pressure of a lawsuit is not the proper time to begin looking for a qualified attorney. It is better to retain an attorney and form a relationship with the attorney well before any litigation is pending. This way school officials will be able to take the time necessary to make sure the attorney hired is the right person for the job.

Choosing an attorney is much like choosing a person to fill any open position in the school district. School officials should examine the attorneys' credentials, seek references from other school districts that have used the attorneys being considered, and interview the candidates that appear most qualified. Choosing an attorney is as important as filling any top-level administrative position in the school district. The process should not be taken lightly.

## SUMMARY

There is an old saying in sports that the best defense is a good offense. The same can be said of special education litigation except that, unlike in sports, it is best to prevent the confrontation from occurring in the first place.

The best way to avoid litigation is to be constantly prepared for it. School districts can reduce their risk of lawsuits by making sure that all employees in the district are well aware of proper procedures. Employees who know and understand the law's requirements are less likely to make legal errors. This is especially true in the field of special education where procedure plays such an important role.

When inevitable conflicts do arise it does not automatically mean that litigation will result. Many conflicts can be solved through more communication between the parties. Misunderstandings can be cleared up and compromises can be negotiated. A formal mediation process can be used to help settle disputes if communication between the parties breaks down.

Finally, when litigation is inevitable, the school officials must not despair. If school employees have followed proper procedure and placement decisions were made in good faith, the school district has little cause for concern. However, when entering the legal battlefield, school officials must come prepared. They must be able to substantiate their actions and recommendations and must be able to justify all placement decisions. A qualified attorney may well be the school district's best asset in a special education lawsuit.

## ENDNOTES

1. 20 U.S.C. § 1415.
2. Zirkel, P. A. & Richardson, S. N. (1989). The "explosion" in education litigation. *Education Law Reporter, 53,* 767–791.
3. Osborne, A. G. (1993). Individuals with Disabilities. In Thomas, S.B. (ed.) *Yearbook of Education Law 1993.* Topeka, KS: National Organization on Legal Problems of Education.
4. Zirkel, P. A. and Osborne, A. G. (1987). Are Damages Available in Special Education Suits? *Education Law Reporter, 42,* 497–508.
5. See Chapter 8 for a complete discussion of the remedies available to parents.
6. Bednar, W. C. (1989). Preventive School Law in Camp, W. E., Underwood, J. K., & Connelly, M. J. (eds.) *Current Issues in School Law.* Topeka, KS: National Organization on Legal Problems of Education.
7. 34 C.F.R. § 300.506 Comment.
8. Goldberg, S. S. (1989). The failure of legalization in education: Alternative dispute resolution and the Education for All Handicapped Children Act of 1975. *Journal of Law and Education, 18,* 441–454.
9. See Chapter 5 for a discussion of standards of appropriateness.
10. Prasse, D. P. (1988). Legal influence and educational policy in special education. *Exceptional Children, 54,* 302–308.

# GLOSSARY

*Administrative appeal*   A quasi-judicial proceeding before an independent hearing officer or administrative law judge.

*Administrative law judge*   An individual presiding at an administrative due process hearing who has the power to administer oaths, hear testimony, rule on questions of evidence, and make determinations of fact. The role of an administrative law judge in IDEA proceedings is identical to that of an independent hearing officer.

*Affirm*   To uphold the decision of a lower court in an appeal.

*Americans with Disabilities Act (ADA)*   A civil rights statute designed to prevent discrimination against individuals with disabilities.

*Amicus curiae*   An individual or organization that is not a party to a lawsuit but is granted permission by the court to submit a brief outlining legal arguments in support of a certain position.

*Annual review*   A review of a student's progress in a special education program and an examination of his or her future special education needs held at least once each year. An annual review may repeat some of the original assessments for purposes of assessing progress but generally is not as thorough as the original evaluation. The student's Individualized Education Program is revised and updated at the annual review conference.

*Appeal*   To request a higher court to review the decision of the lower court.

*Appellant*   The party who appeals a decision of one court to a higher court.

*Appellee*   The party against whom an appeal is made to a higher court.

*Case law*   Law resulting from court opinions.

*Certiorari*   A writ issued by an appeals court indicating that it will review the lower court's decision.

*C.F.R.*   Abbreviation for Code of Federal Regulations. C.F.R. is a publication of the federal government that contains the regulations promulgated by various agencies to implement laws passed by Congress.

*Civil lawsuit*   A noncriminal lawsuit filed to seek redress for an alleged wrong or injury.

*Class action*   A lawsuit brought on behalf of the named plaintiffs as well as others who may be similarly situated.

*Common law*   The body of law that has developed as a result of court decisions, customs, and precedents.

*Compensatory damages*   Compensation for the actual loss suffered by a plaintiff.

*Consent decree*   An agreement by the parties to a lawsuit that is sanctioned by the court that basically settled the dispute between the parties by mutual consent.

*Damages*   A monetary award granted by a court to compensate an injured party. Damages are paid by the party causing the injury.

*Decree*   The judgment of a court that outlines the legal consequences of the facts of the case.

*De facto*   A situation that actually exists, whether or not it is legal.

*Defendant*   The party against whom a lawsuit is brought.

*De jure*   A situation that occurs by sanction of law.

*De minimus*   Small or unimportant, not worthy of the court's concern.

*De novo*   For the second time. A trial de novo refers to a situation where a court hears evidence and testimony that had previously been heard by a lower court or administrative body.

*Dicta*   Statements in a court's opinion that go beyond the facts of the case and are not binding on future cases.

*Due process hearing*   An administrative hearing. A due process or administrative hearing under IDEA is a quasi-judicial proceeding designed to resolve disputes on any matter regarding the provision of a free appropriate public education. The purpose of the hearing is to establish the facts, based on evidence and testimony, and render a decision.

*Education for All Handicapped Children Act*   The original name of the Individuals with Disabilities Education Act.

*En banc*   Refers to a session where the entire membership of a court participates in a decision rather than a single judge or select panel of judges. A rehearing en banc may be granted if a select panel of judges has rendered a decision that is contrary to decisions rendered by similar courts.

*Equity*   Fairness.

*Et seq.*   An abbreviation for a Latin term that means "and following." Generally used in a citation to indicate "and the sections that follow."

*Evaluation team*   A group of individuals who perform assessments on the student to determine if the student has a disability and, if so, what special education and related services he or she will require. The evaluation team is composed of individuals such as the classroom teacher, a special education teacher, an administrator, a psychologist, the parents of the student (and in some cases the student), and other specialists. Different states have various names for the evaluation team such as multidisciplinary team, committee on special education, pupil personnel services team, or pupil placement team.

*Expulsion*   A long-term exclusion from school, generally for disciplinary purposes. Usually any disciplinary exclusion of more than 10 days is considered an expulsion.

*Holding*  The part of the court's decision that applies the law to the facts of the case.

*Independent hearing officer*  An impartial person who conducts an administrative hearing and renders a decision on the merits of the dispute.

*Individualized Education Program (IEP)*  A document outlining the specific special education and related services to be provided a student with disabilities. The IEP also states the student's current level of functioning, specifies the goals and objectives of the instructional program, and outlines the criteria for assessing progress.

*Individuals with Disabilities Education Act (IDEA)*  The federal special education law, codified at 20 U.S.C. § 1400 et seq. Originally titled the Education for All Handicapped Children Act, it was enacted by Congress as P.L. 94-142.

*In forma pauperis*  When the court grants an indigent person permission to proceed without incurring court costs or fees.

*Injunction*  An order issued by the court forbidding a party to take some contemplated action, or restraining the party from continuing an action, or requiring the party to take some action.

*In re*  A Latin term used in case names meaning "in the matter of."

*Mainstreaming*  The practice of educating students with disabilities in a setting with students who do not have disabilities.

*Mediation*  A process whereby a neutral party attempts to negotiate a settlement in a dispute by persuading the parties to adjust their positions.

*Moot*  When a live controversy no longer exists. A lawsuit will become moot if there is no longer any dispute.

*On remand*  When a lower court has rendered a decision after having had the case returned to it for further action by an appellate court.

*Opinion*  A court's statement of its decision in a lawsuit.

*Per curiam*  An unsigned decision of the court as opposed to one signed by a specific judge.

*P.L.*  An abbreviation for Public Law. A Public Law is a statute passed by Congress.

*Plaintiff*  The party bringing a lawsuit to a court of law.

*Preponderance of the evidence*  The level of proof required in a civil lawsuit; evidence that has the greater weight or is more convincing.

*Pro se*  On one's own behalf. Generally refers to a person who represents himself or herself in court.

*Prospective*  Looking toward the future; prospective relief provides a remedy in the future.

*Punitive damages*  Compensation awarded to a plaintiff that is over and above the actual loss suffered; designed to punish the defendant for wrongful action and to act as an incentive to prevent similar action in the future.

*Reevaluation*  A complete and thorough reassessment of the student. Generally, all of the original assessments will be repeated, but additional assessments must be completed if necessary. A reevaluation must take place at least every three years.

*Regulations*  Specific guidelines for implementation of a statute issued by the agency charged with the responsibility for overseeing the statute.

*Related services*  Developmental, corrective, or supportive services that may be required for a student with disabilities to benefit from his or her special education program.

*Remand*  To send a case back to the lower court, usually with specific instructions for further action.

*Res judicata*  A rule that a final judgment of a court is conclusive and acts to prevent subsequent action on the same claim.

*Reverse*  To revoke the lower court's decision in an appeal.

*Sectarian*  Of or relating to a sect. In education law sectarian usually refers to a school or institution that is religiously affiliated, such as a parochial school.

*Section 504*  Section 504 of the Rehabilitation Act of 1973, codified at 29 U.S.C. § 794. A civil rights statute prohibiting discrimination against individuals with disabilities by recipients of federal funds.

*Secular*  Not pertaining to or relating to a religious sect.

*Settlement agreement*  An out-of-court agreement made by the parties to a lawsuit to settle the case by resolving the major issues that initiated the litigation.

*Sovereign immunity*  A legal prohibition against suing the government without its consent.

*Special education*  Instruction specifically designed to meet the unique needs of a student with disabilities.

*Standing*  An individual's right to bring a lawsuit before the court. To have standing an individual must be directly affected by the issues litigated.

*State-level review officer (panel)*  An impartial person (or panel of usually three or more persons) who reviews the decisions of an independent hearing officer from an administrative due process proceeding under IDEA. IDEA provides that if administrative due process hearings are held at the local school district level, provisions must be made for an appeal at the state level [20 U.S.C. § 1415(c)].

*Statute of limitations*  A law that specifies the period of time within which a lawsuit must be filed.

*Students with disabilities*  Students who require special education services due to having an impairment as defined by IDEA. It includes those who are mentally retarded, hearing impaired, visually impaired, seriously emotionally disturbed, orthopedically impaired, speech impaired, other health impaired, or learning disabled.

*Sub nom.*  Abbreviation of a Latin term meaning that a case was decided on appeal under a different name than the one used at the lower court level.

*Suspect class*  A suspect class is a group that has been denied equal protection on the basis of membership in the group. Suspect class status may be based on race, national origin, gender, or some other characteristic.

*Suspension*  A short-term exclusion from school, usually for disciplinary purposes.

*Tort*  A civil wrong committed by one person against another.

*Vacate*  To set aside the lower court's decision in an appeal.

# TABLE OF CASES

The following cases have been cited within the text. The numbers in italics following the case citations indicate the pages in the text in which the case has been referenced. In cases that were affirmed on appeal, the lower court decision also has been cited. The procedural history has been given for cases that were reversed on appeal if the lower court decision was instructive.

# SUBJECT AND AUTHOR INDEX

# ABOUT THE AUTHOR

Dr. Allan G. Osborne, Jr. is the assistant principal of the Snug Harbor Community School in Quincy, Massachusetts, a nationally recognized Blue Ribbon School of Excellence. He is also a visiting associate professor at Bridgewater State College where he teaches courses in educational research, behavioral interventions, and school law. He is a frequent adjunct lecturer in the doctoral program in educational administration at Boston College. A former special education administrator, he has twenty-one years of experience in the field of special education. Osborne received his doctorate in educational leadership from Boston College and a master's degree in special education from Fitchburg State College.

Osborne is a nationally recognized expert on legal and public policy issues in special education. He is the author of *Complete Legal Guide to Special Education Services* published by Parker Publishing Company and co-author of *Effective Management of Special Education Programs* with Philip DiMattia and Francis X. Curran, published by Teachers College Press. Since 1990 he also has written the "Individuals with Disabilities" chapter of the *Yearbook of Education Law* published by the National Organization on Legal Problems of Education. The author of over 50 articles that have appeared in special education and school law journals, Osborne is a frequent speaker at national conferences for educators, lawyers, and federal judges. He is on the editorial boards of several special education and school law journals.